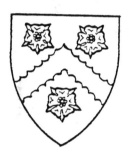

THE GIFT OF
THOMAS JOSEPH WHITE
M.D., L.H.D., F.A.C.P.
TO THE LIBRARY OF
CABRINI COLLEGE
1981

THE AUTOBIOGRAPHY
OF A CURMUDGEON

The Curmudgeon Himself

HAROLD L. ICKES

The Autobiography of a
CURMUDGEON

BY HAROLD L. ICKES

★ ★

★

REYNAL & HITCHCOCK
NEW YORK

Second Printing

PRINTED IN THE UNITED STATES OF AMERICA
BY THE CORNWALL PRESS, CORNWALL, N. Y.

If to anyone,
of course
to
JANE

CONTENTS

CHAPTER	PAGE
Introduction	*ix*
I. A Blessed Event?	*1*
II. An Assistant Druggist's Assistant	*14*
III. Newshawk	*27*
IV. Add "Newshawk"	*44*
V. Public Weal	*72*
VI. A Hardy Perennial	*89*
VII. Two Damn Fools	*115*
VIII. Big Stick	*145*
IX. The Last Sad Rites	*169*
X. Guns Abroad	*184*
XI. "No!"	*216*
XII. From Elephant to Donkey	*240*
XIII. A Chinaman's Chance	*258*
XIV. Mr. I. Goes to ▬▬▬▬	*272*
XV. We Gird for War	*279*
XVI. "The Oily Boid"	*299*
XVII. "Hearts and Flowers"	*312*
XVIII. A People's Peace	*325*

INTRODUCTION

$\mathcal{T}$HE WAR and the task of preserving our liberties are so engrossing and so demanding that I have sought surcease recently by letting my mind wander vagrantly into the past whenever it had a few minutes to spare. It is good for one to occupy his thoughts, even if intermittently, with more agreeable matters than the torpedoing of ships, the bombing of civilian populations, and rape and murder and horrible destruction.

I have not only turned my thoughts loose in such intervals as I could take out from pressing official duties, I have had as an aid in that regard notes that I jotted down before I ever had a thought that, someday, I would find myself occupying a Government position. So it has been a comparatively simple matter to rearrange and amplify certain of these notes into such of a permanent record as is represented by this volume.

A "five-foot shelf" could easily be filled with the books that have been published about Washington during the past few years. We have had Washington served up to us in every style. Then the war came along to increase the already abundant harvest of tomes, documented and otherwise, about Washington people, past and present, Washington events, and Washington as a city. Some versatile authors, who write more dogmatically when not inconvenienced by facts, haven't even felt it necessary to come to Washington in order to equip themselves to discuss "intimately" the backstage of the Nation's Capital.

This, *The Autobiography of a Curmudgeon,* perversely, and therefore characteristically, is not "just another" book about Washington. I would be temerarious indeed if I undertook to compete with all of the good, bad, and indifferent efforts that have been made to portray the American scene as it unfolds at the seat of our Government.

We do not have tea at the White House with Dolly Madison; nor roam about, stiff-necked, with Grandfather John Adams or Grandson John Quincy. We do not share the anxieties of nor attempt to say what Abraham Lincoln should have done in the circumstances. We do not skylark with Peggy O'Neill Eaton or luxuriate in shirt-sleeved democracy with the terrible-tempered Mr. Jackson. We do not frolic all over the White House with the first brood of Roosevelts, nor take mile upon mile of snapshots of the eagerly peripatetic members of the second. We do not slip into 1600 Pennsylvania Avenue with something on the hip to meet the Ohio gang, nor laugh with Taft, nor eat sausages and buckwheat cakes at public expense with the parsimonious Coolidge, nor yawn with Hoover.

The Autobiography of a Curmudgeon represents an attempt—feeble and jaundiced though it may be—to give a candid exposition of certain trends and episodes that particularly relate to newspapers and politics as I have encountered them, not only during the past ten years in Washington, but previously in Chicago and other heterogeneous centers.

(Forgive the repetitious personal pronoun "I," but frankly I don't know how to write an autobiography without it. "The 'great I,'" wrote Stephen Spender, "is an unfortunate intruder.")

If, in these pages, I have hurled an insult at anyone, be it known that such was my deliberate intent, and I may as well state flatly now that it will be useless and a waste of time to ask me to say that I am sorry.

To paraphrase a familiar epitaph:

> Unhonored by his fellows he grew old
>   And trod the path to hell,
> But there were many things he might have told
>   And did not tell.

HAROLD L. ICKES.

Headwaters Farm,
Olney, Maryland.

CHAPTER ONE

A BLESSED EVENT?

Love your life, poor as it is. You may perhaps have some
pleasant, thrilling, glorious hours, even in a poorhouse.
—HENRY DAVID THOREAU.

As THIS TALE of mine unfolds, provided that you will have
the appetite and the endurance to stick to it, it will
be made clear enough what a curmudgeon is—therefore what
I am—and you will discover why I have appropriated the
label as exclusively my own. No one will ever know what
I have gone through to win it, nor can anyone possibly fore-
tell what I am prepared to undergo in defense of it.

Mouth-to-ear rumors about a public man are almost
without exception so fiercely barbed that most people would
hesitate to repeat them out loud if they should be said of a
private citizen. The private citizen has easy recourse to the
courts—protection under the law. So, too, I grant you, in
theory, has the public man, but the more public he is, the
greater the probability that should he prove that he didn't
actually commit the crime, the publicity that he would get
would leave the world convinced that he was in the neighborhood when it occurred. In other words, the people can
believe virtually anything concerning a man in public life
provided that it is sufficiently unbelievable.

1

To illustrate what I mean—should someone start a report that I squirt boiling oil on a visitor whom I wish to run out of my office, few people would doubt it. In fact, they would prefer to think it not at all improbable. Let it be whispered that I frequently order the Department of the Interior elevators shut down and all steps and landings thoroughly greased just before quitting time, and before you can repeat the second verse of the national anthem the story has become a part of my public reputation. The relish that the average individual seems to have for such exhibitions of depravity lends support to any statement about a public official, no matter how grotesque it may be.

Some people don't like the pitch of a public man's voice. It's raspy, or too loud, or unmanly, or too sugary. In private life, the same voice may have the sedative qualities of Lawrence Tibbett's baritone, but coming out of a public man it is unendurable. Thank God it's a simple matter to switch off the radio!

Conservatives kick a public man's repute on the basis of what they deplore as his liberalism. Liberals construct the reputation of the same man on the strength of what they scorn as his conservatism. It doesn't make much difference what a public man holds to or does—he's damned in any case. Thomas Hardy wrote about "the shabby corner of God's allotment where He lets the nettles grow, and where all unbaptized infants, notorious drunkards, suicides, and other conjecturally damned are laid." That men and women in public life are the *"others"* who are "conjecturally damned," I have no serious doubt.

The dictionary says that a curmudgeon is "an avaricious, grasping fellow; a churl." I am that—and more. Besides, I am a *self-made* one. My handiwork takes on added interest when it is borne in mind that I have had few patterns to go by and was in fact well on my way to curmudgeonery before I realized the course that I was taking.

As I have scanned the pages of literature and history, I have found them crowded with accounts of curmudgeons. But on analysis they prove not to have been *self-made*. Ebenezer Scrooge was one so long as he was on his own. Dr. Jekyll was another after he had mastered magic in ten easy lessons. Queen Elizabeth was a fair sort of curmudgeon for a woman, although outranked by Catherine the Great and the De' Medici female, to say nothing of one or two contemporary members of the "gentle" sex that I could—and may before I finish—name. Then there were also Bluebeard and Danton and Samuel Johnson and Morgan the Pirate and Henry VIII and Billy the Kid—and now Harold Ickes. It may be that most of us in this line have been misunderstood and, as a consequence, misjudged. For the others, I offer no defense. I speak only for myself as a once shy, modest (who is there to believe it today?) boy, who never chewed tobacco after the first trial "chaw," who never smoked until he had finished college, or knew the taste of beer until he was twenty-three, or ventured to kiss a girl until it dawned on him that he might be missing something.[1]

To be a self-made anything, especially if it is done "the hard way," is in the true American tradition—although not in

---

[1] I had no social graces. There were no parties or dancing schools into which I entered. Social life revolved principally about the church. There was the big annual Sunday-school picnic held up in some delightful mountain spot and to which we carted enough food to gorge the A.E.F. We invariably returned retchingly miserable from having tried to do all that the A.E.F. would have done to the provender after a day of exhausting maneuvers. I don't know how my mother stood up under the burden of our annual picnics, which were not picnics at all so much as they were gluttonous Bacchanalia. We really played a mean knife and fork in those days—or rather claws and fangs.

that so benignly exploited by Oliver Optic. It would take the
pen of a Voynich to do me full justice. In the absence of
a Voynich I shall undertake to do the job myself. I shall by
my own hand be revealed in all the glory of America's No. 1
Curmudgeon, or Sour Puss. I want the account to be an inspiration to all of those who may aspire to grouse their way
through life or, what is even more complicated, through
public life. I want them to believe me when I say that I have
had a scrumptious time learning the ropes myself. I want
them to profit by my experience, and though some may hope
to excel me in curmudgeonly achievements, I think that it
were better for their complexes if they did not aim quite so
high.

Unlike most boys, I never wanted to be a policeman or a
fireman, but I did have a vagrant ambition to be a carpenter.
I probably wouldn't have succeeded as a carpenter. Besides,
a carpenter builds instead of tearing down. There was a time
when I was, owing to my mother, in danger of becoming, if
not exactly a mellow and urbane human being, at least a
reasonable facsimile thereof. How I escaped developing into
an ordinary soul doomed to pass the collection plate on a
Sunday and go to lodge meeting on Monday night, I will
never know. The toils with which a devoted mother surrounded me almost destroyed my future. It would have been
a simple matter, as I review my career, to have grown up a
panty-waist. I claim sole credit for having rescued myself
from such a ghastly fate. "There, but by the grace of God,
go I!"

I shudder to think how I was raised to dust and sweep and
wash dishes and knead dough and baste the beef and turn
(and burn) the toast and flip flapjacks, and of the hours
that I spent with my flowers and my chickens!! I was even

brought up to do a fairly good job of ironing except for the fancier stuff. I was pinch-hit nursemaid, wood-chopper, fire-builder and tender, chicken-executioner—more useful than ornamental, I think, was my reputation in those formative years.

However, my public repute today does not stem from the activities of my youth. Does anyone care that at the age of sixteen I had read almost fifteen hundred books, including theological tomes which were the tools of an elder deceased cousin when he was a student at the Morgan Park Theological Seminary? Is there anyone interested in knowing that among the fifteen hundred books were the Bible, which I read from "kiver to kiver," and Prescott's many-volumed history of the United States? No—thrice no! I also read *Heaven and Hell,* and *Immersion vs. Sprinkling,* in the hope that the former might at least be lurid. It wasn't. For the information of its publishers I may say that it made absolutely no contri-bution to my career as a curmudgeon. But *I. vs. S.* did, be-cause it was passionately controversial. I will charge the publishers of it nothing for this plug.

But why so fast? No authentic biography, even that of a sour ball, can be written without an accouchement to begin with. I must, before I write anything more, be authentically and officially born, which I may say I was on March 15, 1874, to Jesse B. W. and Martha Ann (McEwen) McCune Ickes, the second of seven children. Yes, figure it out for yourself if you want to, but take my word for it, any way you subtract, it leaves me sixty-nine in the red as of today. The sprouting of this seedling thistle was accomplished in a commodious and comfortable farmhouse in Frankstown Township, Blair County, Pennsylvania, which happened to be the home of his maternal grandfather, in which his mother herself had been born.

Originally, the Ickeses got themselves out of Germany, which is even a better place to get out of today than it was then. This may account for at least some of the idiosyncrasies out of which my reputation has been contrived. Eight or ten generations ago we Ickeses settled in Montgomery County, Pennsylvania, where one of us caught up with a young Swedish-Finnish lass in New Sweden, on the Delaware River, and married her. Another ancestor intermarried with a French family. Some time later another Ickes managed to get into the Revolutionary War by sneaking under the tent as a bountyman at the age of sixteen.

On my mother's side I spring from a line of Scots who, before Revolutionary times, hit the trail along the Juniata River up into the eastern slopes of the Allegheny Mountains of Pennsylvania, where the Ickeses were to overtake them. Grandfather (McEwen) McCune was a member of the State Legislature, and his father was, for twenty-seven years, the nonlegal member of the County Court of three in original Huntingdon County. Which probably accounts for some of my lifelong preference for politics.

Grandparents on both sides, I am told, were in better than comfortable circumstances. I never had any visible proof of it, having come along a half of a century too late. There are other family legends which, as in most cases, are highly unreliable even as a basis for such a loosely built lean-to as a public repute—self-glorifying expressions designed to refurbish prestige or hide soup stains.

Neither side of the family was widely traveled. Having crossed the Atlantic when it was tortuous going, they were only too glad to settle down and stay put. On the average, in both lines, they received as good educations as were to be had in those days. A respectable number of us loved books and read whatever came to hand. Here and there were a few professional men—doctors and preachers—but generally speaking, we were of the soil and proud of it. Mother had ambitions for me along theological lines—Presbyterian, to be specific. Lacking any milk of human kindness in my mental udders, I would have been foredoomed to failure. Far better to be a highly successful curmudgeon than an indifferent preacher. I thought so then, and I think so today.

My father was raised a Baptist; my mother a Presbyterian. The original Ickeses were strict German Lutherans who contributed to the building of the Swamp Lutheran Church, the first edifice of its kind in America. This solidly built church still stands, and its well-populated graveyard contains hundreds of tombstones, many of them now crumbling, on which the bones in the graves that they mark are identified in German script. (My better judgment tells me that the less said about this, the better. Some columnist will be giving it out that behind my disagreeable exterior lurks a Nazi sympathizer.)

Somewhere in the Swamp Lutheran Church graveyard lie my great-great-grandparents, who, happily for them, were laid there before their grandson—my grandfather—was immersed into the Baptist Church. Some of my curmudgeonish disposition is very likely a hangover from this wayward Lutheran, who took fiendish delight in assuring my very strict Calvinistic mother that the floor of hell was paved with Presbyterians.

My earliest recollections as a boy in Altoona go back to the "green corner," a big frame building owned by Grandfather Ickes. It was there that my father was set up in business as the proprietor of a notions store, but father had "notions" of his own that ran to play more than to work, and of course the business folded up. Father played on the town baseball team, and when he quit playing he took to umpiring. He was an industrious "jiner." He was seldom, if ever, home of an evening. So far as his family was concerned he was a pleasant, though scarcely more than a casual, acquaintance.

Among other things, father joined the volunteer fire department, and continued his membership in it even after we had moved so far away from the engine house that it was physically impossible for him to get to it before the fire had burned itself out, or had succumbed to the efforts of the other members of the troop. It was a major family feat, I assure you, to get my father up from a warm bed, dressed, and on his way to a night fire that was already lighting the sky. I can see him now, leaving the house at a canter, helmet awry, adjusting himself to the complicated outfit for a set-to with the flame that was either spent or under control long before his arrival.

While I was a boy at home, I never knew my father to go to church unless there was a funeral on tap, for which gala event he presented himself in one of his choicest and most elaborate secret-order regalias. Not long after my mother's death, and to the utter amazement of everyone in town, he up and joined the Second Presbyterian Church, to which my mother had long loyally belonged. What his father must have said to St. Peter!

I was taught to believe that Presbyterianism was the quickest and the only sure way to grace. There might be other roads to Heaven, but why run the risk? We might tolerate Methodists but we were not encouraged to think much, or too well, of Baptists. But there could be little danger of my wandering after false gods. I had been brought up altogether too strictly for that. I could not doubt that the Presbyterian Church was the straightest, if indeed not the sole, portal to an eternal life where I would at last sprout wings and put in my time playing a harp.

Politically, we were Republicans on both sides. Once my father was, briefly, an aberrant Greenbacker, and the family never quite lived down the disgrace of it. Our house was bright with lights and gay with bunting when a Republican torchlight procession passed. It was a complete blackout, however, when the unspeakable Democrats tramped by.

Father ran for the select council once in a strongly Democratic ward and was licked by four votes. And I had peddled his cards! One of the kindest things some people say of me is that I have shown an uncanny ability to pick losers! Why, bless you, many times I have supported a candidate, knowing from the very outset that he couldn't win. To lose with a candidate you believe in gives one something to grumble about. Picking a winner is, after all, no great shucks. Going down with a candidate that you swear by, rather than swear at, is much better for your disposition, particularly if you are dead set upon swimming against the current. I have never in my life supported a man because and only because I thought that he was sure to win. That would have put me in the uncomfortable position of having to defend when I have always preferred to attack. As a delegate to the Republican National Convention in Chicago in 1920, I yelled "No" —one of two or three in that vast crowd to do so—on the motion to make the nomination of Warren Harding unanimous. Was I wrong? Well, at any rate, I lived to stick out my tongue at my erstwhile Progressive comrades who had scurried into the "normalcy" camp.

One factor that may have contributed to my father's defeat was the influence of the Pennsylvania Railroad over the politics, as well as over the business life, of the City of Altoona. The "railroad set" didn't seem to care much for Jesse Ickes, although later he was elected and re-elected City Comptroller and died during that incumbency.

From certain points of view, my boyhood was interesting, but not exciting. I took prizes for regular attendance at Sunday school and church, for reciting the shorter catechism, and for memorizing the minister's texts for a year. I joined up with the YPSCE (my first alphabetical venture), escorted my mother to prayer meeting every Wednesday night, helped with the housework, and read everything that I could get hold of, including the "begat" chapters of Deuteronomy. Who would have dreamed that a curmudgeon would grow out of such fertilizer as this? When the time came that I must decide upon a career, my problem was to choose one where there would be little and feeble competition. It took me a long time to decide that I ought to excel as a curmudgeon, and I leave it to 134,000,000 Americans to say with what degree of success I have carried out my design.

I was sixteen years old when my mother died. My Aunt Julia had come on from Pittsburgh and to her my mother had confided her hope that her eldest sister, my favorite, Aunt Ada, who was on her way from Chicago, would take back with her as her own my little sister Mary. Aunt Ada responded with great generosity. She not only undertook Mary, but after communicating with Uncle Felix, she decided that I must also go back with her to Chicago. In the circumstances, there was nothing that I so much desired, and yet it was a heavy-hearted young man that Aunt Ada took with her, along with my sister Mary, to the wicked metropolis of Illinois shortly after the funeral.

My Uncle Felix and Aunt Ada owned a drugstore in Englewood. Now a drugstore was my dish, because I had worked for two months in one in Altoona, where, uncensored, I one day dispensed laudanum for paregoric. Fortunately, the life of the child to whom the laudanum was administered was saved. I have no doubt that I was actually nearer death from fright than the child was from laudanum poisoning. That a druggist should permit a greenhorn kid to choose between two bottles, as alike as peas, standing side by side and bearing Latin labels of striking similarity, when one of them contained poison, was enough to start one off on a career of perversity, if there had been nothing else to give it impetus.

This was in the summer of 1890. It was the Chicago of horsecars and cable cars. The Auditorium, the pride of the city, with its wonderful audience hall, now marked for demolition, had just been completed. The South Side elevated was being built. The University of Chicago, which I was later to attend, may have been a dream in the mind of William Rainey Harper, that truly prodigious man among educators, but no one else knew anything about it. The "filthy rich" drove behind high-stepping horses drawing ornate equipages from which tall-hatted coachmen and footmen surveyed their surroundings with a truly devastating scorn. Michigan Avenue, on the South Side, was fronted on both sides by the extravagantly built and maintained mansions of the first or second generations of families that had ventured into the dangerous wilds of the West to carve out fortunes.

And had they brought home the bacon! To say nothing of sleeping cars!

Bicycles were beginning to multiply. They became so much of a menace to life and limb that the City Council paused long enough in the routine of voting juicy franchises to Charles T. Yerkes, an ex-convict from Philadelphia, and his associates, to impose speed restrictions. It was the day of full-length and ample skirts, of long mutton-leg-sleeve waists that terminated in high collars. In time it would not be a sin, or even an immodesty, to wear divided skirts while riding a tandem bicycle with a swain who imagined that he was in hot pursuit. If a girl wanted to swim in the lake, custom required that she be fully and completely clothed, even to a skirt covering the full bloomers underneath. If a man had ventured to the lake shore in trunks, he would have been hauled in for indecency.

I didn't like any of it. The Simon Legree in me had not yet developed to a point where the bile that I generated was sufficient unto itself. I missed my mother and my friends. I longed for Altoona. It was three years before I would admit that the skyscrapers of Chicago were as big and as architecturally satisfying as the three-story wooden buildings fronting on Altoona's own main street; that the homes of Chicago were as comfortable or as well built as those of the city from which I had come; or that even the wide spaces, the beautiful parks, or Lake Michigan itself could compare with the steep hills, the faraway mountains, or the artificial lagoon of Lakemont Park that lay midway between Altoona and Holidaysburg.

Here were the intangible ingredients out of which a careful architect was to build a robust curmudgeonly character. The start may have been as unconscious to me as it was unperceived by others, but as the structure took form I was able to evolve a code that I have hoped would guide others who might attempt, even if in vain, to emulate me. And I still hope so.

CHAPTER TWO

AN ASSISTANT DRUGGIST'S ASSISTANT

Much may be made of a Scotchman if he be caught young.
—SAMUEL JOHNSON.

NO DELEGATION of bluenoses with a police escort met the sprouting curmudgeon from Altoona when he landed in Chicago on that hot July day in 1890 under the wing of his Aunt Ada. If old Mayor DeWitt C. Creiger knew that a sixteen-year locust was blowing into his bailiwick, he didn't get excited. But the time was to come when this same youngster, sweet-tempered enough to begin with, was to have to wear a false beard to escape delegations of city fathers come to meet the Public Works Administrator (a horny crustacean by then!) who had acquired the penultimate say as to what towns and counties and states might have Federal funds for projects, and how much.

The adolescent Harold Perverse had no inkling of such a future. The dispirited youngster who tumbled off the train at the straggling Englewood station, clinging desperately to his aunt, had no notion that he was headed for pre-eminence among Scrooges. If he had, it might have made him feel that he had something to live for after all.

Had it not been for his Aunt Ada, who was one of those

members of the family who loved books and who swore by education, our young gadfly might have abandoned his schooling then and there. My Uncle Felix had not gone beyond the eighth grade himself, and it was his opinion that this was far enough for all practical purposes—his purposes, anyway. But he didn't happen to be the boss, even in his drugstore. It was my aunt who had attended a school of pharmacy and who held a diploma as a druggist. My uncle was by rank the assistant. The store did not produce enough income to support a clerk, so that my uncle was willing to suffer the presence of a hard-working nephew so long as he was willing to open up at six in the morning and stay with it until ten at night. Aunt Ada's conviction that I should go to school prevailed over the contrary opinion of the assistant pharmacist that I was a better investment as a clerk than as a scholar.

When I graduated from the eighth grade in Altoona it had taken me a year longer than I would have gone through in normal course because a peppery teacher (a pretty good amateur female curmudgeon, I have since concluded, she must have been) set me back because I had laughed uproariously at the wrong time. From this experience I learned not to laugh, particularly at the wrong person, except at the right time if there should be one. This was education in reverse. I was to learn that politicians and scriveners don't like to be laughed at either.

Englewood High School admitted me on certificate, and for three years I was to tramp back and forth the weary mile that stretched between the drugstore and the school. At the beginning of the second year, I fell under the spell of the second of the four remarkable women who have had such an influence on my life that, if it had not been for intrinsic churlish qualities that I clung to desperately, might have turned me out a Casper Milquetoast instead of a hellhound. This young lady, Agnes Rogers—lovely, young, and pretty—I mistook for a member of the senior class before I learned that she was indeed a member of the faculty. It was she who stirred in me the ambition to go to college and convinced me that, by hook or by crook, it could be managed. She recommended Cornell, her own Alma Mater. I acquired a catalogue but that was as near as I got to Ithaca, entirely because of financial exigencies. The new University of Chicago, in an environment familiar to me, made me change my course, if not my purpose.

With college ahead of me, I decided to negotiate the four years of high school in three. My inspiration undertook, on her own time out of hours, to give me first- and second-year Greek. During the summer between my second and third years I wrote out in English the four orations of Cicero that were the required third-year Latin. My purpose, which I later carried out, was to attend Cicero classes and at the same time carry Vergil. I could not have done both of these Latin courses without predigesting one of them, considering the other extra work that I had to do.

I continued to open the drugstore at six, washing the showcases, the bottles, and the windows, and sweeping the floors and making and keeping the fires when those cold winds blew down from Medicine Hat and points northwest. I churned the ice cream. Those were the days when a drugstore was a place that sold drugs—not a bastard mountebank restaurant, hardware emporium, and branch library. I dispensed simple medicines, and in time came to fill prescriptions. My frightening experience with *tr.opii* in Altoona had taught me such a lesson that I never made a mistake during the three years that I worked in my uncle's drugstore—which was long enough to qualify me for certification as a pharmacist's assistant had my ambitions lain in that direction. During the summers, and in sufficient quantities for the inevitable winters that were to follow, I filled by hand thousands of quinine capsules of varying sizes. I knew how to put up citrate of magnesia and concoct Seidlitz powders.

To show that I overlooked no opportunity of self-development along the line of the career that, even if nebulously, I must already have decided upon for myself, I early learned that a Seidlitz powder can be an offensive thing. When a customer whom I favored, or who was merely neutral to me, sought the relief that such an imbibition would give him, I would dissolve each powder in the smallest amount of water possible. That made it easy to take. When a pet aversion applied, I—the burgeoning killjoy—used a lot of water in a bigger glass, in which case the mixture drizzled down the shirt front and exploded into the nostrils and the eyes of my victim. Besides which, he had to pay for the treatment.

For two full weeks during my third and last year I substituted in high school for one of the teachers of Cicero. I had entered as a member of the class, over which I temporarily presided, as a freshman. I can remember the joy with which, the first morning, erstwhile classmates hailed my induction behind the teacher's desk by the principal of the school. They thought that they were going to have a lot of fun with me. But they didn't. I am not the kind that people can have fun with.

An ambitious classmate had started a weekly magazine which he allowed me to edit—as in most of my enterprises, without compensation—when his hands were otherwise too full. I became the president of the senior class, a circumstance that is easily understood when I reveal that I had jumped into it surreptitiously from behind. Not being a contemporary, I was little known. My nomination might have been in the nature of a joke, but it turned out to be a poor one for my opponent.

At graduation, I sang high tenor—or as high as I could get, which, I fear, wasn't high enough—on the male octet. I also delivered the "welcoming" address. Even when I think back now in the darkness of the night, I am able to blush at the memory of that oratorical effort. What a speech!

Nothing short of a cutaway suit would serve on so memorable an occasion. So my aunt wrote to my father and I bombarded him for weeks. My father had sent me no money at all during the three years that I had been away from him, and I was still wearing the meager clothes with which I had left Altoona, except for bare replacements of parts, such as shoes, underwear, socks, shirts, and so on. Another uncle, Samuel (McEwen) McCune, had agreed to supply these incidentals and I have never forgotten the satisfaction that I felt when I returned to him every one of the approximately $125 that he had advanced to keep me groomed; an average of $42 a year.

It almost required a Presidential order to get that cutaway, but in the end my father did come across and I was able to appear in a becoming, if unfamiliar and unusual, manner upon the platform of the Englewood Presbyterian Church, where the graduation exercises were held.

Although president of my class, I was still on the shy side. I knew most of my classmates only casually. If I had had more experience, I would have realized that I shouldn't have accepted the presidency. To the very end there was a group that resented me as a carpetbagging intruder. Yes, even then!

This group had had a candidate of its own. This was the first of my dead-cat-throwing following, which was to increase with time.

Typhoid fever was epidemic in Chicago in 1893 and I was one of its many victims. Of it I nearly died, but I managed to disappoint my opponents and recover in time to return to high school with thinning hair, but with all of my lessons made up so that I could graduate with my class. My recollection is that, scholastically, I ranked within the first ten of my class of seventy-two. I believe this to be so, as well as that my general average for the three years was well above ninety, although these again may come under the heading of family legends.

That summer of 1893 I went back to Altoona for the first time since I had left it following my mother's death. I wanted to see what was left of my family and friends. The unpretentious frame home on a twenty-five-foot lot at 1518 Fifth Avenue, which we had built after Grandfather Ickes died, and which contained a bathroom but no sanitary plumbing, seemed quite different and strange. My sister Julia and I were alone in it except that, familiarly, my father ate and slept there. I luxuriated in freedom from school tasks and drugstore drudgery. I had determined to go to college and I did not believe that I could combine college and drugstore as I had high school and drugstore. Besides, I preferred some other way—an easier way if you will—of financing my higher education.

My father was not interested in my ambition and turned a stony ear to any and all appeals for help. I was never much at appeals, even then. I have since learned to say it more effectively with brickbats. I was easy to turn down because I was sensitive. Not yet was I an accomplished curmudgeon by any stretch of the imagination. Nor had I been kicked about enough for my own good. If I could have reached into the future for such an assortment of language as I came to acquire later, I might have been able to rattle a few reluctant dollars out of the pockets of a casehardened parent.

I found old friends in Altoona and I made new ones. I began to know girls for the first time, and I soon learned that I could get along with them in a comradely sort of way. But they were generally too smart for me. They cut circles around me. What later was to develop into a sporting event called "necking" was then in its puling infancy as "spooning." But although I was nineteen years old and had at least a beginning of the savoir faire that one is supposed to acquire in a big city, the time was still to come when I could put my arm around a girl, or even timidly clutch her hand.

Back in Chicago again, I was fortunate to discover a school friend whose father knew President Harper of the newly opened University of Chicago. The father was willing to introduce me and explain my situation. I have always been grateful for the friendly interview that President Harper gave me. He was kindness itself, and gave no indication that I was imposing upon valuable time. He told me that I would be given remunerative work and he indicated that if the paying of tuition became too much of a load, I would be carried on the books of the university until I could repay, an arrangement that was resorted to for part of my tuition and which was a lifesaver for me. I employed my talents as well as I could, whether in my uncle's drugstore, where I was still in charge of the mop pail and the cleaning rags, or whether teaching night school or doing odd jobs around the university, such as screwing little rubber cushions on the feet of the

My mother at the age
of 16. I was very fond
of her.

And my father, who didn't
give one a chance to decide
whether to be fond of him
or not.

The Ickes domicile at 1518—5th Avenue, Altoona, Pa., after it had been built as a one-family mansion. I didn't happen to be on the front porch at the time the above picture was taken, but the ones you see there belonged to the brood of seven little Ickeses. The boyish picture, I blushingly admit, is of me. And I call your particular attention to the subject of a high school oration! Who, indeed, is man but a boy grown up!

classroom chairs. Not an inspiring job, but it helped to do the business.

The seven years that I spent in Chicago in labor, sweat, and occasional tears before I was able to acquire my A.B. at the University of Chicago were a gradual metamorphosis into a radically different spiritual and emotional life. During the three years that I made my home with Uncle Felix and Aunt Ada I continued to attend church and Sunday school regularly. My Aunt Ada had been brought up in the same strict Presbyterianism as my mother, but while she never deviated from the sure tenets of that faith, she had, probably as a result of wider social contacts in a larger city, become just a little less strait-laced. This is not to be understood as implying that she did not keep my feet, as well as those of Mary and her own two stepdaughters, from straying from the only true path. There were times when Uncle Felix would decide to set a public example by decking himself out in his "funeral suit" and shiny high silk hat and going to church. At such times I would be left behind to tend store. But usually Uncle Felix excused himself on the plea that he could not possibly be spared, and then Aunt Ada herded her entire younger flock to church.

I wasn't one who found it easy, or even possible, to discuss intellectual quandaries or emotional crises with my elders. I had begun to be aware of the pretended adult certainty that was so often merely a protective dogmatism. And so, after I had been at college for perhaps two years, I found myself beset with doubts about the religious sanctions with which my elders had tried to fortify me. I had to work altogether too hard to find it possible to attend church regularly, or even to go to Sunday school, which was more to my liking. The Englewood church seemed rather far away when I was living in Hyde Park near the university, and that meant carfare, which was scarce. I ventured into the Hyde Park Presbyterian Church once or twice only to come away with a feeling that I had been trespassing on the privacy of an aristocratic and private club whose members were not used to rubbing elbows with commoners.

Finally I could no longer whistle to heel the serious questions that the pursuit of knowledge—especially in the fields of anthropology and ethnology, in which I was specializing—assailed me. So I had to go into a life-and-death struggle with my religious beliefs. I was not sure but that God would strike me down for venturing to question articles of faith that I had accepted as implicitly as I had my own being. But I could no longer refrain from questioning certain Calvinistic theories that seemed hard and cruel. It was strangely impossible to believe that some such could be justified by the life and teachings of Jesus Christ.

And so I came to have little active interest and practically no personal participation in any formal religion. Ritualism has never appealed to me. And, having disengaged myself from the strait jacket of Calvinism, I found that I could be really tolerant of other religions and of other denominational concepts. However, I still admire the strength and character of Calvinism. But I came to feel that the core of real Christianity, as it is the heart of true religion, lies in that noble utterance of Jesus Christ, "Therefore all things whatsoever ye would that men should do to you, do ye even so to them." My belief is that the Sermon on the Mount is good enough and sufficient for any man to live by or to die by. And so, after great spiritual travail, I have come to have peace of mind so far as religion is concerned.

My main source of income while at college was as a teacher

on the night shift of the public schools. I taught English to a class of adult Scandinavians, mainly Swedes, who had come recently to America. How earnest they were and how assiduous to learn a language that, evidently, was very difficult for them! I had taken an open examination to qualify myself as a teacher, and was bitterly disappointed that my name was not on the first list. I learned later that this was due to my youth.

In this case there was the unexpected interposition of fate in the person of a young girl whom I did not even know by sight. She had entered high school after I had, and I knew her brother. Her father had to do with the hiring and firing of night-school teachers. It was years after that I learned from her brother how she had plagued her father without surcease until he had given me the job without which I would have failed in my ambition.

Under the regulations, a night-school class was kept going only so long as the attendance averaged forty. It was difficult to hold even a band of earnest Scandinavians together when spring moved in. Nor, at best, did the night schools stay open for a longer period than six months. This would mean, at the maximum, an income of $240 a year during the first two years. For the third year the salary was $45 a month, and thereafter $50. I taught for four years, but none of them was for a full year, so that my income was small indeed when it is considered that my tuition at first was $90 a year, later to be raised to $100, and that I had to eat, buy books, pay fees, and purchase at least replacements of my barely minimum clothing. And when I say "minimum" I mean *minimum*. I had just enough to keep me covered and out of jail. I did tutoring and odd jobs to piece out, but it was all hard work and poor pay. I would have borrowed money if I could, but two or three timid overtures made in directions that might and could have helped without feeling it fell flat, and I was forced to continue on my own. I have been glad of it since. I didn't have to feel kindly toward anybody.

At the end of the third year I needed to make up work that I had missed during my first year while out toiling for my bread and occasional butter. To do this, I decided to continue during the summer, thus making an unbroken attendance from October of my junior year to my graduation in June of my senior year. But to do this, I had to have some help. Once again I undertook to assay my father for gold. There was mighty little gold for me in "them thar" pockets. After much effort I persuaded him to pledge me $10 a month for six months, to be sent to me semimonthly. I never knew, however, when the "gusher" would dry up.

During that last summer I was able to live on father's $10 monthly remittance. The university was taking care of my tuition, either by credits for services performed or by means of a debit to be carried on the books until I was able to repay, which I did, in full, shortly after graduation. I was living double in a single room in Snell Hall with an equally impecunious classmate and my room rent was cared for similarly. But I had to eat, pay laundry bills, buy books and supplies, and take care of some carfare and other inescapable miscellaneous items. I solved the problem by managing to live on one 15-cent meal a day throughout the three summer months, with, customarily, Sunday supper, manfully walked for, at the Adkinsons. To Mrs. Ingham's "shanty," across Fifty-seventh Street from my room in Snell Hall, I would go the middle of each day and get the greatest quantity of provender that 15 cents would buy. Fortunately, Mrs. Ingham's food was good, and there was no ceiling on bread and butter.

My customary diet was fried ham. My roommate, Billy (William Otis) Wilson, also put on the feed bag at "Mother" Ingham's, but we never went together. Each was too proud to display his poverty to the other. Later, he was to have a distinguished legal career in Wyoming, where he served as Attorney General.

In my senior year, while carrying an extra course in order to have enough credits for my diploma, I engaged in a number of extracurricular activities. I was on the track team as a performer in the mile walk, now as mercifully extinct as the dodo. Amos Alonzo Stagg coached the team. I was editor in chief of the college weekly; manager of the university tennis team; organizer and manager of the Western Intercollegiate Tennis Association; president of the Republican Club; treasurer of the American Republican College League; a member of the senior class executive committee; and a member of the debating team. I even took the time to become a charter member of my college fraternity, Phi Delta Theta. All of this on a foundation of 15 cents' worth of fried ham a day!

On a certain dearly prized day in June of 1897, I did not go up to the platform to receive my sheepskin from President Harper. My clothes were too shabby and worn. Diplomas could not be had on tick, and that hard-to-come-by $10 had put me on the ragged edge of bankruptcy.

At that time I must have been a sorry-looking specimen of curmudgeonery. I still had a viewpoint that was a combination of hope and air castles. Newspapers hadn't poisoned my life or destroyed any of my pet illusions. I was still ignorant as to what extent corruption was rampant in public life. I had yet to learn what a pitiless pounding a man takes when, witnessing an underdog being kicked about, he raises hell, or when he goes into the service of the public. Don't misunderstand me—I'm not complaining. If I were to do it again, I would tread the same road, and, except for a few details, have it come out substantially as it has.

However, I don't mind saying that there were a few things that I would ask to have changed—for others, as well as for myself. I wouldn't want again to wear ear muffs, a heavy ulster, and gloves when studying—a practice that I had to follow more than once during some of the bitter cold months when I was on my own and away from my aunt's roof. I hope never again to have to break the ice in the pitcher for my morning ablutions. I wouldn't want to have to depend, as I did, on newspapers—especially the *Chicago Tribune*—to keep me warm, putting layers of them over my mattress and between the covers. They served the useful purpose then of keeping me from freezing stiff. Later they were to burn me up on more than one occasion.

If there is anyone still following me who really wants to acquire a curmudgeonly disposition, let him limit himself to 15 cents' worth of food (mostly fried ham) a day, or live in Chicago for even one cold winter in a heatless, bare shell of a house. I promise him that, in no time, he will be able to curdle the sweetest milk that ever came off the farm, merely by looking at it.

Add to such Spartan living politics and newspapers and columnists, as I later did, and—well, we're coming to that.

CHAPTER THREE

NEWSHAWK

Some day I'll pass by the Great Gates of Gold,
And see a man pass through unquestioned and bold.
"A Saint?" I'll ask, and old Peter'll reply:
"No, he carries a pass—he's a newspaper guy."
                                        —EDWIN MEADE ROBINSON.

THERE WAS NO ONE to whom I could turn for a job when I needed one that would support me even in the style to which I had become inured after seven years of lean living and uneven thinking. But a job I had to have. I had learned to exist sparingly enough, but I found that it took *some* money to do even that. A friend on the university faculty thought that I might make a good teacher. Accordingly, I posted my name and qualifications with an agency. A high school in Aurora, Illinois, nibbled at but found no savor in me, and no one else was interested. With my capacity for insufferableness, what a teacher I would have made—in a reform school!

At this point, I rubbed up a very attenuated acquaintance with an editorial writer on the *Chicago Record* who had played on the football team. He introduced me to the city editor, who allowed, without enthusiasm, that he would try me out as a space writer. Five dollars a column for what might get by the crabbed copyreader! That wouldn't cost anything—at least not enough to worry the cashier—because I would be given no assignment that a regular staff man could cover. Even with this connection, therefore, I still had one foot on the brink of starvation and the other on a banana peel.

The *Record's* city editor wore a shiny Prince Albert coat, the collar and shoulders of which were white with dandruff from his too-long hair. He had a forelock that he kept tossing mournfully out of his eyes. He gave me only one admonition, and that was on no account ever to turn in a story in which I described a person as an "old veteran." It was his theory that a "veteran" was ipso facto "old" and that the two words in that juxtaposition represented tautology at its worst, rivaling "two twins" or "present incumbent." It took me years to get it straightened out in my head that a "veteran" may be a very young person indeed.

Equipped with this comprehensive course in journalism, I felt ready to tackle any assignment. I should not have been surprised that the first chore given to me was to run out to the university for an interview with President Harper on some trivial matter. Perhaps I wasn't, but at any rate that's where I went and, as luck would have it, a few minutes after I had turned in my copy, the mane-waving editor came into the city room calling loudly for my blood for having sinned the deadly sin of using the expression "old veteran."

I earned 75 cents of Publisher Victor Lawson's millions that week, which didn't make me feel either sorry for Lawson or confident that I was substantially on the way to wealth or fame. I was trying to balance on the foot that was standing on the banana skin. Fortunately, I never had a desire for wealth—at least not such a desire as would lead me to make its acquisition the chief end and aim of my existence. And

as to fame, I had never given it a thought. What is fame anyway but, as Mr. Dooley once said, "what somewan writes on
yer tombstone."

At the end of the several weeks that followed I managed
to nick Victor Lawson for a few emaciated dollars—just
enough to keep my body and what remained of my soul in
one piece. Then one afternoon the shaggy city editor came in
looking more shaggy and more downhearted than usual. My
wistful self was sitting alone in the city room. There being
no one else present to abuse, he let me have it.

"Ickes," he said dolefully, "if things don't pick up around
here pretty soon there is going to be a shaking up of dry
bones and you will be one of the dry bones."

What cheerful news on an empty stomach! But luck, unlike the Hoover prosperity of the future, was really around
the corner, although not quite ready to reveal itself. It
wasn't enough to furnish a chicken for every pot, but it was
going to be enough to permit me to eat more regularly at
Kohlsaat's justly celebrated one-arm lunchroom. (If Kohlsaat had not later come to fancy himself as a great publisher
and editor, he might have continued indefinitely to earn big
money by dishing out a quarter of an apple pie for a nickel
and a sturdy helping of doughnuts and coffee for a dime.)

My skulking city editor, during the days that followed,
gave me some assignments that I suspect in his heart he
hoped and believed would be as sterile as a china egg. But I
was feeling too keenly the pangs of hunger not to put all of
the drive that I had left into them. Besides, I developed and
followed leads of my own, with the result that, in the course
of two weeks of hard work and hunger, I had produced three
beats. They weren't stories of the first magnitude, but enterprising newspapermen in those days set great store by scoops

of whatever importance and sought by their persistence and ingenuity to achieve them. They were not satisfied then merely to avoid being scooped. We had not yet reached the time when, what with the press services and the radio, a man can't be scooped, try he ever so hard. Great things—scoops! Or they used to be.

Once again the apparition that was my city editor shambled into the city room. Once again he addressed me, this time with: "Ickes, you have been doing better lately," which I already knew. "I like scoops," he continued. "How would you like to go on the regular staff at $12 a week?"

How would I like to earn a steady $12 a week! How would I like to sit down in front of a thick steak! Silly question! Perversely, I did not accept right out of hand. I needed money and $12 a week, coming regularly into the Ickes till, would be a bigger income than I had ever had in my life. It actually represented the colossal sum of $624 a year. Nevertheless, I clutched at my middle and told the mangy one that I would consider it—or was it he who, not wishing to commit the paper irrevocably to another heavy fixed weekly charge of $12, suggested that I think it over? Anyway, I was in a nervous sweat for fear the offer might be withdrawn.

Richard Henry ("Dick") Little—long, lean, popular reporter on the *Tribune,* and later to occupy the chair of Bert Leston Taylor as editor of the *Tribune's* "Line o' Type or Two"—was a friend and fraternity brother of mine. So was Sherman R. Duffy, assistant sporting editor of the *Tribune,* and, by the way, still going strong on the *Chicago Sun.* I can only account for the presence of such good fellows on the *Tribune* staff on the ground that in those days the *Tribune* was a fairly decent and respectable paper. Bertie McCormick had not yet inherited it.

I told Little and Duffy what the *Record* cornucopia was willing to pour into my lap each week. With the irreverence of scoffing, hard-boiled newspapermen they referred to Victor Lawson as a goddamned skinflint. And they spoke most irreverently of my moth-eaten city editor. They said that I could do better—much better—on the *Tribune,* and so over to the *Tribune* I went, with their assistance, as a space writer. I did manage to do pretty well, too, as they had predicted. One week I earned $35—a king's ransom in my little world. As a matter of fact, $35 a week wasn't hay among regular newspaper reporters in those days, and I felt that I was getting into the upper brackets. I foresaw that I was about to arrive.

I happened to be working for the *Tribune* when the occasion of its annual "Family Dinner" arrived, and I was invited to the feast, following which hired men were wont to glorify the *Tribune* with slobbering eloquence. I have never been quite sure whether the young chap sitting next to me was Joe Patterson or Bertie McCormick, although I suspect glumly that it was the latter, because he was distinctly snooty, in a McCormick sort of way, and didn't let me forget that he was a "Yale man." (I have always kind of had it in for Yale ever since.) If it was Bertie, as I have since nearly convinced myself, what an opportunity I had to poison his soup! And I missed it! And each succeeding course was an opening of a lifetime which I neglected, to my shame. There, indeed, was my chance to perform a service for humanity that I doubt not might have inspired Frank Knox and Marshall Field to perpetuate my memory in bronze.

Teddy Beck[1] had just been promoted to city editor of

---

[1] I received the news of Edward N. Beck's recent death with deepest regret. He was a fine fellow, a superior newspaperman, and a friend.

the *Tribune*. Teddy was another grand person—as good as they come—and many times have I wondered how he has been able all of these years to breathe, without succumbing to it, the mephetic air that permeates the Tribune Tower. There are others, too, who it seems to me must work in gas masks.

Teddy had gone out one afternoon to the university to hear a lecture by Richard Mansfield, the actor. I had drawn this assignment. Teddy had ordered my copy brought to him. He pronounced it a good story, according to the grapevine in the person of the inimitable and unequaled Jimmy Durkin, and made no changes. Small wonder that I was beginning to feel my oats as a "journalist" when the quavering gentleman who was still shaking his mane over the city desk of the *Record* sent for me. He was on the hunt for an assistant sporting editor, and the job was mine at $20 a week! After I had been seduced by the *Record,* I was told by Sherman Duffy that I could have had a job on the regular staff of the *Tribune* (will the *Washington Times-Herald* please copy?). Beck hadn't liked my going, and for years I imagined that he neglected to recognize me when he saw me.

So, assistant sporting editor I became—and was. Overnight I blossomed into a football "expert," swelling with inside knowledge of the gridiron. I wrote Monday-morning comment on Saturday's games under a by-line. The sporting editor, the late Harvey T. Woodruff, was a college friend and fraternity brother, and we got along together famously. John D. Hertz, who later was to pile up millions by means of a fleet of taxicabs, was our "pug" specialist. Edna (Teddy) Bean, short-haired ahead of the times, was—it's true!—bicycle editor!

A vacancy occurred in the post of assistant political editor.

I applied for it and so did Frederic W. Wile, who a short time later went to Berlin for the Lawson foreign service. I got the job, probably because the paper already had made other plans for Wile. Malcolm McDowell, one of the finest human beings whom I have ever known, was my immediate chief. When, a few weeks ago, he died, I lost a true and loyal friend and an able member of my staff.

To write politics for a metropolitan newspaper gave me my first real opportunity to barb my disposition—and in the shortest time. I didn't neglect it. I embraced it stranglingly. No longer was I in danger of growing up to be an all-day sucker. There was nothing gentle about big city politics in those days, even from the standpoint of one who was only writing about it. It was the plug-ugly, the heavy-handed manipulator of ballots, the man who could smell out the loot and get to it first, who was in the saddle. He played the tune to which the "businessman in politics" and the stuffed shirts danced, and for which they paid. No softy could meet him or give him orders except on his own terms. Here was my chance, since I wanted, more than anything, to be a success at throwing typographical brickbats. So I began the accumulation of a sizable explosive vocabulary, which I soon trained myself to mix more or less judiciously and to hurl at any convenient target. The fatter the political cat, the louder the wail.

I learned to be a realist. I discovered, from my place in the press box, that the ebb and flow of surface political sentiment did not then—nor does it today—give any true indication of the violent crosscurrents that run just a little deeper. I became cynically wise to the selfishness and meanness of men when their appetites are involved. (I was to learn later that, absorbed in political fortunes of their own, women can be just as selfish and just as mean.) I found out, too, that there are men and women who often serve the common good at great self-sacrifice and without any hope of or desire for political reward or even without any, except condemnatory, public recognition of themselves.

As a Republican, but as independent as a hog on ice, my chief interest was in the Republicans. It happened that the Republicans, at the time that I went to work for the *Record,* were being welded into a strong and militant machine under questionable but able leadership. Four men stood out— William Lorimer, who had worked his way up from driving a streetcar to dominate the Republican organization in the West Side wards that included the Democratic strongholds; Henry L. Hertz, a Danish immigrant who had become the political overlord of the Republican Northwest Side wards where the Scandinavian elements were most in evidence; James Pease, who was in control in Lake View, which was overwhelmingly native Republican; and T. N. ("Doc") Jamieson, who ran things in the equally strong independent Republican territory of Hyde Park where I lived.

In the lesser rank of political leaders were Fred A. Busse, later Mayor of Chicago, whose power was confined to the near North Side; Charles S. Deneen, soon to be State's Attorney and then Governor and United States Senator, a Lorimer lieutenant who was rapidly building a political principality in the Englewood wards; Tom Braden and Arthur Dixon, who had entrenched themselves in the near South Side wards embracing the "black belt"; Fred Blount, vice-president of John R. Walsh's Chicago National Bank, who represented the financial and business interests, but who was an active politician in his own right; John M. Smyth, who owned a big department store in West Madison Street, and Graeme

Stewart, a wholesale grocer, who was useful chiefly as window
dressing—one of those typical American citizens of business
and social standing who occasionally is in politics but seldom
of it, who thinks that he is on the inside, who is ostenta-
tiously consulted, and who is pushed forward when the elec-
torate becomes restless and good-government-minded, but
who really knows very little, and, in the end, is without
influence.

On the other side of the political fence, the Democrats
were enjoying the leadership and control which the election
of Carter H. Harrison [1] as Mayor in 1897 had given them.
Harrison was a respectable figure. Born to the purple, he was
a descendant of the old and honorable Harrison family of
Virginia, and was distantly related to President Benjamin
Harrison. His organization was dominated by Robert E.
("Bobby") Burke. Burke was built like a hogshead—as round
and not much, if any, taller. He was secretary of the county
committee, of which Tom Gahan was chairman and Fred
Eldred treasurer. Tom Carey, from "back of the yards,"
"Hinky Dink" Kenna, "Bathhouse" John Coughlin, Jimmy
Quinn, and others of their stripe were prominent in the
group. They were, believe me, cash-value realists. Politics
was their living, their fortunes—yes, their very lives. They
collected graft from gambling, from vice, from prostitution,
and from contractors. These wolves and jackals Mayor Harrison, generally speaking, permitted to roam unmolested in
the highways and byways of the city to pick up anything that
wasn't nailed down, although the Mayor himself was not

---

[1] Carter H. Harrison, Sr., and Carter H. Harrison, Jr., were each elected
five times as Mayor of Chicago. Harrison the elder was assassinated in 1893.
His son first went into the office in 1897.

guilty, I am convinced, of ever having taken a thing that didn't belong to him.

While a bright sun shone upon the Democratic party of Chicago after the 1897 mayoralty election, there was discernible in the sky a cloud that was plainly visible even to such a freshman political writer as I was. The component parts of that cloud were Roger C. Sullivan, John P. Hopkins, and George E. Brennan. Sullivan and Brennan were to grow to great political stature. I think that it is fair to say that it was Sullivan's switch at the right time in the Democratic National Convention of 1912 that made Woodrow Wilson the party nominee and President for two terms.

This was the political setting when I took over my new duties as a political newshawk. Life was relatively easy. I reported for work at one o'clock in the afternoon and wandered over to the City Hall and the County Building, where I dropped in at intervals at the offices of the Mayor, the Sheriff, the County Treasurer, and other principal officials. I would accept the almost daily invitation to "have a cigar" (only sissies smoked cigarettes in those days) and then would put my feet on the desk to join company with the feet of "mine host" while we chewed the political fat. On these rounds I would ultimately meet up with the political reporters of the other papers—Lane of the *Inter-Ocean,* Mullaney of the *Times-Herald,* Gregory of the *Tribune,* Stowe of the *Chronicle,* Fargo of the *Post,* Armstrong of the *News*—who were similarly trying to make themselves believe that they were not only working but working hard. It was a rare day when all of us did not find ourselves in late afternoon in the office of John P. Hopkins.

Hopkins was handsome, unmarried, and rich. When Carter Harrison the elder was assassinated in 1893, a special election

My three pet Chicago mayoralty candidates, of whom only one, Judge William E. Dever *(left)* made the grade.

The other two, Charles E. Merriam *(left)* and John M. Harlan *(above)* made several unsuccessful bids, and as a result Chicago deprived itself of what I still insist would have been first-class administrating.

On the way to the Republican National Convention at Philadelphia, 1900. I am the third one from the left, not counting the monument—the young man with the boiled shirt front. Malcolm McDowell is on my right.

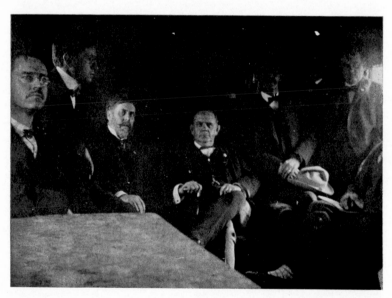

Harold L. Ickes *(second from left)*, reporter on the *Daily Record* (Chicago), interviewing Mark Hanna *(center)*.

had been held and Hopkins was chosen to fill out the unexpired term. It was a political slipover. The term lasted long enough for John and his friends to participate richly in the Ogden gas-franchise steal. But he destroyed himself politically, except that he continued to be a powerful figure in the inner circle of the Sullivan-Hopkins-Brennan clique, of which he was the chief financial bulwark.

Hopkins' offices were on the second floor of an old building on the south side of Monroe Street, between Dearborn and Clark. The ground floor was occupied by the Monroe Street Restaurant. Here, practically every afternoon, in addition to the reporters, would gather Hopkins, Sullivan, George and John Brennan (no relation), "Red" and "Black" O'Malley, occasionally Ross Hall, and others. Here we would sit and listen to Hopkins and Sullivan curse Carter Harrison and all of his works. And what lurid expletives for eager ears! Not only had Harrison barred them all from real participation in the political affairs of the city, he had also made it impossible for their followers to collect graft in their own right.

During this same period I also came to know intimately the leaders of the so-called reform element in Chicago. All of these men had followed John Maynard Harlan in his forlorn-hope campaign, as I had, and of this and other Harlan campaigns I shall have something to say. All of the "reformers" were devoted to the common good. Their rallying point was the Municipal Voters' League. I do not know whose idea the League was, but Victor Lawson supported it liberally from the start. His regular contribution was $10,000 a year.

In virtually every ward, movements were developing to send honest and able men to the City Council in place of the crooks who had been hogging the jobs, and waxing fat on graft. Citizens were thronging the gallery of the City Council chamber. On one occasion, when a particularly offensive ordinance that Yerkes wanted was up for consideration, and it was doubtful whether it might not be passed even over Mayor Harrison's veto, a group of citizens from the then 33d Ward, one of whose aldermen was wobbly, occupied conspicuous seats in the front row of the gallery from which they dangled a rope that ended in a significant slip noose.

My association with the men who were interested in cleaning up politics in Chicago became intimate and close. Not only was my employer a strong supporter of the reform movement; even before I had hired out to him, I discovered that at heart I, too, belonged to it. When I tried to help my paper run the crooks out of the city I wrote out of conviction, and I wrote with all of the vigor and ability that I had. From that day to this I have been accounted a political reformer. And yet I have never lost my friendly personal contacts with many of the more decent active politicians as well as with some whom I knew to be crooked. I confess that I liked and enjoyed the company of the crooks. They had real human qualities—most of them.

The reformers were aloof and austere. They had a veneer that was like the polish on a slab of granite, and contrasted unfavorably with the warm joviality of the Irish political chieftains. I am grateful that I was never in a position where I felt that I had to go either to the politicians or to the reformers for help. But had I needed help I am sure that I would have been more certain of getting it from the politicians.

By the time that the political frolic of 1900 began, I had cut my eyeteeth, if not all of my wisdom teeth, as a political reporter, although I was probably not unlike most young men who engage in newspaper life.

I had covered a number of local conventions—ward, city, and county—for in those days even aldermen were nominated by conventions, mostly packed. Political reporting was one merry round of them, and from these I had come to understand fairly accurately the psychology of the professional politician. Naturally, I was looking forward eagerly to the 1900 campaigns when the country would be filling most of its top offices, including the Presidency.

The campaigning that year didn't bore me. Newspapermen, you know, are supposed to take on an air of ennui along with everything else. This may only prove that I was not a newspaperman after all, because I was interested genuinely in everything that went on.

Judge Orrin N. Carter, Republican County Judge, decided to become a candidate for the Republican nomination for Governor with the support of the independent Republicans generally, as well as that of the independent press.

Judge Elbridge Hanecy, an able but hard-boiled political judge, was the entry of the Lorimer-Jamieson faction.

Downstate produced two other candidates—Congressman Reeves of Streator, a run-of-the-mill politician with a decent but colorless record, who had the support of the so-called Federal machine; and Richard Yates of Jacksonville, the son of Illinois' Civil War Governor, who had served a term in Congress. From my vantage place as an "old veteran" journalist it did not appear that Yates would have more than two or three county delegations with him, including that of his own county of Morgan.

Hanecy had a sharp tongue and an acid disposition. I may have learned some of my tricks from him. I was putting in some good licks for Carter because to me he represented the decent element in Chicago politics, and besides, my boss wanted him elected if possible. Accordingly, I lost no opportunity to scratch the sensitive hide of Hanecy with a pen that was becoming sharper with practice. The result was that at his press conferences Hanecy would tongue-lash both my paper and me. This was foolish of him, as it is of anybody, and I ought to know, because I have been on both sides of the press-conference table. I have written and been written about, and, offhand, I am not prepared to say out of which end of it I have had the most fun.

The Republican State Convention in 1900 was held at Peoria. It is still one of the highlights in the political history of Illinois.

So bitter had been the fight in Cook County that there was little likelihood that Carter delegates would ever desert to Hanecy or vice versa. Cook County had almost half of the total number. It was the hope of the Reeves crowd that Carter or Hanecy could be persuaded to swing to its side, and accordingly its policy was to curry favor with both. Yates was regarded as a negligible quantity. He had only a handful of delegates, and no one paid much attention to him or to what he was doing. His time was consumed in flirting with delegates, avoiding making enemies and hoping against hope that, in the end, he might come up with the medallion.

We correspondents were seated at our tables on the platform in the convention hall wondering whether and whence the break would come. We had even begun to speculate as to the possibility that the convention might not adjourn in time to let us get to Philadelphia, where the Republicans, in a few days, were expecting to choose a national ticket.

It was about eleven o'clock one morning when the band

began to blare and wild excitement was noted among the handful of Yates delegates. It was clear that something had happened to "coke" them up. All through the convention hall there was a spirit as of something important impending. Even the delegates had no inkling of what it was, and they were just beginning to wonder, after the manner of politicians, if they ought to look about for the bandwagon and scramble aboard, when down the center aisle came a procession with a Yates banner borne aloft at its head.

To the amazement of the newshounds, Billy Lorimer was carrying the banner, with Judge Hanecy at his side. Stepping on their heels were John M. Smyth, Fred Blount, "Doc" Jamieson, and others of greater or lesser importance in the machine. Lorimer, Hanecy, and as many others as could possibly squeeze themselves onto the platform, stood yelling for Yates, while their henchmen circulated among the delegates, lining up votes. I do not remember how long the demonstration continued. It may have been fifteen minutes or a half an hour, but it went on until Lorimer was convinced that the convention was sufficiently impressed with the fact that Yates was the fair-haired boy.

At the proper moment Lorimer and his stooges withdrew from the front of the platform. Order was restored, another roll call, and Yates was nominated. Personally I was crestfallen. However, it was not my first defeat, nor by any means my last.

Yates was a weak, easy-going nonentity with few ideas, no real purpose, and little character. On the platform he was a shoddy sentimentalist. I had heard him speak at the Hamilton Club of Chicago during the campaign and I conceived a thorough disgust for him. He carefully avoided discussing any controversial political, social, or economic issue. He would become lyrical over Illinois or Grant or Logan or Lincoln and, at an appropriate place in virtually every speech, he would ask his auditors to take their handkerchiefs from their pockets and wave them as he uttered a maudlin sentiment about some national hero or party saint who had been dead and buried long enough to be a perfectly safe topic for discussion. I think that, almost without exception, the newspapermen were thoroughly disillusioned as to Yates and disgusted with the manner in which his nomination had been achieved. I made up my mind then and there to vote for Samuel Alschuler of Aurora if he should be nominated at the forthcoming Democratic convention. I was finding it increasingly difficult to be a Republican.

The night following his nomination, Yates held a jubilee at his headquarters. I went over because I wanted to ask him whether Lorimer would handle his patronage if he should be elected. Just a simple, polite query! I asked my question, which greatly disturbed him. Drawing me aside, he said with "tears" in his voice: "I hope you are not going to start in to hammer me." He was as plaintive as a child. He was conciliatory, too, and I formed an aversion for him that, while it softened somewhat as I grew older, never entirely disappeared.

My recollection is that Malcolm McDowell and I went direct from Peoria to Springfield, where the Democrats nominated Alschuler, a young Jew who had made a very good record as a member of the General Assembly and who was later to be appointed to the Federal bench by President Wilson.

With the lines drawn in the state, we headed for Philadelphia, bumping and swaying on the Baltimore & Ohio Railroad, which, in those days, was the butt of every poor railroad joke in vaudeville. The *Record's* staff was much enlarged for the occasion. William E. Curtis, the Washington correspondent of the *Record,* joined us, as did also George Ade and John T. McCutcheon.

I had written to my father that I would be in Philadelphia, and I offered to get him a ticket of admission. Father was at that time City Comptroller of Altoona. He met me and witnessed the "deliberations" that resulted in the nomination of McKinley for a second term, and of Theodore Roosevelt as his running mate. That was the last time that I saw my father alive. A Philadelphia cousin procured for me a guest card to the Union League. But I believe that I have lived that down in the intervening forty-two years.

It was a foregone conclusion that McKinley would be nominated. He was an uninspiring individual, and none of us felt much interest either in him or in what was going on. I did not attend any more of the proceedings than I felt that I had to. The real news was outside of the convention, which of itself was a drab affair that did not even furnish local color, with one exception. That exception was the hard-riding, hard-biting Theodore Roosevelt.

CHAPTER FOUR

ADD "NEWSHAWK"

The newspapers! Sir, they are the most villainous, licentious, abominable, infernal—Not that I ever read them! No, I make it a rule never to look into a newspaper.
—RICHARD BRINSLEY SHERIDAN.

IT WAS DUE to Theodore Roosevelt's foresight while serving as Assistant Secretary of the Navy that Admiral Dewey was on hand, "set and ready to go," when the Spanish fleet showed up, looking for a fight, although not ready for it, at the Philippine Islands in 1898. Unwilling, however, to sit at a desk in Washington with a war going on, even although he was in effect running the Navy, Roosevelt resigned to go to Cuba as Lieutenant Colonel under Colonel Leonard Wood of the Rough Riders.

I do not know how important the Battle of San Juan Hill was as a military engagement. Compared with the battles that are staged today it may have been on a par with a tug of war between the fat men and the lean men at the annual outing of the I.O.O.F. Nevertheless, Theodore Roosevelt made it, for at least two generations, one of the notable events in American history. He knew what to do with a talent—no napkin-wrapper, he.

Returning from Cuba, Roosevelt became the Republican

candidate for Governor of New York. There has always been
a question as to whether he was a legal resident of the state
at that time. There were those who were interested in making it appear that he had renounced his citizenship, although
he still owned an estate at Oyster Bay, to which he returned
after he had vacated the White House.

Tom Platt, the easy-going Republican boss of New York,
was opposed to Roosevelt and all of his works, both legitimate and adopted. But since public enthusiasm was running
high for the hero of San Juan, who was Tom Platt to oppose
him?

As Governor, Roosevelt had continued to grow in public
estimation. Always a forceful and picturesque figure, he had
added a soldier's uniform to his stage props. The people
liked his vigorous personality that was such a contrast to
that of the tepid McKinley. Except for the hog-tied delegates
from south of the Mason and Dixon line, there can hardly be
any doubt that Roosevelt would have been swept into the
Presidency in 1900 if it had not been thought that McKinley
should have the conventional two terms. But habit is strong.
It has become almost traditional that a President, however
disappointing his first administration, is entitled to a renomination. Moreover, it is almost impossible to refuse it,
because the President, with his prestige and his vast patronage, is difficult to defeat, as witness 1912 when Taft was
renominated over the more popular Teddy Roosevelt. Even
Harding might have been the party candidate again in 1924
had he lived. Hoover won renomination in 1932, and that
was following tradition at its best—or at its worst.

The important men in the Republican national organization in 1900 were Platt of New York; Matthew S. Quay, the
smooth and unscrupulous Senator from Pennsylvania; and

Murray Crane, the equally adroit Senator from Massachusetts. (Reed Smoot of Utah didn't trail much.) These three men formed a political triumvirate of great power. They represented acquisitive big business when huge agglomerations of wealth were being built up. Money was the country's god, and mere bigness, either of individual fortune or of business enterprise, was the thing to which to salaam. These men never lacked funds. Mark Hanna was top man with McKinley, as he had been in 1896. Boies Penrose was just burgeoning into full bloom as a politician of power and influence, but he was not to reach the heights until after the disappearance from the scene of his political mentor, Matthew Stanley Quay.

These men, for all of their power and money, feared Roosevelt. There was actually some apprehension that Teddy might stampede the convention and make off with the nomination. Bryan and the Democratic convention of 1896, still fresh in their memories, sent goose pimples running up and down tough hides that had long been immune to apprehensions. The bosses could not handle Roosevelt. He was a new type. They did not know what to do with him, but they knew that they ought to do something. And so they decided to make a Throttlebottom out of him. That would be burying him alive, with a vengeance. They were in Philadelphia for that purpose, and that was the only interesting news that the convention produced.

Could Roosevelt flirt with the Vice-Presidency to the point of endearing himself to the delegates, with an eye on 1904, without finding himself married to a bride that he did not want? It was a difficult role, and Roosevelt was not particularly cunning. He was too forthright. In the end he was, luckily for him, outplayed. It was so perfectly obvious that

the overwhelming sentiment of the convention was for him
for Vice-President that he dared not stubbornly refuse the
nomination. If he had he would have run the risk of impair-
ing seriously, and perhaps even of destroying, his popularity
with the country.

From Philadelphia we journeyed wearily to Kansas City.
The weather was getting hotter and hotter. It was a certainty that Bryan would be renominated by the Democrats,
because the free coinage of silver was still a big issue, with
imperialism peeking through the keyhole, and the party had
no other leader who could compete with the silver-tongued
Nebraskan.

Kansas City had never had a big convention and was not
equipped to entertain one. Hotel accommodations were inadequate. The *Record* had even a larger staff at Kansas City
than it had had at Philadelphia. We could not get sufficient
sleeping quarters and so we had to bed down many of our
people in one big room on the ground floor of the hotel
which was ordinarily a dining room or a parlor. Into this
room we ran our special telegraph wires and here several of
us slept—if we could with typewriters and telegraph instruments clattering. It was sweltering. I was so hot, so uncomfortable, and so overworked that I have never had a desire
since to see Kansas City.

The atmosphere in the convention hall was enough to
smother any less self-absorbed creatures than the professional
politicians who gathered there and were used to it. How they
love sweat and tobacco smoke! Bryan was in absolute control. The only fight concerned the platform. What emphasis
should be placed upon the free coinage of silver, and what
other issues should play second string? From his earliest days,
Bryan had been passionate on the money question, but his

thinking along economic lines was confused and naïve. But there cannot be the slightest doubt that he meant well or that our political life is the better for his having lived. He caused people to realize that money and property ought not to be the sole concerns of government, but that social well-being and individual happiness are also entitled to the consideration of the political and governing classes.

The fight over the platform was long-drawn-out. I remember standing wearily against the door hour after hour with my ear glued to the crack trying to pick up something of what was going on inside of the room where the committee on resolutions was hard at work over the money plank. In the end, the will of Bryan prevailed. While maintaining his principles, he made sufficient concessions so that the third-party movement died. On the surface, the Democratic party was again united. The Palmer-Buckner insurgency of four years earlier was sprinkled with embalming fluid.

We were a crew of weary reporters when we returned to Chicago. We had had a full month of conventions, long hours, bad food, stuffy halls, poor beds, nauseating politicians.

There was no thought of President McKinley's making an active canvass. It had become the custom for a President seeking re-election to sit, encased in several layers of dignity, on his front porch, aloof from the actual hostilities. McKinley hadn't even taken to the stump in 1896, on account of his own free-silver past, and if he had good reasons for keeping off it then, he had better reasons four years later. It was decided by the Republican high command that Roosevelt would kick off, and St. Paul, Minnesota, was chosen for the first meeting. I was detailed by my paper to cover it.

Bernard J. Mullaney in those days was, and for several

years had been, the top political reporter on the *Chicago
Times-Herald.* Mullaney was an able newspaperman, a close
friend of John P. Hopkins and Roger C. Sullivan, and a conservative. Republican Mayor Busse made him his secretary
and in later years he became a close associate of Samuel Insull, who had him elected a vice-president of the Peoples
Gas, Light & Coke Company. Mullaney, who did not like
Roosevelt, was also covering the St. Paul meeting.

As Mullaney and I loitered in the broad gallery of the
hotel that overlooked the foyer, arm-swinging Roosevelt
came striding toward us. He was alone, and we stopped him
on the chance of getting something to write about. Besides,
I had never met him. When Roosevelt had gone on his way,
Mullaney turned to me and said: "That man's crazy, and it
would be just his luck if McKinley should die and he became President." When McKinley fell before an assassin's
bullet early in his second term, Mullaney's words rang in my
memory.

During this campaign my main duty was covering headquarters as well as doing my share of the meetings.
McDowell and I divided the job between us. Generally
speaking, he took care of the Republican and I of the Democratic headquarters, although this was by no means a hard
and fast rule. Mark Hanna was spending a good deal of his
time in Chicago, and Bryan was there whenever he was not
actually on the stump.

As in 1896, Bryan had little money to spend. His headquarters were bare and shy of personnel. He spoke everywhere—to smaller crowds in halls or to gigantic ones
outdoors. He had to keep expenses down. With the newspapers of the country generally against him, Bryan knew
that it was his personal contact with the people that would

put him across if anything could do it. It came to be a truism that while Bryan got the crowds, the Republicans would have the votes. And so it proved again to be. Mrs. Bryan usually traveled with her husband and was a good deal at headquarters when he was. They were not able to tour the country in private trains in the manner of the Republicans.

Roosevelt was always particularly strong in the West. This was largely due to the fact that he had owned and operated a ranch in the Bad Lands country on the Little Missouri near Medora, North Dakota. His breezy, friendly manner was much more Western than Eastern, and so was his wide-brimmed felt hat. What appealed to the West often fell flat in the East. Some there even regarded him as a poseur. So it was determined to send him on a special tour of the Great Plains country. I had hoped to be assigned to this trip, but another got it, much to my disappointment.

I did not regret it subsequently, however, because, late in the campaign, Mark Hanna decided that he was going out to face his critics and traducers in the West. I drew the assignment to go with him. Personally, Hanna was a likable man—short and squat, with a round, friendly face. The most distinguishing of his features were his eyes. They were full of life and vitality and power.

Many years later, in 1912, when Mark Hanna's daughter, Ruth, as the wife of Medill McCormick and subsequently in her own right, became prominent in national politics, it was said of her on a number of occasions that she had learned her politics at her father's ample knee. I have seen it in print that she was confidant, adviser, and constant companion of her father during his campaign for McKinley, but I can say truthfully that I not only never saw her, I never heard her name mentioned throughout the 1900 campaign. And in 1896 she was a mere child.

In addition to Hanna himself, his party included, besides newspaper correspondents, Elmer Dover, his secretary, Senator William P. Frye of Maine, and Victor Dolliver, brother of the Iowa Senator, both typical campaign spellbinders who were taken along to do the main part of the vocal slugging because Hanna himself had little aptitude for it and no training. Senator Frye came into the correspondents' car unexpectedly on one occasion and caught me delivering his own speech, with appropriate gesticulations and vocalizations, to an appreciative audience. He was not pleased.

I have never had any doubt that Hanna, as a result of this tour, contributed substantially to the Republican victory. We made many stops, and Frye or Dolliver would hold the crowd until there were only a few minutes left and then Hanna would appear on the rear platform of the train. So anxious were people to see this much-advertised political devil that they would drive great distances—"great distances" in those days being, say, twenty-five to forty miles by horse and buggy or fifty miles on horseback.

Hanna handled his crowds adroitly. He would lean against the rear brass railing of the observation car waiting for the applause to die down. Generally he did not have to wait very long. The crowds to start with were either against or at least curious about him. He would stand before them, in a friendly, human way, and then he would say something like this:

"I have come out here, friends, to prove to you that I have neither horns nor a tail. You don't see any horns on me or any tail, do you? Nor is my suit covered with dollar marks. (He referred to Davenport's savage cartoons in the Hearst press.) I am just a plain American citizen like yourselves, interested in my country and trying to keep it from falling into the hands of people who would destroy our prosperity and reduce the economic condition of the workers and the farmers to that of the peasant classes in Europe."

Then he would discuss briefly one or two issues of the campaign, referring especially to the tariff, to which he attributed America's "prosperity," and, more often than not, he would close with his favorite exhortation not to "change horses in the middle of the stream."

Leaving Chicago, we had swung up into Wisconsin along the Mississippi and then over into Minnesota, which we toured for the better part of two days. From Minnesota we crossed into South Dakota, where big crowds turned out to see the political desperado from Ohio. Next we hit the trail across Iowa into Nebraska. The trip ended at Lincoln. There Hanna was scheduled to make two appearances, one in the biggest auditorium in the city and the other in a small hall in a laboring community. The small meeting was to be held first.

Now I never shirked my work, nor did I ever willingly leave anything to chance. I always insisted upon hearing with my own ears and seeing with my own eyes. I knew that the big meeting would be late and, as I was sending my dispatches to both the *Record* and the *New York Herald,* I wanted to top off a successful road trip with a good story. I assumed that, as usual, Hanna would make precisely the same speech at each meeting, so I suggested to Barney Mullaney, who was also with the party, that I would cover the first meeting if he would take the second. I thought this a clever maneuver and a timesaver for both me and my papers. Mullaney agreed. So out I went to the first meeting, and by the time that I had pounded out and filed Hanna's cut-and-dried speech with as much local color as I could collect, the other boys were back in our private train from the big meeting.

I noticed that Mullaney and the rest of them were hurried and preoccupied. Mullaney had barely spoken to me as he rushed to his typewriter, and I became anxious. I made him tell me what was up. I learned that at the auditorium Hanna had let go of a bitter personal attack on Bryan. He had done nothing of this sort on the entire trip, so that it definitely came under the heading of news, and big news at that. Lincoln was Bryan's home city. For four years Bryan had spared no pains to acquaint the country with the fact that he had a very low opinion of Hanna. He painted him, as no doubt he believed him to be, as the evil and sinister representative of the great financial and business interests of the country that did not scruple to pour endless money into the campaigns of the Republican candidates whose masters they were. A brilliant speaker with the widest audiences that any man in America had had up to that time, he had spread far and wide his highly unfavorable views of Hanna and what he stood for in American public life.

Although Hanna had submitted to Bryan's attacks in silence, undoubtedly he had been badly cut by them. Hanna did not regard the prodigal use of money in campaigns as anything improper, especially if it were Republican money. He might, however, have perceived a scandal if the Democrats had had the bigger pork barrel. He was "saving" America from the dangerous radicals of the day, just as other representatives of privilege, both before and since, have justified corruption and bribery to maintain the established order as "a patriotic deed" in the "public interest." But the Bryan attacks had cut deep and festered. Whether it was in the back of Hanna's mind all along to assail Bryan in his home city, I do not know. He always said what little he had to say extemporaneously, so that we never had advance copies of his talks, which made it all the more necessary for us to cover his meetings.

In any event, he did go after Bryan with all that he had at the meeting which I did not attend. And there was I, a distraught correspondent who had missed the boat, having already filed with his two papers a perfectly conventional story covering an earlier meeting!

In my mind's eye I pictured the wrath that would descend upon me from my managing editor when he compared my product the following morning with the real story as it would appear in the other Chicago papers. I had a healthy respect for Charles H. Dennis, a distinguished journalist who, in an even, quiet tone and with carefully selected and expurgated words, could make one feel more like a worm than a loud voice and choice billingsgate could ever have accomplished. So I made Mullaney pause long enough to give me some of the highlights, and with that material, plus what I was able to worm out of the other correspondents, I contrived to work out a new lead for my own story which at least would spare me the ignominy of being scooped. Apparently, it did the business, because I heard no word of criticism upon my return to Chicago. But it taught me the risk of taking chances, even in a good cause.

The campaign resulted as all of us had every reason to believe that it would. There was little enthusiasm for McKinley, but Roosevelt, the national hero, stirred up considerable genuine cheering for the Republican ticket, with the result that it was safely elected.

Persistent stories had filtered into the newspaper offices

from the Roosevelt trip that the Vice-Presidential candidate was actually drunk a good part of the time. I think that these were the first of a long series of calumnies which circulated for years and which finally ended, along about 1913, in an action for libel by Roosevelt against the editor of a small Michigan newspaper. There was never any basis for the stories. In later years I saw a good deal of Roosevelt. I was with him on occasions when there were no restraints upon his drinking more than was good for him if that had been his disposition. I can say truthfully, based upon my own association with him, that Roosevelt was a temperate man in everything but the expenditure of his energy.

One particularly insidious story had come out of Minnesota. It was to the effect that at the town of Red Wing, Roosevelt had been so drunk that he had had to clutch the railing to keep himself from falling. The Hanna party stopped at this same Red Wing and it happened that we struck it at about the same time of day that Roosevelt had. A temporary platform had been built and was also used by Hanna. In the middle of the afternoon, which was the time of both meetings, a glaring sun struck full into the eyes of the speakers. I questioned closely some of the local people about the alleged intoxication of our candidate for Vice-President and the convincing explanation was that the sun was shining brightly in his eyes while he was speaking so that he had to twist and squirm to avoid the glare, especially since his eyes were weak and he wore unusually heavy lenses. My informants were quite positive that Roosevelt had not had a single drink that day and that he "hung onto the railing" because it hurt his eyes to attempt to stare the sun out of countenance.

After the election, but before the Republicans had closed

their national headquarters in Chicago, Hanna sent for all of the reporters who had customarily covered his beat and gave each of us an enlarged photograph of himself. Previously he had given scarfpins to the correspondents who had been with him on the trip. Mine was a sapphire, surrounded by small diamonds, and I still treasure it as a memento of a most interesting experience.

My newspaper career was nearly over. In December 1900, I was sent to Ann Arbor, Michigan, to cover a meeting which was addressed by the one-time President, Benjamin Harrison, who attacked the McKinley Administration for taking the position that the Constitution did not "follow the flag" to Puerto Rico and the Philippine Islands. Harrison, a distinguished lawyer, maintained that the islands were a part of the United States and that the Constitution extended to them notwithstanding treaties or legislation. This address was a prepared magazine article that already had been copyrighted. The *New York Herald* had wired to the *Record* that one of its best reporters should be sent, because the report of the speech would have to be in indirect discourse. It had to be and it was. This was the only occasion that I ever saw Benjamin Harrison. This was his last public utterance. He died the following March in Indianapolis.

* * * * * *

Certain of my ill-wishers are kicking against the pricks by alleging that I have no right to boast (if that's the word) that I was once a newspaperman. As a matter of fact, I am rather partial to the theory that I must have been a precocious lad to have earned a political assignment on the *Chicago Record* right next to the political editor so soon after leaving the classroom. I was covering national conventions three years after graduating. There are those who will stick up their noses at this bit of personal appreciation, but I offer it more in an attempt to put them down than to raise myself up. I hope that it nauseates them as they do me.

Having established by the record that I really was once a newspaperman, whether the *Washington Times-Herald* likes it or not, I hope that I may be regarded as something of an authority when I express an opinion as to certain newspapers and certain of the newspaper gentry. Whether so or not, here goes.

Let me say, first of all, that I have no patience with those men and women in public life who abasingly try to curry favor with the newspapers, either because they are too cowardly to fight or because of a desire to build up reputations as benign, clever, and humane statesmen. I maintain that it is far more self-respecting to be a curmudgeon—and a mean one—than a newspaperman's doormat. Only a certain type of moronic journalist will have any admiration for the public official who crawls around on his belly before glorified printers' devils. But how some of them love it!

There is no gainsaying that the newspapers, as a class, have done something through the years to make me what I am. The newspaper industry took me in when I needed a job. Of this I am neither unmindful nor ungrateful. My impression is that I became a pretty good newspaperman, but then, as someone has suggested, "what is one man's opinion?" Be that as it may, I can survey the field as one who has been on both sides of the fence. Whereas I was once a prideful newspaperman, wedded to my job, enthusiastic, impressed by the importance of keeping the world informed, or reformed, now I can't even read some newspapers without nausea.

Foremost, of course, and almost in a class by itself among

newspapers that are allergic to me (and to which I am allergic), is the *Chicago Tribune*—good old WGN, run by good old Robert Rutherford McCormick, a man of many marvelous self-acclaimed military "exploits." [1]

Bertie modestly claims, among other things, that he introduced the R.O.T.C. into the schools; that he introduced machine guns into the Army; that he introduced mechanization, and automatic rifles; that he was the first ground officer to go up in the air (I wonder what makes him think that he ever came down) to observe artillery fire. He says that he was the first to advocate an alliance with Canada, and that he forced the acquisition of bases in the Atlantic Ocean.

He admits, however, that there were some things that even he couldn't do. He was unsuccessful in obtaining the fortification of Guam, for instance, and in preventing the division of the Navy between two oceans. (If he had come along in paleozoic times, he might have simplified the problem by fixing it so that we wouldn't have had two oceans.) Bertie

---

[1] Quoting directly and in full from Bertie McCormick's letter dated February 20 last to J. H. Sawyer, Jr., 333 North Michigan Avenue, Chicago: "Thank you for your very temperate letter. What the most powerful propaganda organization in the world has misled you into believing was a campaign of hatred, has really been a constructive campaign without which this country would be lost. You do not know it, but the fact is that I introduced the R.O.T.C. into the schools; that I introduced machine guns into the army; that I introduced mechanization; I introduced automatic rifles; I was the first ground officer to go up in the air and observe artillery fire. Now I have succeeded in making that the regular practice in the army. I was the first to advocate an alliance with Canada. I forced the acquiring of the bases in the Atlantic Ocean. On the other hand I was unsuccessful in obtaining the fortification of Guam; in preventing the division of the navy into two oceans. I was unable to persuade the navy and the administration that airplanes could destroy battleships. I did get the marines out of Shanghai, but was unsuccessful in trying to get the army out of the Philippines. Campaigns such as I have carried on inevitably meet resistance, and great persistence is necessary to achieve results. The opposition resorts to such tactics as charging me with hatred and so forth, but in view of the accomplishment I can bear up under it." Whatta man, indeed! And, I might add, horse feathers!

confesses that he was unable to get the Army out of the Philippines, although he did get the marines out of Shanghai. Perhaps it isn't too late for him to get the Japs out.

Summarizing his own achievements in that characteristic but refreshingly modest way of his, Bertie has himself rounded them up under the general heading of "a constructive campaign without which this country would be lost." (And to think that once I sat so close to him at a banquet table that I might have dropped ground glass into his soup; and would have done so had I known then what I know now!)

For years I have been in this great man's hair all over his head. (At some point later in this narrative I shall attempt to offer a reason for Bertie's aversion to anything and everything pertaining to me.) I have been running off of his presses regularly and faster, and ever faster, since I came to Washington. God willing, it will be forever thus, for life would otherwise be empty and dull. Bertie and his *Tribune* hate me for myself and myself alone. Even when I get mixed up and do the right thing, which they say is a rare occasion, the *Tribune* manages to find something wrong with it.

Out of this relationship with the *Tribune* has sprung one of the happiest and most satisfying feuds of my turbulent career. As high priest in the cult of "attack first and investigate later, but never retract," McCormick has really done the lion's share in making me the biggest mote in the public eye and in pitting me against the newspaper industry.

Let me be quoted as saying that I think there is a safe, practical, and economical method of controlling the external parasites of fish, and good old Bertie will stop his thundering presses while he jams in an editorial by which he hopes to prove that Ickes is another.

Should I say that the Statue of Liberty is a grand old lady, permanent may her wave be, the *Tribune* will accuse me of using abusive language and it will observe that I am, as always, in poor taste and speaking disrespectfully of a member of the weaker sex.

If I am quoted as saying that the Isle Royale is God's own country where the deer and the bull moose play, the *Tribune* will devote a column of wide measure to proving that I am a cheap nature faker. It will insist that I am pretending to be a conservationist, but that in fact I am playing politics with the great outdoors and acting as though it belonged to me.

Charming fellow, Bertie McCormick, who, if he had been blessed with any sense of humor, would have died long ago of laughing at himself.

> There is a news fellow named Bert,
> To whom Ickes is just a hair shirt;
> Like a pig to his sty,
> He runs straight as a die
> To get him more handfuls of dirt.

I often wonder if Bertie knows that I once did space writing for his paper, or that I collected as much as $35, as aforesaid, in one week for my efforts. If he doesn't, I'd like to be a little bird—near an open window to be sure—when he hears the news. If Bertie begrudges me what I so hardly earned, I will be glad to reimburse his paper. It's on my conscience anyway.

Throughout the years that I have been at odds with the *Tribune,* my one regret has been that there hasn't been an evening edition to quarrel with, too. All of this time I might have been having twice as much fun.

The revulsion of feeling which the *Chicago Tribune* has

for me is reflected, in a bungling fashion, in the not-so-well-known *Washington Times-Herald,* which has been particularly insistent among newspapers that I was never in the game myself. The *Times-Herald* is second on my list of newspapers whose unfriendliness I prize highly and would not change to love if I could.

Cissie Patterson, who flutters, like a plucked bird, over the *Times-Herald,* is a cousin of Bertie McCormick's. This accounts for a lot of things. Neither used to boast of the relationship, but now each is the other's own best tout. What Bertie or his intellectual vassals think and say of me become the thoughts and the words of Cissie just as soon as a copy of the *Tribune* reaches her desk—unless, of course, the *New York Daily News,* run by her brother, Captain Joe Patterson, gets there first, in which case Cissie applies shears and paste to the leading editorial and rushes to press.

I used to theorize that a little sweet feminine influence, much as I would regret it, might have a salutary effect on dear old WGN, and then Cissie got tired of herself and decided that she might as well lose money on a newspaper as to pay it out in income taxes to be spent by an administration that she and her cousin Bertie had made up their minds to be against, whate'er might betide. So I was forced to modify my belief that a woman's influence couldn't be anything but good, and note a large exception in Cissie's case.

Some heat but no light is thrown on the complexes that beset Cissie and Bertie (with brother-cousin Joe Patterson thrown in for the record) as we thumb through the files of the *Tribune,* the *Times-Herald* and the *News* and note their editorial opposition to even the suggestion of getting ready for the present war. They assured us that Japan would not and could not attack us—Bertie spoke pontifically out of the amplitude of a personal experience that, he says, included his personal feat of getting the marines out of Shanghai—and they threw bombs weighted with their best assorted language into the fight to prevent any possibility of getting ready. The Japanese attack on Pearl Harbor was extremely embarrassing to Cissie and Bertie and Joe, who are now trying daily to cover up their own telltale trails by criticizing the Administration because the country is not so well prepared as it might have been if "Col. McComic," with admiring cousinly support, had furnished the Army and the Navy with one of the masterly strategic blueprints that he now works out daily for our military leaders. Doubtless he's the same big help to them in wartime that he has been to me in peacetime.

Speaking of feminine influence in high newspaper rank, I am reminded that, in the race among members of the press who hate Ickes, the *New York Herald Tribune* is also well out in front. I hope that Ogden Mills Reid and his estimable wife will be able to bear up under the shocking news that that paper—then the *New York Herald*—printed more than one important story that it bought from the old *Chicago Record* which had been written by a certain struggling and hungry young curmudgeon by the name of Ickes.

When I walk out of the Department of the Interior Building for the last time to return to the dreaded peace and quiet of private life, I will be surprised and disappointed if I don't discover Bertie and Cissie in the front row hissing me and with their feet stretched into the aisle hoping that I'll stumble over them. However he might feel, Oggie would be too well-bred to act the hooligan.[1]

There have been other examples of unrestrained dislike for me among newspapers. Recently I ran across my knife-scarred name at the end of a "civic-spirited" editorial in the

now defunct *Kansas City Journal*. It had been put there by a
certain Harry Newman (is he the Harry Newman, do you
suppose, who formerly sojourned in Chicago?) who by-lined
himself proudly as the *Journal's* new editor.

In announcing the paper's change in management, Editor
Newman conveyed its high regard for the *Journal's* adver-
tisers and paid-up subscribers, for the city, the county, and
the state in which it was located, and then concluded with
this line:

WE DO NOT LIKE THE WEATHER WE HAVE BEEN HAV-
ING NOR HAROLD ICKES.

So help me! There it was! Just like that, Editor Newman
had made up his mind that "we" didn't like Harold Ickes,
whom he probably had never seen, and the end of a goodwill
editorial seemed as good a place as any to announce it. In
this casual and informal way it thus became the *Journal's*
official opinion of a man whom it didn't know, and a contribution to his reputation in that area.[2]

Not that it matters now—the *Journal* is gone and Newman
with it, I presume, (in view of Newman's paean of goodwill
in his first issue after taking over, I wish that I could have
seen his reference to me when the *Journal* blew up in his
face and he had to write its obituary), but it still stands as a

---

[1] I am often asked: "What are you going to do when you finish as Secretary of the Interior?" It's a nebulous question (so is the answer), like the one
in the old song, "What're you going to do when the rent comes round?" It's
hard to say. My offhand answer has been that I'll probably rest on my oars
for a few knots, and then (if the war's over) I may write some of the things
that at the moment are "verboten." I may even "do" a newspaper column.
(Customers will please form a line on the right.) It would entertain Horrendous Harold to be present when a Cabinet officer was writhing in agony
and not be that Cabinet officer.

[2] Imagine my amazement when, on October 9 last, Harry Newman wrote
me a letter "to offer my most humble apology for the inaccuracy and un-
truthfulness I have written about you. . . . I am ashamed that I allowed my-

typical and not uncommon example of what sometimes goes into the making of a public man's repute.

Still more recently the *Seattle Times* told its readers that "we have yet to hear that Mr. Ickes has a friend in Alaska." Of course the *Times* is closer to Alaska than I have been for some time, and probably has checked the matter more carefully than I have been able to do, but I am wondering if it surveyed the territory adjacent to Woodchopper just south of Mastodon and the Porcupine River. The reason that I ask is that I understood indirectly that there was a fellow right in there who claimed to be my friend, and I am curious to know if something happened to him. I sincerely hope that he got what he so richly deserved.

A Washington correspondent recently wrote home that Ickes is "the most personally unpopular person in the Roosevelt dynasty."

Now that's a strong statement to make, and without meaning to drag any of my associates down into the mire with me I feel that I should remind this correspondent that the so-called Roosevelt dynasty covers a lot of ground and is bound to be inhabited by many unpopular and disagreeable persons. What dynasty isn't? If I, then, am the most unpopular one in it, of what am I trying to convince you? Haven't I

self to write as I frequently did. . . . I have attempted to prepare an article of some 6,000 words critical of your motives and of your ability and . . . that I might be accurate, I was more than ordinarily careful in my research. That research makes it necessary for me to write exactly the opposite kind of article and to state that the care with which that research was conducted changed a highly critical attitude to one of sincere admiration for your human qualities, your respect for your high office, your integrity and loyalty to just causes." I am almost sorry (Ickes speaking) that the *Kansas City Journal* folded up. And I am glad that this letter was not received until the manuscript for this opus was about complete. It might have discouraged me utterly. My hat is off to Newman, but I hope that no one is looking.

been saying that I am the outstanding curmudgeon of my time?

In the final analysis it is the printed word—the "opinions" of the Newmans and the *Seattle Timeses* and the Washington correspondents—that goes into the reputations by which public officials are invariably judged. Consider the Coolidge myth as a shining example of what the newspapers can do when they really apply themselves to a job. In my case they at least have something to go on. It was when I discovered that the newspaper editors—comrades once!—and the writers of the country were going to parade me as a contumelious and oppugnant ingrowing hair on the body politic, whether I deserved it or not, that I finally determined to let nothing divert me from carrying out my grim intention to become the most industrious skipper in the Washington cheese.

If, in accomplishing my design, I have on occasion made suckers out of the newspapers and the columnists by inducing them, unwittingly, to add to my unhappy reputation, I nonetheless am grateful to them for their generous contributions to what has been our joint cause.

Among other things that I have learned "the hard way" about newspapers, in the almost ten years that I have been in Washington, is that the smaller the newspaper, the deadlier its bite can be. I thank my stars that I haven't had to read all of the many thousands of weeklies and smaller dailies that strut regularly before their readers and preen themselves upon how much they know about something that probably wasn't so to begin with. Give any bilious boiler-plate editor a broken-down typewriter and an even start and he'll outdo any of the hired hands of the Bertie-Cissie-Joey axis.

Some of the hand-set editorials that have been written about me have scorched the varnish right off me. After reading them I have wondered what was holding me up. I finally had to stop them, as well as those of my three pet aversions, from coming to my office. My insurance company was threatening to cancel my policies or else raise the rates on me. The smell of something burning used to cling to my clothes for days.[1]

To each member of the fraternity, of whatever size or sex, I doff my hat in grateful acknowledgment of every barbed boost that has been shot at me. Without the help of newspapers that made it possible for me to eat, I might not be here today, and without their help since I left their ranks, I might be unknown or merely taken for granted. And that would never have done.

As my daily good deed in reverse English, and without seeking credit for it, I propose that the newspapers of the country throw out the truck that so many of them carry in their mastheads and substitute the following as their North Star of editorial policy:

> Who steals my purse steals trash . . .
> But he that filches from me my good name
> Robs me of that which not enriches him,
> And makes me poor indeed.

The question What would you do without free speech? has been asked me so many times of late that I am beginning to wonder if someone isn't trying to kid an expert. Maybe

---

[1] "Misrepresentation of facts is the common practice of the writers of newspapers," according to the Duke of Wellington (from the biography *Wellington* by Philip Guedalla). "If I possess any advantages in point of character," the author quotes the Duke as saying, "I consider myself bound to set the example to others of a determination to prevent the blackguard editors of papers from depriving us of our reputation by their vulgar insinuations. The truth is, I refused to employ a relation of the editor of 'The Times' in my family, and that is the reason he has accused me of corruption, but that is no reason why I should bear it."

there is a quiet move on foot to abridge Article I of the Bill of Rights as to H. L. Ickes and this is a subtle way of telling me about it.

I won't deny that I have exercised my constitutional privileges as much as the next one. I won't deny it because the scrapbook will show that I have done my share of talking. If I were to be put on a speech meter, my monthly bill would run high. Or if talk were to be rationed to me, an "A" card wouldn't last me as long as it would take me to get home. But free speech is one of the many grand prizes that I drew along with millions of other Americans when I had the good sense and the foresight to be born in this country, so what the hell?

If it is being hinted that the time is coming when I or anyone else in the United States will speak only when given permission, let me be among the first to say that this is what is known in the trade as Japanazi bull. Some people know it as Axis bushwa. I just want to be around when someone— *anyone*—tries to shush the American people. What a time he's going to have! He should come prepared for trouble. Thumb through any issue of the obtuse *Congressional Record,* scan the pages of the first newspaper that comes to hand, tune your radio to any station, and you will be convinced quickly that Article I of the Bill of Rights still lives and that, if anything, it is being used more today than ever in the hundred and fifty-one years that it has been in force.

Recently an American newspaper editorial entitled "Free Speech in England" was called to my notice. It wasn't what the editorial said but what it didn't say that took my breath away. The implications which I got from a reading of it were so startling that I think it is worth while to reproduce it here in its entirety. I have since seen it in at least three representative newspapers which, presumably, were willing that it should go into the record as their official opinion. Herewith then the editorial—"Free Speech in England":

If the ears of Harold Ickes, Senator Barkley and sundry other public servants happened to have been cocked in the direction of Leeds, England, the other day they might have heard a primer lesson in democracy of which, their recent utterances testify, they are sorely in need.

Commander R. T. Bower is a member of Parliament. He is also a member of the Coastal Command of the RAF. It was in Leeds that Commander Bower rose up and delivered himself of his smoldering wrath against His Majesty's War Government's administration of the war.

Churchill, he said, is akin to the fabled comedian who eats his heart out longing to star in tragic roles. . . . "We are a democracy. True democracies should be suspicious of so-called great men. . . . The Fuehrer principle is not for us." Finally: "I sometimes suspect Churchill himself would rather go down on the sinking ship than see someone else bring it safely to port."

There are millions of Englishmen who will testify that Commander Bower is totally and utterly wrong. But that isn't the point. The wrathful commander's blast is a prime example of one of the great principles for which the United Nations fight— the freedom of the individual to criticize by the spoken or printed word.

For more than two years England has lived in peril of her life. She has skirted the abyss of obliteration and looked into its measureless depths. Yet today a member of both Parliament and the armed forces still can, with impunity, blisteringly criticize the head of the Government, drawing in reprisal only the equally vituperative maledictions of his equally free-speaking political opponents.

Washington papers, please copy.

If most readers don't get from this that we in America no longer enjoy—if we ever did—the right to criticize freely, at least not to the same extent that the privilege is enjoyed in

England, then I have missed the point entirely. I must be slipping. To me it says as clearly as possible that what Commander R. T. Bower said at Leeds was something that no one in this country would dare to say in a comparable situation. Either the man who wrote the editorial is crazy—or I am.

Just for the fun of it I made it my business to have checked one day's crop of American newspaper clippings—one day's crop, mind you!—to discover, if I could, to what extent the right to criticize the Government and everybody in it is being lost in this country. Shooting balling irons! The report that came back to me was enough to make a sensitive public official rush home and beat up his family if the output for that particular twenty-four hours is typical of what rolls off of our newspaper presses every day. And I have a pretty good reason for believing that it is.

That was the day that Jouett Shouse jumped down the throat of the Administration and said that it was short-sighted, "lamentably weak," "confusing and contradictory," not frank.

That was the day that Walter Trohan reported in the *Chicago Tribune* that jealousy in high places was endangering the war effort.

That was the day that the *Washington News* observed that we had learned nothing since Pearl Harbor; that there was a complete lack of unity between the various divisions of the Government.

That was the day that the same *Washington News* devoted the biggest part of one of its tabloid pages to an interview with a half-baked crackpot described as "an ex-D.C. raid warden" who predicted "bloody revolt" among us, the "shooting of Gentiles," "a war-guilt trial and punishment for the President," and "a dictator occupying the White House within three years." (And that's what some editors call *news!*)

That was the day that twelve Democratic United States Senators flayed the "Administration's conduct of the war," charging "confusion worse confounded," and "intolerable arrogance on the part of bureaucrats who have been vested with dictatorial power."

That was the day that Lawrence Dane quoted Alexander P. de Seversky in the *Boston Herald* as saying that "stupidity, rather than criminal intent, caused American military and naval chiefs to insist upon the construction of obsolete planes by industry."

That was the day that Bill Cunningham had a piece in the *Boston Herald* accusing the Senate of "dawdling" in the face of a crisis, and urging that "bewildered politicians be discarded for real leaders."

That was the day that the *Rapid City* (S.D.) *Journal* said that "this war is a picnic for a vast host of New Dealers." (Here was one of the unkindest cuts of all, because it plainly suggested that some of us in Washington were getting so much fun out of the war that we wouldn't end it if we could. The man who wrote it must have a beautiful disposition.)

That was the day that the *Ogden* (Utah) *Standard-Examiner* said that "Washington's public relations are deteriorating so rapidly as to constitute a menace to public morals."

That was the day that Dr. George N. Shuster, as president of Hunter College, called for a Congress that would curb the Administration, and suggested that "we might be willing to take a somewhat weaker President if we could have a much greater Congress."

That was the day that the *Cedar Rapids* (Iowa) *Gazette* printed an article by a Harry Boyd that took everyone in official Washington by the scruff of his neck and shook him until his back teeth rattled.

By this time I had seen enough to convince me that if free speech means criticism run riot, and if criticism run riot is the true measure of a democracy, then we have a democracy in America as no other country has or ever will have it. Also that we have more free speech in one state than is to be had in the whole British Empire. Commander Bower would be a squeak-mouse over here.

The one batch of clippings that was consulted represented the harvest from not more than twenty-five newspapers out of a total of more than two thousand dailies and ten thousand weeklies! Can you imagine what the score would look like if it were possible to go through all of them?

"Free Speech in England" my eye! As though we didn't have it in America!

Not that I think that it should be checked or that it covers too much ground. I'm merely relating the facts. I agree wholeheartedly with the late Colonel Henry Watterson, who, when rebuked for criticizing the Governor of Kentucky, wrote: "Things have come to a heluva pass, when a man can't cudgel his own jackass."

Having convinced myself all over again that free speech in America is here and isn't being threatened, let me return to the original question—what would I, of all people, do without it? That's an easy one.

I'd shoot myself.

CHAPTER FIVE

PUBLIC WEAL

They have such refined and delicate palates
That they can discover no one worthy of their ballots,
And then when someone terrible gets elected
They say, There, that's just what I expected!

—OGDEN NASH.

ALL OF MY LIFE I have been interested in politics and public affairs. Whatever since schooldays my hands have found to do, it has in some respect, slight or otherwise, been related to politics. My mother took her politics just as intensely as she took her religion, or her children took her prize gingerbread, and nothing could have been more intense than that. Being a Pennsylvania Scotch Presbyterian, she couldn't have been anything but an ardent Republican. Her father, as I have previously mentioned, had served in the State Legislature of Pennsylvania—for several terms—and there was a favorite fable in the family, probably unfounded, that he might have become Governor had he not sickened of the whole business and gone back to his farm and his gristmill. Considering some Governors whom I have known, I am not disposed to brag about this. On the contrary, I have seen days when I was convinced that we may have narrowly escaped having another nasty skeleton rattling about the house.

I recall the bitterness of my mother's feeling toward
Grover Cleveland, even if he was a Presbyterian, and her enthusiasm for Blaine. I have no doubt that if my mother had
been born a man she would have been up to her ears in politics, but no woman of her day could even take part in an
informal political discussion, except with her close friends or
members of her family.

Dr. George Ickes, my father's cousin, was a Democrat and
lived in 'the west end of Altoona, which, by the way, was
overwhelmingly Republican. I recollect vividly that he and
my mother engaged in a lively political discussion one afternoon on the subject of Grover Cleveland. How his ears must
have burned that day! Although taught that children were to
keep their teeth tightly clenched in the presence of their
elders, I interrupted the discussion to say pertly that "Cleveland was no good anyhow; he could take off his collar without unbuttoning it." This perfectly innocuous observation
of·a nine-year-old, which I had picked up somewhere, cut my
cousin to the quick, and I have thought of it since very frequently as the type of argument that an immature child or
a moronic adult will advance as a conclusive reason against
a candidate for office. How many thousands of times since
that day have I heard equally profound and devastating argu-
ments during a political controversy, with no more foundation or sense to them than that "Cleveland can take off his
collar without unbuttoning it"!!

My mother cried when the returns showed conclusively
that Cleveland had been elected. I know now that while
Blaine's election would have been a cause for at least temporary rejoicing among us Republicans, his political character
and public career were such that he was not fit to be President of the United States. It was far better for the country

that my mother should cry her eyes out because Blaine was defeated than for the havoc that he might have wrought as President.

The funeral train that bore the body of President Garfield back to Ohio passed through Altoona, and I made up one of the large crowd gathered at the station to pay tribute to the nation's martyr. That was in 1881, when I was seven years old.

When, in 1890, I left Altoona in the custody of my aunt to go and live in Chicago, I was a Black Republican without knowing why except that my mother—and also my father, save for his brief straying into Greenbackism—were Black Republicans. In becoming a member of my aunt's household, I continued to be among Black Republicans. I doubt if any one of them ever voted other than the straight Republican ticket, whether it was good or bad. Their justification was that the worst Republican was better than the best Democrat—soothing syrup, that, for a stomach in revolt! Later, I was to hear Senator Albert Cummins of Iowa enunciate the same "principle" in a campaign speech in Chicago.

When I entered the Englewood High School in the fall of 1890, the principal was Orville T. Bright. In 1892 he became a candidate on the Republican ticket for county superintendent of schools. There was a good deal of interest in his candidacy, and because he was popular with both teachers and students, there was a general clamor to do something for him. Mr. Adkinson proposed that I make a speech for our candidate at a Republican rally in a hall in Wentworth Avenue near my uncle's drugstore. I have been grateful that none of the few who heard that speech ever held it against me. It is a bit of luck that no gibbering columnist can get hold of it. I was intensely embarrassed and self-conscious. In the circumstances I probably did all that any normal person could have done to defeat him, but the fact is that Bright was elected.

Neither Uncle Felix Wheeler nor Uncle Sam McCune took the slightest personal interest in politics. The contrary was true of Elmer W. Adkinson, one of the salt of the earth, whose friendship I acquired through my close association with his son Henry at the Englewood High School. Mr. Adkinson had been interested in local politics before Englewood became a part of Chicago. I suppose that at one time he was the dominant Republican influence in that restricted area. Then Charles S. Deneen, who landed in Chicago about the same time that I did, settled in Englewood and set out to make a political career for himself. He prospered at it. Mr. Adkinson, like every other political leader, resented new and, particularly, aggressive rivalry that threatened his own position. He tried to block Deneen's rise, but unsuccessfully. The result was that although, when I knew him, Mr. Adkinson was president of his ward club, he was gradually being forced to the rear. This he resented. Quiet and mild-mannered man that he was, he hated Deneen to the end of his days. I think that if he had not been so stubborn, if he had accepted gracefully the situation that he could not change, he might have gone on the bench—where he belonged and where I tried to put him in 1912 via the Progressive party.

Gradually I began to overcome the unreasoning partisan viewpoint. I don't know what caused this and I don't know the date of my first slight deviation from the political path that my feet had always trod. Certainly the change in me was not due to any of my associates or to any of the members of my family. We had always read the *Tribune* in the Wheeler family, but after I entered college in 1893 I switched to the *Record*. In the first place, the *Record* was cheaper (in price) than the *Tribune*. I soon began to like the *Record* and to absorb its independent political point of view.

At any rate, whether from the inside or from the outside, or from a combination of both, my spirit began to throw off the shackles of blind partisanship, although I still accounted myself a Republican with the seed of the unborn Progressive in me. In due course I became a member of the University of Chicago Republican Club. The women students took no interest at all in the organization, and the men took little more. It was a pretty slim affair. Sometimes it would go into a state of coma for a considerable period. Then someone would take an interest in it and the corpse would be regalvanized.

L. Brent Vaughan, a classmate of mine, was such a one. He resuscitated the club and asked me to join. I consented. Vaughan was elected president and I was chosen treasurer, with nothing to treasure. This was along in 1896, just prior to the Presidential campaign of that year. I think that Vaughan revived the club because the Republican leaders were trying to stir up interest among college students who were old enough to vote. A meeting of the Intercollegiate Republican League was held early that summer in Grand Rapids, Michigan. Vaughan and I were sent (or did we choose ourselves, if indeed there was anyone else in the organization to say us nay?) to represent the Republican Club of the University of Chicago. I don't know how our expenses were managed, but Vaughan arranged it, probably through some Republican committee.

I met a number of interesting young men at the Grand Rapids meeting, among them one by the name of Deberville from the University of Vermont who, when he found that I was not a fraternity man, suggested that I organize a chapter of Alpha Tau Omega at Chicago. I was soon let in on the secret that Vaughan went to Grand Rapids with an ambition to be elected president of the League. I, of course, was for him, and supported his candidacy, but he was licked in advance. However, to my great surprise and despite the fact that I was not a candidate for anything, I found myself elected treasurer—still with nothing to treasure.

Vaughan was not pleased, either with his defeat or with my success. Shortly after our return to Chicago the time came to elect the officers of our local club and Vaughan had a candidate for the top job. Budding curmudgeon that I was, I decided that I too wanted to be president, and so told one or two of my friends (those were the days when I had 'em). I made no campaign but I won by a very close margin. So far I was batting 1,000 per cent. I had been in three elections— one for the principal of the Englewood High School, and two for myself, and I had been on the winning side each time.

I managed to get my hands on a ticket of admission to the Democratic National Convention which met in 1896 in the old Coliseum, a relic of the World's Fair that later was destroyed by fire. William Jennings Bryan was known to me slightly by name, but that was all. My seat in the convention hall was a poor one. It was way back and way up in the topmost gallery. If there had been anything nearer the rafters, I would have been in it. The acoustics were terrible. Those of us who were in the gallery had great difficulty in hearing, so much so that we adopted the habit of shaping huge ear trumpets out of newspapers (they do have their uses), and there we would sit by the hour with the trumpets leveled toward the speakers on the floor below. It must have been a weird sight from the main floor to see no faces but only row upon row of newspaper cones in the galleries.

There were many outstanding national figures among the delegates—David B. Hill, Senator Gorman of Maryland, Senator Teller, the great silver advocate, of Colorado, who had been a Republican, and many others, including a young free-silver enthusiast from Virginia named Carter Glass. What went on did not mean much to me, and since I couldn't hear well, even with my trumpet, I had to be content with watching, from afar off, generally indistinguishable figures acting in what to me was a historic pantomime.

Then one day Bryan asked for and obtained the floor. He began his famous "Cross of Gold and Crown of Thorns" speech. His wonderful voice filled the auditorium. His was the only speech that could be heard in every nook and corner of the building. One by one the paper ear trumpets were dropped, and the audience, spellbound, sat with eyes intent upon this bold and eloquent young Congressman from Nebraska.

I comprehended only vaguely the money issue in that campaign. As a traditional Republican, I was unquestioningly a gold man, in addition to which, for such reasons as I could understand, I believed in the gold cause. But this speech of Bryan's thrilled me just as a speech. Everybody knows what it did to the convention. During the short time needed for its delivery, Bryan became the top man of the Democratic party, and for years thereafter held its leadership. Defeated three times for the Presidency, he was nonetheless a great man whose life added up on the asset side of the national ledger. He was also one of the greatest orators of all time.

The strategy of the Republican managers in 1896 would not permit William McKinley, the Republican candidate, to

leave his home in Canton, Ohio. Unhappily for him, Mc-
Kinley had been, as a member of Congress, more than kind
toward silver. The Republican platform committed him to
gold, and McKinley, being what he was, had no difficulty in
about-facing and becoming an ardent advocate of the gold
standard. But if he had wandered away from home base, he
might have found himself in the West, which was rabid for
silver. Consequently, he conducted the first front-porch campaign in the history of American politics. Instead of his going out to meet the people, delegations were taken to Canton
from all parts of the country to meet him. No hand-picked,
expenses-paid member of a delegation would venture to ask
embarrassing questions.

A man by the name of Kelso at the University of Chicago
conceived the idea of turning an honest penny by selling bas-
reliefs of the Republican candidate. The Scotch in a man
is bound to come out. In order to advertise his wares, he
cooked a plan whereby the Republican Club would send a
delegation to Canton to present Governor McKinley with
one of the bas-reliefs of himself cast in bronze. Kelso suggested the junket to me and I fell for it. I was too much of
a greenhorn even to suspect that I was being used. I did not
know, until a friend put me wise later, of the scheme to
market the article, but in my wide-eyed innocence thought
that the plan was an expression of generous enthusiasm for
a great cause. So the sucker accepted, and a hand-picked delegation, consisting of Gus Axelson, Kelso, and me, one night
boarded a train for Canton. Our trip was financed, but not
on a very generous scale. While Axelson and I jimmied ourselves into one upper berth, Kelso slept comfortably below
with the bust. (If he had had even the vestigial remains of a
conscience, he would not have been comfortable.) But I was

young, and the prospect of meeting a live Presidential candidate was enough to make up for all discomforts.

Arriving in Canton, we found our way to Major McKinley's home, where I presented him with the bas-relief in a few as well-chosen words as I was capable of stringing together. He accepted in appropriate language and then we had a brief general chat. He was friendly and affable, as candidates are wont to be, especially before elections, but I decided later that he had not made a profound impression on me. During the interview the editor of the *Canton Evening Repository* (still the leading newspaper of the town and then McKinley's favorite journal) was introduced to me, and I mumbled the assurance that I had been getting the "Suppository" right along, as indeed I had (free), because it was the party's official newspaper in that campaign. I was frightfully embarrassed by the unfortunate slip of the tongue, but not so Major McKinley. He enjoyed it immensely. The editor didn't, although he managed a sour smile.

The campaign was hard-fought and very exciting. Bryan set the country on fire, but he had no money. Mark Hanna had plenty of money for McKinley. Never had money flowed so freely. The precedent set by Hanna in 1896 was a bad one that has had a malevolent effect upon American politics ever since. As a matter of course, he corrupted states that have been corrupt ever since. I have never doubted that if the Democrats had been able to raise enough money, even for legitimate purposes, Bryan would have been elected.

As evidencing the profligate spending by the Republicans, I was advised to canvass the university students to find out how many who were for McKinley would be willing to go home to vote on election day if they were furnished railroad transportation. Round-trip tickets would be provided. Many students took advantage of this splendid offer of a free ride home at no other cost than a vote for McKinley. (The day before election I found on hand an uncalled-for return ticket to some point in Nebraska. I did not want to see this go to waste. My closest friend, Stacy C. Mosser, had never been in those parts and so, at my suggestion, he set out to enjoy a twenty-four-hour trip in a day coach.) I do not believe that in any other campaign since has this wholesale and expensive method of rounding up votes been resorted to, even by the Republicans. Many years later, it was to be made unnecessary as states began to adopt absentee-voter laws.

My first Presidential vote was cast in this election and, while I put it on the line for the Republican ticket, it was without any enthusiasm. However, in the same election I voted for John P. Altgeld, who was running for re-election as Governor of Illinois on the Democratic ticket. I felt that he had been a greatly traduced man. How the *Chicago Tribune* and others had smeared this humane and courageous man because he had fought for the underdog, and especially because he had pardoned those who still lived of the innocent victims who had been railroaded to the penitentiary after the Haymarket riot! So far as I could see, Altgeld stood about where I wanted to stand on social questions. I had never met him, nor had I ever heard him speak. (Later I had a most interesting interview with him for my paper.)

On the other hand, Altgeld's Republican opponent, John R. Tanner, did not appeal to me, so I started my active political life by voting at the same election for a conservative Republican candidate for President and a radical Democratic candidate for Governor. Thus I was well launched upon the independent political career that I have ever since followed. Altgeld was defeated, lowering my average slightly, with a total of four victories against one defeat. Not bad for one who was just getting dried off behind the ears!

In the spring of 1897 there was a mayoralty contest in Chicago. The year before there had been elected, as a member of the City Council from the Twenty-first Ward, an aggressive young lawyer by the name of John Maynard Harlan. Harlan was then in his early thirties. He stood six feet tall, all bone and muscle. He had played center at Princeton and was boxing regularly two or three times a week to keep himself in perfect physical condition. He was the youngest son of Justice John Marshall Harlan of the Supreme Court of the United States.

The Chicago City Council at the time of Harlan's election to it had been sinking to depths that were lower and lower. It was forever on the auction block—ready to go to the highest bidder. So besodden was it of prostitution that it would rather have offered its favors free of cost than vote in the public interest. The leader of the gang that controlled the Council and the man who was supposed to ladle in the gravy for an "equitable" distribution among his second-story men was Martin B. Madden, a Republican alderman from the Second Ward. Madden was in the stone business by daylight. Later in his life, when he tried to jump from the festering Chicago City Council to the United States Senate with the support of Lorimer and his gang, the public revulsion was so spontaneous that the attempt was abandoned. Still later, he did venture to run for the House of Representatives and he made it. He had the right kind of a district, plenty of money, and no scruples about using it where it would do him the most good. In time he rose to a position of great power and influence, as chairman of the Appropriations Committee, a position that he held at his death.

But at the time of which I write, Madden was just the un-scrupulous captain of a crew of piratical racketeers. "Gray Wolves" was the name given them by the brilliant William Kent (later a Congressman from California), who had gone into the Council as a Republican the year before Harlan be-came a member. Harlan and Kent, flanked by two or three others, made a valiant stand against this chain gang. "Pay-as-you-go" Charles T. Yerkes, to whom I have previously referred—a precursor of such men as Samuel Insull and James A. Simpson—was the chief corrupter, but he did not pay alone. He controlled the North and West Side traction systems. Having served a term in the penitentiary for corrupt practices while a citizen of Philadelphia, he moved to Chi-cago, secured control of the two main traction lines, and proceeded to mop up. He was willing to share his loot with his cash-register aldermen, whose "fares" he rang up as they passed him with eagerly outstretched hands.

Yerkes wanted extensions of his franchises. He was willing, as always, to pay for what he wanted, and from 1896 on, the fight that he made to obtain legislation at Springfield per-mitting the City Council to give him longer than twenty-year franchises raged. He felt sure of his Council if it could only get an enabling act. Concurrent with leveling his financial batteries upon the State Legislature, he opened a similar of-fensive against the City Council, but there he ran into Harlan and Kent. Kent did not rank high in debate or upon the platform but he could push a punishing pen. Harlan was one of the most effective men on his feet that I have ever known. He not only had the moral courage to say what he thought, he had the physical courage to back it up if neces-sary. As Allen B. Pond once put it, "John Harlan doesn't call a spade a spade; he calls it a dirty shovel."

Such a fight, of course, meant headlines in the newspapers, of which in those days I was merely one of tens of thousands of readers. Through the columns of the *Record* I followed the assault on Yerkes in the Council, and when the Municipal Voters' League was organized to lend support to Alderman Harlan, who was leading the fight, I filled in a membership blank with my name and address and dropped it in the mail. That was my first protest of record against corruption in public office.

The 1897 mayoralty fight was a crucial one in Chicago's history. It was to be waged upon the traction issue, with ex-convict Yerkes as the chief point of attack. It was a chapter in the timeless story of a public utility gouging, biting, and slugging the public by whose favor it existed, and of corrupting that public's "servants." I was to engage in many such battles during my life. There could be no career based upon public favor in such a course. But it could make a nutmeg-grater of the most angelic disposition.

The Republicans, fearing Harlan, reached into the Circuit Court and chose as their candidate a highly respectable citizen, able lawyer, and good judge—Nathaniel C. Sears. His selection was no doubt predicated on the proposition that, if elected, he would be "safe."

The Democrats nominated Carter H. Harrison the younger, a name to conjure with in those days. It was said and believed for many years that Harrison had made terms with Yerkes. It is not improbable that Harrison's active managers made representations and promises, but if Yerkes ever drew any checks against Harrison, they were not honored. In any case, Yerkes supported Harrison. Anyone rather than the "dangerous" Harlan.

Opposed to Sears because they sensed no people's cham-

pion in him, and to Harrison because they were suspicious
of Yerkes' influence, were many thousands of independents
and reformers and just plain people. A movement, encouraged and supported by Lawson's *Record* and *News*, sprang
into being almost overnight intent upon running knight-
errant Harlan as an independent candidate. Civic enthusiasm
shot up. Nominating petitions were circulated and signed in
vast numbers, and Harlan entered the race as an independent
Republican.

I was thrilled. Some months before, I had heard Harlan
address a meeting at the Marquette Club, and then and
there, convinced of his political integrity and high courage,
I fell hard for him. Moreover, I was in no doubt as to his
ability to fight. Naturally I became an eager adherent of the
independent cause. Through Professor William Hill, of the
department of political economy at the University of Chicago, I took on some of the work of building up Harlan sentiment on the campus. Hill was one of Harlan's inside men
—a man of little experience or force, but sincerely independent and brave.

The *Record* printed a call for volunteers. The treasury
was low. In fact, it was said that there wasn't enough money
to carry the campaign to its close, and so volunteers—willing
hearts and hands—were called for. I dropped everything and
sought out Professor Hill, who took me down to Harlan's
headquarters, where I met the candidate's brother, James S.
Harlan, later successively to be Attorney General of Puerto
Rico and a member of the Interstate Commerce Commission.

It must have been perfectly clear to Brother James and
everybody else that I was without experience, but so badly
manned were the headquarters that I was actually put in
charge of assigning watchers and challengers to serve on elec-

tion day at the polling places. There was no money with which to pay anyone, but for two weeks, day after day, I stood callowly behind a counter and as men came in to offer their services, consulted my records and maps, assigned them to the proper precincts, and made arrangements for their credentials. So few people were willing to work for the love of it that I took anyone who offered, and I haven't any doubt now, based on what I have since learned of the ways of machine politics, that many of the volunteers that I mustered for duty for Harlan had been sent in by Republican and Democratic leaders. In other words, I was probably accepting men upon whom the two old organizations were confidently relying to help to defeat a troublesome political upstart.

I managed to slip away from headquarters once or twice to hear the candidate, who was still a stranger to me. Harlan conceived the plan of holding noonday meetings in Central Music Hall, which then stood in State Street near Washington, on the site now occupied by the great Marshall Field store. No one had ever heard of noonday political meetings, and Harlan's close advisers opposed the strange notion. He made the point that the downtown area was the nerve center of Chicago, to which he would attract thousands of men who would leave the meetings not only as converts to the cause, but as flaming apostles for it. So, on Harlan's judgment alone, the meetings were undertaken, and similar ones have been held in downtown Chicago theaters in every campaign since. Some years later, when "Billy" Kent persuaded me to go to New York to help a bunch of Yale amateurs to organize in support of Otto T. Bannard for mayor against Judge Gaynor, I introduced the noonday political meeting idea there. But it did not take. New York greatly differs physically from Chicago.

Central Music Hall wasn't big enough by far to accommodate the crowds that stormed to hear Harlan smash out at the corrupt gang led by Yerkes and Madden. Nor was he content to assail the gangsters alone. He secured a list of the directors of the Yerkes traction companies—a coterie of prominent businessmen among whom was the original Marshall Field himself. He would read this list and then demand that the men on it assume some responsibility for Yerkes's crooked practices. But none of them ever so much as intimated, at least publicly, that he felt any responsibility for "Pay-as-you-go" Yerkes.

Harlan sentiment surged high. He barnstormed the city, making one of the most vigorous one-man campaigns that I have ever witnessed. It became evident that Sears couldn't finish better than third. The question was whether Harlan could beat Harrison. In a situation like this, the thing happened that always happens when crooked politicians get together. At heart all professional political gangs are the same. If necessary, they will combine to elect a hairless Mexican dog in order to defeat the forces of good government. If they can prevail by delivering themselves to the other fellow, that's what they will do. So in this case, when it became clear to the "Gray Wolves" that Sears was going to bring up the rear, they ran to Harrison, regardless of party label. It didn't cost him a dime. Here was a case of political prostitutes offering themselves freely. We saw it coming and felt our stomachs beginning to curl. Our ideals and hopes were curdling.

My position at headquarters entitled me to a seat on the platform of the Auditorium, where the final Harlan rally was to be held. It was ten o'clock when the vigorous, strongly

built candidate pushed his way through the thronging crowd
that had been waiting since early evening. I had never seen
anywhere else a crowd brought, wildly cheering, to its feet as
John Harlan lifted that crowd out of its seats that night.
Even Bryan, with his impassioned "Cross of Gold and Crown
of Thorns" plea, had not equaled it. My backbone had never
had such a workout as that scene gave it. How I envied Harlan his power, which was the power of sincerity and truth
—the power to advocate boldly the just cause—in strong,
forceful speech, expressed in brilliant phrases and beautiful
English.

The people of Chicago flocked to the polls and elected
Carter H. Harrison for his initial term. Harlan was second,
and Sears a poor third. Thus ended the reading of the first
Harlan lesson.

I went back to the university to pick up my work where I
had dropped it and to graduate the following June.

CHAPTER SIX

A HARDY PERENNIAL

It seems to me, when it cannot be help'd, that defeat is great.
—WALT WHITMAN.

MAYOR HARRISON made such a good record, especially in resisting the attempted raids of Yerkes and his gang, that his re-election in 1899 was conceded. The Republicans had Zina R. Carter, faithful retainer of "Boss" Lorimer, for their candidate, but Harrison's popularity plus the Yerkes blight was too tough a combination even for the crooks. (And I still accounted myself a Republican!)

Harlan had retired from the Council at the end of his first term in 1897, and was at this time inactive politically, although he continued to be a potential candidate and a constant threat to the politicians until his final nomination and defeat in 1905.

In 1901, Harrison, running for his third consecutive term, defeated my old hard-boiled "friend" Judge Hanecy, whose failure to secure the Republican nomination for Governor at Peoria in 1900 had made him even more embittered and cynical. Personally, Harrison was a respectable figure, and no one ever accused him of dipping his fingers into the graft till. But the Democratic machine, under the leadership of

89

Bobby Burke, was a pretty unsavory institution. It was a political cesspool that no amount of activated sludge treatment could deodorize. There was graft and plenty of it, much of it the meanest and most sordid kind—from gambling, from tax-fixing, from saloons, from prostitution, from illicit drugs, from vice of every description. Even children were encouraged to gamble. What part of the rake-off didn't go into the party's war chest was appropriated by or distributed among the plug-uglies in proportion to their influence or their cupidity. I recall that during one of the campaigns we reporters fell to speculating how much money Harrison's managers probably had for his expenses and where it had come from. I asked John P. Hopkins how much could be collected in twenty-four hours. He readily named the figure of $1,000,000. As the city grew and working arrangements between politics and the underworld and the contractors were perfected, I have no doubt that much larger sums found their way into the pockets of the grafters.

Harlan wanted more than anything in the world to be Mayor of Chicago. Having made such a good showing in 1897, it was natural that it should seem to him and his friends that the mayoralty was within his grasp. He didn't realize, of course, that the regulars never forget nor forgive political irregularity. Ordinarily, the insurgent may as well leave all ambition behind. The organization will, under compulsion, as in 1905 it did with Harlan, take as its candidate for office a man it can't get rid of in any other way, but its revenge is usually certain in the end.

During my tenancy in the job of assistant political editor of the *Record* I had come to know John Harlan. I saw him frequently and he wore well. In time we became inseparable friends. I wanted to see him in the driver's seat. To those of us who had our eyes still glued to the traction issue Harrison was a strictly laissez-faire mayor, without any inclination for an offensive fight—a policy that was not particularly distasteful either to the traction interests, provided that nothing worse befell, or to other sinister influences that flourish on political inertia.

After the 1901 election, Harlan decided to make a try for the regular Republican nomination two years later. Only a few of us were in on this decision. It was realized that the ground would have to be prepared well in advance of 1903 if he were to have a chance. Harlan had no political organization nor the means or capacity to put one together. Four friends contributed $10,000 each to a fund to do spadework during the next two years—Victor C. Lawson, Delavan Smith, publisher of the *Indianapolis News,* and Thomas and David Jones, Princeton alumni who had large interests in the American Zinc Company.

Meanwhile, Victor Lawson had sold the *Record* to H. H. Kohlsaat, the apple-pie-and-coffee man, and it had been merged with the *Herald.* In the mixup, with the unexpected help of Roger C. Sullivan and Fred M. Blount (strange bedfellows for me), I found myself on John R. Walsh's *Chronicle*—altogether unhappy and ill at ease, working out of the city room on run-of-the-mine assignments. When Harlan asked me to give up my newspaper job and undertake to watch the political situation for him for the ensuing two years, I almost choked in my eagerness.

That Harlan could not indefinitely be kept in leash, the organization regretfully realized. He wanted to be Mayor and he was capable of fighting for it. He believed that he could do great things for his city, and I am sure that if, in the full flush of his youthful idealism, he had found himself responsible for the social and political welfare of the people of Chicago, he would have distinguished himself. Probably a great public career would have opened itself to him.

I rented an office in an old building that fronted on the east side of Dearborn Street, between Madison and Washington. My space overlooked the alley, so that the rent was lower and I could be inconspicuous. My name appeared nowhere in the building, and I had no telephone. A bare handful knew what I was doing. My friends at the university thought that I had some kind of a job downtown, and people downtown thought that I was doing something at the university. It worked beautifully; for two full years I was a political ghost.

My main job was to keep in close touch with developments in the traction situation. I clipped everything that had to do with this and local politics appearing in the newspapers, and before I knew it I had more than a dozen huge scrapbooks filled and cross-indexed in a card-catalogue file that made specific information instantly available. I also spent a great deal of time on the beat that I had traveled while reporting for the *Record*—circulating among the city and county officials and political leaders. The politicians took me for granted and, while occasionally an interest was expressed as to what I was doing with myself, no one pressed the inquiry to a point where it became embarrassing. I became a human sponge.

Harlan's ward was controlled by Fred Busse, who was then one of the second-string bosses in the Republican organization. As a member of the State Senate, Busse was an insider in the small group of three that ruled that august body. This meant control of legislation as well as control of the cash register. Thus he was a power, although ranking below Lorimer, Jamieson, Hertz, and Pease. His domain lay just south of the territory dominated by Pease, which made him and Pease natural allies.

The east portion of Busse's ward embraced the Lake Shore Drive; the west side was composed largely of slums, pockmarked by saloons, gambling houses, and brothels. Tough gangs roamed here and serious crimes, including murders, were numerous. The streets were not safe at night, nor the alleys in the daytime. It was Busse's job to keep tight rein on those born to the calico and deliver their votes at the proper time in the necessary quantity, while east of Clark Street he had to keep the "Gold Coast" convinced that, while he was a rough-and-ready politician, he understood the problems and aspirations of those born to the purple and fine linen.

In a saloon in the no-man's land connecting, but at the same time separating, these two widely divergent sections, Busse and Federal Judge George A. Carpenter, scion of an old, rich, and respectable Chicago family, used to fraternize with "the boys," until the Judge was caught at it.

Busse was also adroit in currying favor with the newspapers, especially the *Tribune*. Victor Lawson, Herman Kohlsaat, Joe Patterson, and Bertie McCormick all lived in Busse's ward. Caressingly, he stroked the silky flanks of Patterson and McCormick, with the result that the *Tribune* stood by Busse when it attacked others who were more worthy of support. Even Lawson and Kohlsaat were not too censorious where Busse was concerned.

Harlan also lived in Busse's ward, and since he could emit political lightning flashes of high voltage, Busse thought it wise to give him his head. As a matter of fact, he had supported Harlan when Harlan ran for the Council, and the two had never broken, although Busse remained regular and was for Judge Sears in 1897. A man who was clever enough to control a ward as mixed as Busse's was too smart not to get along with even a rampant young crusader, at least up to a certain point. It developed later that it was none other than Busse who, after the 1901 election, had suggested to Harlan that he get ready for 1903. He advised Harlan to begin laying his foundation, and he also suggested that I be engaged to carry the hod. Accordingly, Busse knew of my relationship to Harlan, but he discreetly kept the knowledge to himself. An admission that he knew might be regarded as a commitment, and Busse was too shrewd to implicate himself so far in advance. I dealt with him on the theory that, in good time, he would declare for Harlan, and I looked upon him as the strongest factor in Harlan's favor.

Harlan and Busse kept in close touch with each other through me. It was well along in 1902 that I became suspicious of Busse. Word reached me that he was laying wires for the nomination of Graeme Stewart, a partner in the wholesale grocery firm of W. M. Hoyt & Company. Stewart was an active and prominent member of the organization in Busse's ward—an attractive personality, but a stuffed shirt. A regular of regulars, he instinctively knew when to look the other way with pious disregard of dubious goings-on. He craved the prominence and acclaim that go with high political position, but he knew very little about issues and cared less—a "dependable" man. The support that Stewart could muster was the kind that controls nominations, via the soapbox-selected delegates, whereas Harlan's strength lay in his popular appeal to the inarticulate rank and file of the voters.

At first I said nothing to Harlan about my suspicion that Busse had run out on us. I wanted to be sure of my ground, besides which I was certain that Harlan wouldn't believe me.

He wouldn't want to. But the more I probed, the more I became convinced that Busse in his heart had already betrayed Harlan. So one day I told Harlan of my fears, and, as I expected, he stormed at me. Any suggestion that his plausible friend and supporter Busse might betray him was little short of an outrageous slander. The best that I could get out of him was a promise to keep his eyes and ears functioning and to be careful in what he said to Busse.

From that time on my principal job consisted in trying to convince Harlan that Busse was his enemy, a Judas whose price, one could bet, was more than thirty pieces of silver. I began to test my theories on Busse. I found that he was less accessible. I discovered that it was more and more difficult to have a word with him in private and that when I did get inside of his back room he was no longer frank and open with me, but distinctly evasive.

I finally gnawed a promise out of Harlan that, at the first opportunity, he would confront Busse and force a showdown and, if possible, in my presence. Then to Harlan's surprise he found that he couldn't get an appointment. He couldn't even get Busse on the telephone. But his chance came. One day on our way back to the office after lunch, Harlan and I caught sight of Busse going into the Central Trust Company of his friend Charles G. Dawes, and we followed. Harlan was not lacking in courage or forthrightness. We mounted the steps behind Busse and Harlan faced him. Busse was fundamentally yellow, as most betrayers are. At first he tried to bluff and hedge but finally, under pressure, he admitted the truth of what I had been telling Harlan. Instead of breaking him in two right there, as he could have done, Harlan stung him with a few verbal jabs and we contemptuously left the miserable creature cringing in the middle of the foyer.

Busse's defection was a great shock to Harlan. He naturally began to wonder on what basis he could become a candidate for the Republican nomination when he would not even have the delegates from his own ward. He concluded that it was hopeless. I knew that he was right, but I insisted that he stick to the raft, not because I was getting $25 a week out of my stingy little job, but because I couldn't bear to see Busse and his buzzards get away with it. Harlan pleaded that he had no money to finance a campaign—which I knew. He argued that his wife, who didn't want him to run anyhow, simply would not hear of his being a candidate in the circumstances. I was acquainted with that situation, too. Mrs. Harlan had never been in sympathy with John's interest in public matters. She never helped him in a campaign except to leave the city for its duration.

My rebuttal was that if he quit then he was through forever. I argued that he wasn't deciding whether or not to be Mayor of Chicago in 1903, since by no stretch of the imagination could he hope to be that; that he was facing the bigger issue of whether he was to retire definitely and finally to private life and tie a tin can to the tail of his political ambitions.

I prevailed. Harlan arose from the table at Rector's, where we were Dutch-lunching, and said: "Ickes, you're right. I'll make the fight, but I don't know how I am ever going to square it with Mrs. Harlan."

I don't know how he squared it with Mrs. Harlan, but I do know that he made the fight, and a great and glorious one it was, too. During the bitter cold winter that followed we tramped the streets, attended meetings, rang doorbells, kept the telephone going, cornered politicians in the lower brackets, and then started a speaking campaign right in the middle of the coldest season of the year. Some nights were so cold that our halls were virtually empty when we arrived, ourselves half frozen. At first we ran the campaign from Harlan's office to save expenses, even if it did not do the law business much good. I was campaign manager, press agent, and confidential adviser, from 8 A.M. to 11 P.M. or later. If there had been a band, I would have been it, too. And it would have been brass.

When the last meeting of the day was on the North Side, I would sleep in one of Harlan's beds and when it was on the South Side, he would bunk with me. I rented the halls, arranged for the printing and distribution of handbills, took charge of the publicity, and combed the neighborhoods for influential citizens to preside at meetings. Whenever I failed in that, I introduced Harlan myself. At the outset of our speaking campaign I gave out press releases in the form of excerpts from Harlan's statements. Later, as the campaign steamed up, I prepared advance copies of his speeches, so that before his noonday meetings, which we were then holding in McVicker's Theater, all newspapers were supplied. This method was new then and we got wonderful publicity, especially in the Lawson paper.

In my leisure (!!) moments I busied myself trying to get together some kind of an organization. At first, Harlan was holding one meeting a night. The campaign looked to be about as hopeless an engagement as a man had ever got himself into. Then, to my enthusiastic surprise, with nobody interested in the far-off April election and the weather so cold and inclement that few people would have gone out to hear George Washington repeat his Farewell Address, Harlan told me to put on two meetings a night instead of one. That's the kind of a scrapper he was. It sounded good to me, so I put my other shoulder to the wheel.

Gradually interest was stirred, and in a short time we were holding three, then four, then five, and finally six meetings nightly. We began to fill bigger halls. And did the customers like our bill of fare! We hired Eugene Fletcher to keep open house at headquarters while we scoured the city for workers and votes.

The nominating convention was to be held three or four weeks prior to the election. As his crowds had grown, Harlan had begun to kid himself that he was going to make off with the nomination. "Candidate's psychology," as I had come to call it, is a well-known but necessary disease that keeps a fellow going. For myself, I nursed no illusions. However, I did not by any word of mine take the edge off of his fine fighting spirit, which a realistic analysis of the situation would have done. All that I knew was that we were making a damned good fight that wasn't going to get us anywhere, at least in 1903. But after that—

The preconvention campaign came to a close at a time when Harlan sentiment was mounting magnificently. There came the inevitable day, however, when delegates were to be selected, and when that time did arrive the organization delivered to Graeme Stewart almost as one man. Under the convention system you can't beat an organization that has money. An organization *without* money is tough enough. We had neither an organization *nor* money. If there had been a direct primary, Harlan, I am sure, would have been the nominee, in spite of the organization and all of its money.

However, Harlan had achieved what he went after—he had re-established himself as a force to be reckoned with in the future political life of the city. Harlan was a good sport about it and declared for Stewart, who after all was a decent citizen, even if politically he was a dud. The fight was over, and all elements of the party were united, on the surface at least, behind the candidate that the tricky Busse had succeeded in putting over.

With Stewart nominated I assumed that I was out of a job. During the closing weeks of the campaign I had not been able to draw even the meager salary for which I had been engaged. Our little trickle had run dry. I just didn't say anything to John about it. He had more than enough to worry about. Then Stewart told me that he wanted me to handle his publicity! A job! with pay! The best that I had ever had! Fifty dollars a week maybe! Stewart took me to meet his manager, Alexander H. Revell, proprietor of the largest furniture store in Chicago. Revell had been shoved into the key spot in order to strengthen the illusion that Stewart was the "businessmen's candidate" and that the campaign was being run by "businessmen."

I set to work at once, writing Stewart's speeches and interviews that were given out formally to the newspapers. At an early conference I had reminded Stewart that the important issue was that of traction and asked him what his position was. I was delighted when he said that it was "the same as John Harlan's." It didn't take me long to discover that what Stewart knew about the traction issue you could stick in your eye and not feel it. Stewart rarely, if ever, used the statements on traction that I wrote for him. I doubt if he or Revell ever went to the trouble of reading them, but they got into the papers just the same, because the newspapers never took the trouble to check the release with what the candidate actually said. I consoled myself that if by any chance, which I felt was slim, Stewart should be elected, he would be publicly committed, by the speeches and statements that I had written for him, to the right kind of a traction policy.

I cut at least one good big wisdom tooth in this campaign. Harlan had freely charged that the traction interests customarily put their money on both of the leading candidates if "Barkis was willin'." He believed this, and so did I, but neither of us could have proved it. I was in Revell's office one day when, right under my censorious nose, he dispatched a trusty to Yerkes to tell him that he wanted $14,000 to finish the campaign. And the money was promptly forthcoming. That I know. I felt certain that there had been previous political alms that Yerkes, that goodhearted man, had also kicked in for Harrison's campaign, although in lesser amounts. While it has been the custom in American politics for the public-utility and other privileged interests to give to both major campaign funds, it is as a matter of course that they contribute larger sums to the favored and more pliable candidate, while to the less favored one, if he will accept them, and to the one not likely to win, they make smaller contributions just by way of insurance against a possible mischance at the polls.

It appeared, therefore, that Yerkes was not afraid of Stewart on traction, in spite of what I had been saying in his name in the newspapers daily. Stewart had assured me that Harlan's traction policy was his too, and he had, at least tacitly, adopted the traction principles that I had enunciated for him, day after day. Yet here he was, getting big contributions from the very interests that he was supposed to be against!

I had to go through with it for all I felt that I had been tricked. My loss of confidence in Stewart was so great that on election day I simply could not bring myself to vote for him.

These three Irish cronies were
the delights of my early newspaper and political career.

George E. Brennan
His equal as a politician
I have never met.

John P. Hopkins
Handsome, rich and
single.

Roger C. Sullivan
Who spoke up for Wilson
and, I believe, made him
President.

"ANYBODY ELSE?"

I cast my ballot for Harrison, who won by a scant 8,000 votes. How close to the bull's eye had Billy Loeffler, the shrewd city clerk, come when he predicted the result to me.

With the fourth consecutive election of Harrison, despite his obstinate do-nothing policy on traction, my political activities went into an eclipse. I closed the office which I had been using for Harlan, and again found myself face to face with unemployment.

In this dilemma, I managed to scrape together, by one means or another, enough money and prospects to permit me to enter the University of Chicago Law School, where I landed in the fall of 1903. But I was not to finish my course without another interruption. The Republicans had reached the conclusion that the only way that they could permanently purge their ranks of John Harlan was to make him their candidate in 1905. It would mean two more years of looking into the City Hall from the outside, but it would be worth it to get rid of the troublesome creature who could not be made to understand how little he was wanted. And perhaps it may be guessed from between the lines how much love was lost between the political plug-uglies and this persistent sniffer of gunfire.

Harrison's policy of "do-nothingism" in traction matters finally caught up with him. The voters got tired of seeing him hanging about. A strong municipal-ownership sentiment was growing as one result of the stubborn refusal on the part of the traction interests to accept an ordinance under which the people might get a decent break. The leader of this sentiment on the Democratic side was Judge Edward F. Dunne, who had been on the Circuit Court bench for years and who had a large personal and political following.

Dunne snatched the leadership from Harrison that year, and he did it on the traction issue.

Meanwhile, it became apparent that Harlan could have the Republican torch for the asking. The organization was tired of fighting him face to face. Hypocritically, Republican leaders began to call upon Harlan to assure him of their longing for him for 1905. They literally swarmed his office, stepping on each other's toes to pledge him their support. What they did not tell him was that they were going to use him as an emetic. Even as they protested their eagerness for his leadership, many of them had their tongues in their cheeks. They had made up their minds that a scientific job of encirclement and penetration was the best way to get rid of him.

Harlan fell for their blandishments and called on me again to go down with him. I had no thought even of hesitating. A fight was, after all, a fight and I had not had a good one for a long stretch—two years, in fact. Besides, a miracle might happen. Anyhow, it was now or never for Harlan. The result was that I dropped out of law school in January of 1905 and devoted myself once more to the job of trying to help make Harlan Mayor of Chicago. The perennial traction question was still a question. It still is, but with an apparent chance of being settled after the politicians have had their last fling at it as I write, forty-five years after it first became an issue.

So once again I found myself in the heat and clamor of a mayoralty campaign. With the Republican nomination safely tucked away by Harlan, and with Dunne sure to be chosen by the Democrats, I conceived the plan of jumping the gun by having Harlan grab the traction issue and run with it the night before the Democratic convention. I had to argue with

Harlan to get him to agree, but at last he did so and we rented Orchestra Hall for the coup de main. I insisted that he prepare his speech carefully, even though he knew the subject backwards. There was to be a grave joining of issues and there must be no misunderstanding as to where Harlan stood.

One of the most difficult things in the world was to make Harlan write or dictate a speech. A fluent extemporaneous speaker, he hated the very thought of it. He kept putting this one off until the day arrived on the night of which he was to deliver it. Everything was ready but the speech. At the eleventh hour, by dint of bullying him, Harlan was finally induced to close his office to everyone except me and a court reporter, and he proceeded to dictate a speech which I hoped would close the campaign before it had really opened.

To my horror, a change had come over Harlan, a change that I had not realized until the three of us were alone in his office a few hours before he was to throw down the gage of battle. I had noticed, come to think of it, that he had been talking somewhat differently about traction, but I had paid little attention. I thought that he was merely browsing about the subject, thinking out loud, as he often did, and viewing it from different angles while preparing himself to deliver his knockout punch. I did not know that in his thoughts he had begun to swing away from the strong and popular position that he had occupied for so many years. Instead of taking the aggressive, forthright stand that was to be expected of him, his tone was conciliatory and judicial. I interrupted several times to expostulate with him, but he impatiently shook me off and cautioned me to wait until he had finished.

At last he was through, and he asked me what I thought of it. I assured him that, in my opinion, he would be licked before he started if he delivered that speech. He argued that he hadn't changed. His language to me indicated that he had. And language would count in traction-wise Chicago. My position was that he simply had to take such a stand that Dunne would either have to accept it as his, too, or adopt another that would make his position an impossible one.

We put it up to James S. Harlan, John's older brother, who agreed with me. But John would not give up. He was naturally stubborn, and on this occasion he had a great pride of opinion and an overwhelming confidence in himself. The battle raged until Harlan threw the speech onto his desk and told me to fix it up if I could without changing the thought. I undertook hopelessly to do this, with the time for the meeting almost upon us. Under great pressure I went through the speech, making a little change in the phraseology here and a little there, but attempting nothing drastic except in the peroration. That I rewrote so as to bring it more in line with what Harlan formerly had been advocating. But this made the speech more or less of a hodgepodge. It was not an integrated whole. It faced in two directions—or at least in a direction and a quarter.

Orchestra Hall was crowded that night. As I sat on the platform and studied the audience for the effect of the speech upon it, my heart turned to lead. I knew then that Harlan was a beaten man. In a box I saw Joseph Medill Patterson, one of the two coeditors of the *Tribune*. Patterson, who had called himself a Socialist, was young and enthusiastic and sincere. He had already called on Harlan to say that he would support him if Harlan's position on traction met with his approval. Patterson had gone to Orchestra Hall to satisfy himself on this point. His support would have meant much.

The next day Patterson called on Dunne and pledged him

his support. He campaigned actively for Dunne, assisted substantially in his election, and became Commissioner of Public Works in the Dunne cabinet, a job that he funked when
he had to decide whether to force Marshall Field and Company to disgorge Peck Court, a short street that it had acquired for what many thought an inadequate consideration.

It was during this campaign that I met Frederic A. Delano
for the first time. A fine, public-spirited citizen always, he
had been president of the Wabash Railroad. Even then he
was intensely interested in city planning and came to Harlan
to talk about what could be done for Chicago. Harlan was
greatly taken with Delano and confided to me that, if elected,
he would offer him the Commissionership of Public Works.
On all other possible appointments Harlan's mind was entirely open. He had made no further commitments, even in
his own mind.

At the height of the campaign my brother Felix died of
typhoid fever in Nevada, and I accompanied his body back
to Altoona for burial. I was away from Chicago only two or
three days. When I stepped off of the train upon my return,
a feeling of deep depression came over me. I have always
been highly sensitized during political campaigns. I get a
sense about the result, and it is usually correct. My feeling
that day was that we were on the rocks. When I reached
Harlan's office I told him bluntly that, in my opinion, he
was through. He could take it. He said that if that were true
we would have to fight the harder. That too was like him.
He had admirable courage. Although by now he had veered
back to his old position on traction, he hadn't recovered the
ground that he had surrendered on this supreme issue. He
had created doubts in minds that could not shake themselves
clear.

A few days later we got a real break. Judge Dunne, at a public meeting in the first ward, had put his good right arm about the shoulder of "Hinky Dink" Kenna—a man who voted his people like cattle and who had a grimy grip on his ward through a corrupt association with flophouses, vice, prostitution, and gambling. He called Kenna "his friend" and praised him for his human qualities! He gave his audience to understand that the great and noble Kenna—"Hinky Dink" to you!—would stand close to the throne if he, Dunne, were to be elected. What a chance to take the ball and run through the broken field.

When Harlan reached his office the next morning I was already furiously at work on his noonday speech. I was heaping ridicule, sarcasm, and invective upon the Judge's gray head. It was as outspoken a philippic as I was capable of writing. Harlan approved it enthusiastically and we rushed into the arena.

From that moment we dropped traction; we raised a moral issue instead. Day after day, until election came, we pictured Dunne and the "upstanding" "Hinky Dink" working together in the political vineyard. The campaign immediately took on new life. Instead of Harlan's being on the defensive on traction, he was on the offensive on morals. It was the old John Harlan at his greatest, smashing at corruption and the crooked alliance between politics and the underworld. One could almost see the change taking place. Chicago was being swept by a near tidal wave. But the time was too short. Harlan recovered a tremendous lot of ground, but not enough. Dunne won by 23,000 votes.

Another reason was the Republican machine. It had given Harlan lip service only. Regulars attended Harlan's meetings and cheered his speeches—with murder in their black hearts.

They muttered imprecations and voted for Dunne. And they accomplished their purpose. With the blundering assistance of Harlan himself, the 1905 election effectively disposed of him as a political threat. He might have come back, but he destroyed even that possibility by an unholy hookup on the traction issue as to which he had been the pure knight, *sans peur et sans reproche.*

Dunne honorably tried to carry out his campaign pledges. Raymond Robins, an aggressive, political-minded young social worker of my own age, had supported Harlan, although he was a Democrat. It was during this campaign that I first met Robins, and for many years thereafter we continued to fight side by side, until 1920, when he followed Harding. After Harlan's defeat, Robins had gone over to Dunne. Dunne appointed James Hamilton Lewis Corporation Counsel, and Robins prevailed upon him to appoint a Republican, Walter L. Fisher, later to be Secretary of the Interior under Taft, as Special Traction Counsel. Owing largely to the influence of Robins, Dunne also appointed the best Board of Education that Chicago has ever had, with the possible exception of the one named years later by Mayor Dever. On the Dunne board were such outstanding persons as Jane Addams of Hull House, Mrs. Emmons Blaine, Wiley W. Mills, John J. Sonsteby, and Robins himself.

As I have said, Dunne tried, in all sincerity, to make good on his promises. The first thing that went wrong was traction. Fisher was plainly determined upon making some kind of a settlement that would be a compromise of the position that Dunne had taken in the campaign. He drafted an ordinance which he proposed to put through without benefit of referendum. Dunne had promised the people an opportunity to vote on any settlement. At this stage Robins and a small voluntary group, including myself, although only incidentally, prepared and circulated a petition for a referendum on the pending traction ordinance. It was a big job and an expensive one which Robins himself helped to finance. However, with the aid of the Teachers' Federation, under the leadership of Margaret A. Haley, and the support of labor and other groups, the necessary signatures were secured, the referendum was held, and the ordinance was defeated.

Meanwhile, lines were being laid to defeat Dunne in 1907. Fred A. Busse, the man who had betrayed Harlan, was being groomed for the job and in due course he became the Republican nominee, with Dunne on the Democratic side. For myself, the choice was easy. I was for Dunne on his record as Mayor and against Busse on his personal and public record. I could already savor the salt in Busse's blood.

Busse was really a semi-notorious character, however much the *Chicago Tribune* and such men as Graeme Stewart and Alexander Revell might vouch for his respectability. He was clever, too, in a cunning way. He knew how to attach the gold-coast diggers to himself by running their scions for public office. Both Bertie McCormick and Joe Patterson, among others, had risen to this bait.

Busse's natural associations were in the dives. He was a barroom tough. A woman he had secretly married forced him to recognize her after he became Mayor. Up to that time, he was reputed to be a bachelor, living with his parents in an apartment in Clark Street on the North Side. During the campaign this tough old bird was dramatized by the able Mullaney as a son so devoted to a gentle old mother that on her account he had never married. His father, as County Commissioner some years earlier, had been a boodler, and Fred had been brought up in that school. He was in politics for what he could get out of it, and he got it, too. In private life he was in the teaming and coal business, and most of the coal that he sold was to public institutions or to interests that did business with the city and the county. He had no background of education and no ideals of good citizenship, but his supporters contrived, in spite of it all, to create for him the reputation of a keen, aggressive, competent businessman and able administrator who would give the city just the kind of administration that it needed after the distrait Dunne. To the very end the *Tribune* loyally supported him, despite its certain knowledge as to just what he was. Hadn't he steered Joe and Bert into public office? And mightn't he advance them further?

Dunne was on the defensive from the start. He had to defend on traction, and on the public schools. On both issues he was right. That was the trouble. The majority of the press and of the "respectable" business interests did not want good schools or a fair traction settlement. *Wasn't* I improving my learning, if not my disposition?

I did not take an active part in the campaign. I had just finished my law course,[1] and while I was for Dunne, I hadn't the heart to get into another time-eating free-for-all scrap as I had for Harlan. Toward the end of the campaign, however, when it became evident that the tide was running heavily

---

[1] It was an exercise of the right of free will that took me back to the Law School. I had had an early desire to study law, so here were three pleasant and profitable years. It was good for me that I was thrown into association with men considerably younger than myself—men whose minds were young, alert, and keen. The last that I heard of that Law School class of 1907 was that it was still the best in the school's history. It turned out men like Laird Bell and James B. Blake, who were leaders of the bar in their respective communities of Chicago and Milwaukee, as they were in the classroom.

for Busse, a small group of us independents did try to do something for the Mayor, but to no avail. Busse won by 13,000 votes.

And so Chicago had Busse, the near-hoodlum, as its "business" Mayor. Busse knew his way about politically; he knew how to run with the white rabbits of the Lake Shore Drive and hunt with the jackals of Goose Island. Out of this wisdom he evolved his policies. He knew that the business interests wanted clean streets, good paving, vigilant traffic policemen—in *their* section—and a city safe and attractive to visitors who would spend money. He knew that the householder wanted frequent and regular removals of garbage, well-lighted streets, playgrounds, and bathing beaches, but not for the underdog. He knew that in the twilight zones of the city what was wanted were bigger and more saloons, open all night, gambling houses, and brothels. He knew that the politicians wanted favors and graft and that the contractors wanted to wax fat off of public works. He knew, as did everyone else, what the public utilities wanted. And what these various elements wanted, Busse wanted and knew how to get.

I once heard John P. Hopkins, one-time Mayor, tell the story of a mass meeting of eminent citizens at Central Music Hall to denounce open vice and prostitution and the violation of the Sunday closing laws by the saloons. Every stuffed shirt in Chicago either was there, or had allowed the use of his name. Moral indignation ran high. The Mayor simply had to get busy and clean up the town—or else! How could one doubt the civic virtue and personal sincerity behind this moral outburst? This was of a Sunday night. In his office the next day at City Hall, the first visitor received by the Mayor was the manager of one of Chicago's great department stores who had been at the Central Hall meeting. No one had more loudly declaimed against prevailing moral conditions or more eloquently pleaded that Chicago be made pure and good at whatever cost. What he wanted to say to His Honor in private was that the latter must not take too seriously the protestations of the night before. The deacons and the elders who had almost choked on their vehement words of protest felt that it was necessary to go on record to placate public opinion. But to clean up the town, as had been suggested, would be "bad for business." And that would never do!

It should have been disconcerting to Busse's supporters—the *Tribune* among them—when there was discovered in his safe-deposit box, after his death, a large block of stock in a company that exclusively sold manhole covers to the city. I wonder, though, if anything could disconcert the *Tribune* then—or now—except, of course, some entirely inadvertent act of goodwill on its part in the public interest. There is never any silly season for that hardened sawbug.

I was distinctly *persona non grata* at the City Hall during the Busse regime. Even his secretary—my one-time friend "Barney" Mullaney—refused to speak to me for several years. We did patch up our differences in time, only to have them break out again when Mullaney went over to Samuel Insull, and I went all-out against him. Yerkes, Busse, and Insull helped to sharpen my teeth for Mussolini, Hirohito, and Hitler.

As I have intimated, I went back to my law studies after the Dunne-Harlan battle of 1905, there to attend strictly to my own business. Now and then I would stop in at Harlan's office. On one such occasion he told me that Judge Peter S. Grosscup had offered him a retainer of $10,000 and compensation of $2,000 monthly if he would "represent the people's interests" as "Attorney for the Court, for the People" in the receivership proceedings affecting the Yerkes traction systems then pending in Grosscup's court. Having failed to get the "right" kind of franchise, Yerkes had thrown his lines into the Federal court, where, no one doubted, they would be handled by Grosscup to the advantage of Yerkes and his gang. They finally emerged in 1942 after making a soft living, covering many years, for a great host of lawyers, receivers, masters, experts, public-relations gentry, court reporters, and God knows what else. Grosscup saw in Harlan a "respectable front." The idea of appointing the man who at one time was the outstanding champion of the people's interests was not a bad one, even for His Honor. In fact, it was smart. But it didn't fool all of us.

When Harlan told me of the offer and of his determination to accept it (Harlan was always hard pressed for money), I suffered a real shock. I begged him to refuse. He argued that he had sacrificed much for the people and had received only ingratitude in return. I pleaded with him not to destroy the faith of those thousands of young men and others in the city who had followed him in his fights and who still believed that he had been right. On this subject, I became emotional, because I felt it deeply. Tears trickled down my fast leathering cheeks and I noticed some in my former leader's eyes, too. All afternoon I wrestled with him, but his mind was made up. He had already committed himself to Mrs. Harlan. He assured me that he would continue to fight to protect the people. I told him that he couldn't and at the same time serve his real client—the traction companies. I predicted that he was closing the door, hermetically, upon a promising public career that could be resuscitated unless he himself chose deliberately to stab it to the heart.

From that moment our paths separated. We shook hands

and I went home, greatly disturbed, heartsick, almost ready to give up.

Some time later Harlan sent for me and told me that he had been authorized by Grosscup to offer me a job as publicity man. The very thought that Harlan would even approach me on such a matter made me feel degraded. The gap between us widened. From that time on, as the years passed, I saw less and less of him. Occasionally, I used to run into him at the club or on the street, but there was nothing in common between us. Always it was apparent that he was seeking to justify to himself the course that he had taken, but I could give him no comfort. He became more and more involved in the traction mess, winding up the sorry affair with a lawsuit of his own to recover a big fee from the traction lines, in addition to the subsidy that he had already received from the same client.

From that point on Harlan went into more and more of an eclipse. Even the big interests had no use for him, and kept aloof. A man who betrays himself once rarely has any takers the second time. He struggled to regain a footing. He ran for delegate at large to the Republican National Convention of 1924 and was defeated badly. He went to New York to start all over again, but he made little headway. Scrupulously, as he would, he managed to keep up appearances, and he still presented an imposing figure, but spiritually he was no longer the fine, daring man who had entered the lists in 1897 against the robber barons of Chicago.

When I came to Washington as Secretary of the Interior I found John Harlan living here with his sister. He came to see me on several occasions. His pride in me was touching and pathetic. I felt a resurgence of my old affection for him. Then, in the early spring of 1934, he died suddenly, and one

Sunday afternoon I attended his funeral services in the New York Avenue Presbyterian Church. There was only a handful of us—his widow, his children, his sister, Chief Justice Hughes, the late Justice Sutherland, Frederic A. Delano, and a few old family friends.

> To fret thy soule with crosses and with cares;
> To eate thy heart through comfortlesse dispaires;
> To fawne, to crowche, to waite, to ride, to ronne,
> To spend, to give, to want, to be undonne.
> Unhappie wight, born to desastrous end,
> That doth his life in so long tendance spend.
> —EDMUND SPENSER.

CHAPTER SEVEN

TWO DAMN FOOLS

I'll taunt ye with my latest breath,
And fight ye till I die!
—George Washington Patten.

J STILL CRAVED Fred Busse's blood, while the *Tribune* still salaamed before him. Not that it wouldn't in all probability have poisoned me. Busse had cheated Chicago out of a capable mayor—John Harlan. He had smeared another—Mayor Dunne—and cut short the latter's usefulness in Chicago politics, although in 1912 Dunne was to be elected Governor. By means of cunning propaganda, Busse had been foisted on the people, which was bad for them. Everything worth while had wilted under his slimy touch, although he was careful to keep up superficial appearances. If the *Tribune* was for him, so was the underworld. So, as sometimes happens, were respectable citizens, including the deacons, the elders, and many of the preachers. So were the "interests" that did "business"—funny business mostly—with the city. Truly a formidable combination!

Charles S. Deneen had been renominated and re-elected Governor in 1908. I had been for him when first he ran in 1904. In fact, he had personally offered me a job on his headquarters staff to do publicity and had suggested an appointment in the event of his election. But I had declined because, as I told him, I did not play politics on that basis.

"I am for you for Governor," I had said, "as I was for you for the nomination, and I hope that you will be elected because you are the best candidate. But I am not looking for a political job. In any event, I cannot go to work for you. I am studying law and must not interrupt my studies." Nevertheless, I was to do that very thing the following year for Harlan.

I couldn't even attend the convention that had nominated Deneen in 1904 over the opposition of the notorious—and soon to be the "notoriouser"—William Lorimer, et al. I was in bed at the time, side-stepping temporarily an operation for appendicitis by drinking quarts—yes, quarts—of olive oil cold out of a bottle. What a predicament for a curmudgeon with a good fight going on outside! Getting oiled up, on the q.t. However, with my eyes on the mayoralty election and Harlan in 1905, I had convinced him that he ought to go as a delegate and put up a real fight for Deneen. Busse had put Harlan on his delegation and the latter had been of real help to Deneen.

Deneen gave a satisfactory account of himself during his eight years in office, even from the point of view of an impatient progressive like myself. I never was an enthusiastic Deneen man. I regarded him as too cold and cautious and selfish. He was altogether too conservative to suit me. He rarely took a step forward unless someone pushed him, and then he took only a quarter-step. Notwithstanding, he was a creditable public official and, according to his lights and within his limitations, rendered public service of a high order, excepting only as to his grabbing of fees during his eight

What the well-dressed Y.M.C.A. worker wore in World War I as modeled by Curmudgeon Ickes, shown here with his stepson "over there."

Here I am with Colonel Theodore Roosevelt, snapped in the LaSalle Street Station, in Chicago. In case you can't tell, I am the one under the pancake hat.

—But Honest Harold Can Be Quoted (and Is)

years as State's Attorney—in total a tidy sum that had put him on his feet financially.

As 1911 came on, Busse was in his first—and last—term as Mayor, but it was for four years, instead of two as previously. As it reached the home stretch it found Deneen repeating in the Governor's office; Albert L. Hopkins, of Aurora, hoping in vain for a second term as United States Senator; Richard Yates still (why I never understood) a Congressman at large; and Lorimer and his friends, although embittered by his expulsion from the United States Senate, still a potent factor (but slipping fast) in Chicago politics. The Lorimerites were biding their time and missing no opportunity to punish their enemies or to help their friends. The old Harlan movement had spent its force. However, there were still a considerable number of us who had followed John into battle who were now persisting in keeping a loosely knit liberal organization together as best we could without funds.

It appeared certain that Busse would be a candidate to succeed himself. As a matter of fact, there was no one else in sight. A disheartening situation to a man hungering for a bone to crush, but true. All the time, I had been nursing a secret ambition to be in on the Busse kill whenever it might occur.

Public confidence in Busse had been weakened through an intelligent and forceful fight that was being made on him by a young man who had not been long in the City Council —or even in Chicago—Charles E. Merriam, a junior professor at the University of Chicago. Merriam's was an attractive personality. Born and raised in Iowa, he had attended the University of Berlin and had taken his Ph.D. degree at Columbia. Then he found his way to Chicago, where he joined the department of political science, of which Harry Pratt

Judson, later to be president of the university when William Rainey Harper died, was the ornate façade.

Merriam had gone to the Council with the support of George Sikes and later of Roy O. West. All of his active political life West was a Deneen lieutenant, and was to be, for about eight months, Secretary of the Interior under President Coolidge. West played a clever hand. He was noted for his "affidavit" face, and he knew not only most of the devious tricks of the game but also the language of the political reformer. He could himself pose as a reformer when the stage setting called for it. As had Deneen, he had come to Chicago penniless to seek his fortune, and had done a very good job of it in the dual role of member of the Board of (Tax) Review and lawyer representing business concerns with, incidentally, large taxable interests.

From the beginning, Merriam had taken an active part in Republican politics in his precinct and ward. He wasn't spectacular, but he was forceful and determined. No one could doubt that he was both capable and strong. Some influential party leaders had urged Merriam for a Councilmanic vacancy that had occurred, and West undoubtedly saw a good opportunity to make himself solid with the powerful university community. He always made a point of that, but he did not propose to overdo it.

Returning from Springfield, where we both had been delegates to the 1910 Republican State Convention, Merriam and I fell to discussing the mayoralty situation. We had known each other, but not intimately. Merriam's work in the City Council had given him an opportunity to see much that was passing behind the scenes and to guess at much more. He was a shrewd and able observer. Both of us deplored the loss of John Harlan, but that was a thing of the past and nothing could be done about it. We considered man after man, but none seemed to fill the bill.

Finally I said to Merriam: "It looks to me as if you are the only man in sight." His availability had struck me with great force during our exchange of views, and of course I had followed his career in the City Council closely and approvingly.

Merriam sincerely did not agree. He said that he hadn't been long enough in Chicago; that his only public office had been that of alderman for one term, and that he was in no position to make the kind of a campaign that would be necessary to win. His principal objections were that there was no organization that we could throw into the fight and that the chances of financing an effective campaign were remote, if they existed at all.

I met his points one by one. I assured him that what was left of the old Harlan organization could be put together quickly. I pointed to his record in the City Council as outstanding. I admitted that there might be difficulty in financing a fight against Busse, but I believed that if Charles R. Crane and one or two others would help us, even that could be accomplished. I told him, also, that I thought that the *News* would go for him and that we could count on other newspaper support, even if some of it might be reluctant. I believed Fred Busse to be yellow at heart, and I ventured the prediction that Busse would not run if Merriam became a candidate against him.

Merriam agreed to run on two conditions. The first was that nobody else who might be available could be found to make the try, and the second was that I should manage his campaign. I met the second condition at once. I have come to know Merriam quite well since that day, and I have often wondered why he consented to be the candidate. He is one of the most cautious persons that I know. He isn't the kind of a man who takes chances. He does act on principle, and he will enlist in a lost cause even when he knows that it is lost, but there is a great difference between fighting for a lost cause and offering yourself as a personal sacrifice, as Merriam, in effect, was doing. At any rate, his word was given and he never tried to wriggle out of it. He has never been that kind.

I called a meeting of a few reliables for the Sunday following the Friday of our return from Springfield, at the University Club. I do not now recall the names of all of the men who were there. Merriam himself was not present. I do recollect, however, that William B. Moulton, the first chairman of the state Civil Service under Deneen, Shelby M. Singleton, and John Siman, a fine young citizen of Bohemian birth, were three of those in attendance. Probably James F. Stepina, president of a Bohemian-American bank and a scrapper for a decent city, was present, as usual. There were possibly ten others, and not a professional politician among them. All had been through one or more of the Harlan fights and all of them I knew well.

We went over the situation briefly and agreed that unless Merriam should make the fight, there wouldn't be any. Busse would thus be saddled on the city for another term. I told them, as I had told Merriam himself, that I believed that we could nominate but that we probably could not elect Merriam. I had reason, based upon experience, to expect that if they were licked in the primaries, the Republican "regulars" would rock on their fat bellies into the Democratic tent as they had done when Harlan was a candidate. My thought was that we could force Busse into hiding with Merriam, who had been fighting him so effectively as a member of the City Council. That of itself would be worth the chips. Every man present acquiesced and promised to go along.

We began at once to get the campaign under way. Merriam relied largely upon my judgment as to tactics and methods. He knew that I had been through several city campaigns, while he had never been in a fight outside of his own ward, and never in one in a managerial capacity.

It was my judgment that the first thing to do was to announce Merriam's candidacy promptly and as a surprise. My belief was that the very boldness of such a step would get us off to a good start. In other words, I was suggesting that he jump off the end of the pier without first finding out how cold or how deep the water was. I had to do some tall convincing on this score, but in the end I did persuade him.

While conducting a clandestine canvass to test out sentiment, we were working also on the announcement, which we wanted to have the effect of a bombshell. So, soon after the "off-year" election in November of 1910, the newspapers carried the astonishing announcement of Merriam's candidacy in the forthcoming February primary. They all gave considerable space to the news that this young college professor had thrown down the gauntlet to Busse and the whole Republican organization—the whole fanged pack of them.

I could almost hear the politicians scratching their wooden heads. The boldness of the stroke amazed them, and then they thought that they saw a funny side to it. Something must be wrong with a man, they reasoned, to be going after big game with a peashooter. They finally decided that it was too good a joke to keep, and so they exploded into a good laugh at the expense of the damn-fool professor and his equally damn-fool manager. They reckoned that I could lick

Merriam myself, even if they couldn't, but of course they could and would—plenty!—when they got round to it in their own good time.

Before the laughter had died down I started after two things—an organization and money. The idea was to have Merriam take to the stump at once—it was time, the only thing that we had, against organization. I knew that the crowds at first would be small and that the road was rough and long and cold. But I had seen Harlan travel it and I knew that Merriam could too.

Charles R. Crane, later our Minister to China under President Wilson, was president of the Crane Company, a highly prosperous business that had been built up by his father from the ground. He was a rich man with a rare public spirit. He was the one in a million who would contribute to a cause that he believed in even if he knew that it was hopeless. And he was extremely liberal, not only to local causes but to those outside of the state if they appealed to him. He was a generous contributor to the late Robert M. La Follette and to other fighting liberals. He had long stood behind Jane Addams of Hull House. Nor did he advertise his benefactions.

First I had a talk with Walter S. Rogers, Crane's confidential secretary, who was his outpost in public and charitable matters. I knew Rogers well. I also knew Crane, but not so well. Rogers was a quiet, mild man who knew many people. He knew and admired Merriam and thought well of our plans. He suggested that I meet Crane in his hideaway office in the Fine Arts Building and tackle him myself.

Crane had a curious manner when one was talking to him. He didn't seem to pay attention. At times he appeared to be half-asleep, with his mind anywhere but on the subject at hand. He asked me virtually no questions. When I had finished, he said that he didn't see much chance to defeat Busse, whose measure he had, but he approved of Merriam and would help. He didn't say with how much and I didn't ask him. I knew that he wouldn't be niggardly. He suggested the names of others who might go along.

A generous check came promptly from Crane's office. That gave us a start. Neither Merriam nor I could contribute anything to the treasury. In no campaign have I ever made financial commitments for which I did not have the money in hand or in sure prospect. Neither have I ever left an unpaid bill behind a campaign. Nor have I ever made or been induced by a political promise. (My only promises have been to myself—to get the particular political crook the next time.) On such a basis one can go through a campaign and live to see another day, but not otherwise.

Our first public meeting was held in the latter part of November. Here we broke another precedent. To start a mayoralty campaign before Christmas was almost as asinine an undertaking, in the opinion of the stereotyped, as to try to move Christmas back of the February primary. But we had a long row to hoe and it behooved us to get started. Anyhow, if there was to be a funeral, it would be ours.

Next, we undertook to interest Julius Rosenwald, who was then the active head of Sears, Roebuck & Company. I had never met Rosenwald, but Merriam and Crane knew him and so did Raymond Robins, whose active assistance had already been enlisted. One day we had a small luncheon meeting at the City Club, attended by Merriam, Robins, Crane, Rosenwald, and myself. Although Rosenwald was one of the most generous of souls and a first-rate citizen, when it came to politics he was delightfully naïve. He never seemed to grasp the significance of politics, and I doubt whether, up to the time of our meeting with him, he had ever taken any real interest in it. He was content to drift along with the tide and accept the current conventional view of public officials. That's how he happened to be of the opinion that Busse had given a "good administration" and was entitled to re-election. We soon swept his mind clear of such rubbish.

Rosenwald said that he and Mrs. Rosenwald were going to Europe and that he didn't like to give money when he wasn't going to be about to see how it was being spent. It could be seen that, unlike Crane, he wanted a run for his money. Furthermore, he didn't believe that we could nominate Merriam. Here I assumed the burden and explained why I thought that we could nominate, even if we could not elect, our man. In the end, Rosenwald turned to Crane and said: "Well, Charlie, I am going to Europe but I will make you my agent. You put into this campaign as much money as you want to and when I come back I will send you my check for half of the total."

After the luncheon, as we were waiting for the elevator, Rosenwald said to me: "I still don't think that you can nominate Merriam, but if you do, send me a cablegram and I will come back on the first ship to help elect him. My office will always know where I can be reached."

This was real encouragement that called for real enthusiasm. We opened headquarters on the parlor floor of the old Grand Pacific Hotel. Almost without exception I had been an unpaid volunteer in all of the campaigns in which I had taken a part, but I frankly admitted this time that I couldn't work on such a basis. It would be a long pull, during which I had to live and carry the obligations that I had assumed. By this time Walter Rogers, representing Crane and also in his own right, was sitting in on all conferences, and he agreed that I was worthy of my hire. He suggested $150 a week as being reasonable. Merriam concurred. I told them that I would take $75 a week, and so it was agreed. I could taste Busse in anticipation, and to bite a chunk out of his generous façade would be almost compensation enough.

By the first of the year we were really a going concern, even though the politicians still thought that we were something of a joke. We were holding meetings that were getting bigger, night by night, and organizing, organizing, organizing. Merriam was a convincing speaker. He always knew what he was talking about, and he had a way of inspiring confidence and stirring people's interest.

I was having my greatest difficulty getting together a competent headquarters staff. I was fortunate in securing the services of Charles M. Thomson, who had fought his way into the City Council against the Republican organization of his ward. He was a fine young fellow with plenty of ideals and a high sense of public service. He was very Scotch and very Presbyterian and very honorable. He became my assistant. In 1914, after giving an excellent account of himself as a Progressive member of Congress, with the help of his old comrades-in-arms, he was elected a judge of the Circuit Court of Cook County. There, and on the Appellate Court, he served with distinction until the implacable machine got him in the end.

I took a man who had been active in the Deneen organization to run halls and speakers. He turned out to be not only incompetent, but a first-rate grafter. When I fired him, Walter Rogers took over his work, but Walter wasn't a fine-tooth-comb detail man. So in the end I was running that part of the show, too.

To handle publicity I secured a man who was new to me, Robert Buck of the *News*. He had never been in a campaign, but he thought he knew all about running one. He resented supervision and was indisposed to recognize authority, so we didn't get along any better than a couple of strange goats. When practically all of us went, bag and baggage, into the Progressive party in 1912, Buck contentiously stayed behind to keep "the home fires burning" against our penitential return. He must have run out of fuel by now.

One other person, very insignificant at first, but later to loom importantly, was Mabel Gilmore, a pretty miss of eighteen, fresh out of business college, who applied for a job as stenographer and got it. She was smart, attractive, and a go-getter. She knew how to work with men and still keep them at arms' length respecting her. She worked herself to the front by sheer merit. Mabel was loyal and she could carry out orders, but she also had imagination and initiative. She was not on my personal staff during the Merriam campaign, but later we made her secretary of our executive committee, and, still later, she became my political secretary. She held that job for some time, until we put Charley Ringer across as a member of the Board of County Assessors. Then I virtually coerced Ringer into giving a job to Miss Gilmore, who meanwhile had married George W. Reinecke. Mabel Gilmore was the first woman ever to occupy a key position in the assessor's office, and she made good. Subsequently, she went to Senator Medill McCormick when I departed for France in 1918. Later still, Coolidge made her Internal Revenue Collector at Chicago, the first woman to hold such an office. Again she made good. For several years she has been, competently, the minority member of Chicago's Board of Election Commissioners.

I believe that, without question, we had the finest volunteer organization that has ever been knit together in Chicago —or anywhere else, for that matter. It was built from the ground up after Merriam had become a candidate, and it was composed mainly of volunteers from the ranks of young business and professional men who wanted a change and were willing to work for it.

Early in the contest Roy West came to headquarters to see me. He was sad because he hadn't been consulted! Of course he was for Merriam! But why hadn't we said something to him? Because he would have moved heaven and earth to change or thwart our plans, that's why! Knowing this, we had deliberately kept him in the dark. I listened to him, I hope, without letting my face show what a dissembler I believed him to be. I told him gravely that we had not wished to embarrass him. I had had too much experience with politicians not to know their ways. And, in the end, West double-crossed Merriam! He wasn't even clever about it.

From the time that Merriam announced his candidacy there was interest as to what the professional Republicans would do—those who went from election to election with a "good-fellow" expression on their faces and a dirk up their sleeves. It soon became clear that I had made a shrewd guess as to Busse. He decided not to stand for re-election. He had turned a bilious yellow and had gone under cover. Even the clever "Barney" Mullaney couldn't have contrived an immunity for Busse. Nor found enough disinfectant to make him smell respectable.

Meanwhile, there was much jockeying among the various factions. Unable to make joint cause against Merriam behind a candidate whom they could agree upon, they were losing valuable time. Our faces began to take on the smiles. They could agree on but one thing, and that was that they didn't want Merriam.

Meanwhile, also, our organization was coming along famously, becoming smooth-working and effective. I had hoped that Governor Deneen would be for Merriam and so I had kept out of his wards. He should have been. After all, our kind of people had supported him for Governor in 1904, when without us he could not have been nominated. Deneen came to Chicago from the state capital frequently, and I tried unsuccessfully to see him on a number of occasions. I suspected that he was dodging me, sparring for time. Finally I cornered him.

He mumbled something about the favorable sentiment and growing demand for John F. Smulski, a Polish stuffed shirt who was frequently used as window dressing, and who, once upon a time, had been City Treasurer, and promised me that I would have definite word from him within a week or two. Shortly thereafter, I met him again and he broke the news to me that there was so much popular demand for Smulski that he and his organization had to be for him. He also told me what I already knew; namely, that I was free to step out and organize "his" wards of the city. The only thing about this statement that surprised me was the reference to Smulski's popularity. He was as popular as a waif found on one's front stoop. I assured the Governor that he was committing a blunder and that if I organized against him I would subsequently hold my organization against him. But he stood his ground. So did I, and the next day we started the work of organization in those districts we had held up in deference to the state's chief executive.

From the first, Crane contributed generously for both himself and Rosenwald. Other public-spirited citizens who made

contributions were Cyrus H. McCormick, Harold F. Mc-
Cormick, Mrs. Emmons Blaine (also a McCormick of the
right strain), La Verne Noyes, Victor F. Lawson, Miss Helen
Culver, and William Kent. These gave large amounts and
hundreds of others came in with smaller sums, while thousands sent in their "two bitses." It was the first campaign that
I had been in in which we had all of the money that we could
legitimately use. And for all of that, we ran an economical
one.

Shortly after the turn of the year, the politicians were
laughing out of the other side of their mouths. They decided that they had to do something. They had to do it in a
hurry, too. So they threw a blanket on Smulski and trotted
him around the track. I had not forgotten that in spite of the
Deneen organization, he had run 100,000 behind his ticket
as the party candidate for State Treasurer. I wasn't very
much afraid of him.

Charles W. Vail, another Deneen man, also announced his
candidacy. Deneen tried to dissuade him, but Vail got out
of hand. He too heard the people calling, and couldn't make
out the name.

John R. Thompson was another entry. Thompson hadn't
been in politics very long. He had money of his own, made
in the chain-restaurant business, and he had the questionable
support of the gasping Lorimer-Jamieson faction. He also
had strength of his own in Hyde Park, where he lived in
West's ward, adjoining Merriam's.

All of the time Busse was saying nothing and apparently
doing nothing—at least not openly. However, it became clear
before it was over that he would throw to Thompson. Bar-
ring his own candidacy, that was a natural for him.

The campaign rose to its crescendo. During the last two

weeks we were holding noonday meetings in downtown theaters every day and turning crowds away. In addition, we had as many night meetings as it was humanly possible for Merriam to make. Headquarters became a bedlam. The elusive Roy West had come in much earlier to say that he was off for Europe and to bid me good-by and (with fingers crossed) "good luck." He had left his organization in good shape for Merriam!—so he assured me.

Finally, the climax. Merriam, the young college professor, the first of the two "damn fools" who had so highly amused the politicians with his opening announcement, not only made off with the nomination, he came through with a majority of all the Republican votes cast. Chicago was stunned. The eyes of the professional politicians were bloodshot. The like of it had never happened before.

Henry Bingham, West's chief lieutenant in his end of the Seventh Ward, which was also Merriam's, came in to see me.

"Henry, how did it happen that Smulski got so many votes in your precinct?" I asked. "Not a single Pole lives there. It's an organization precinct, you control it, and you and West were supposed to be for Merriam."

Bingham looked me squarely in the eye as he said: "Orders."

"From Roy West?"

"Yes."

West and his blarney! (*!#″*!#″*!″*) I never let him know that I was on to his spitball outcurves. Years later, as the result of the interest of Edward J. Brundage, at one time Attorney General of Illinois, and of George E. Brennan, I was urged to become a candidate for the Circuit Court bench of Cook County on a coalition ticket. But Roy O. West slipped into the office of Victor C. Lawson, who was willing to support me, and persuaded him that a Lorimer corporal should go on instead—otherwise Lorimer might defeat the entire ticket. Quite a liberal course for anyone in the art of double-crossing!

We carried John R. Thompson's ward, and broke Thompson's heart. We carried the Black Belt, to the amazement of everybody. And apparently the people did not know that their hearts were breaking for Smulski. We carried every Deneen ward in the city with one exception, that containing the stockyards, which was heavily Democratic and therefore more susceptible to machine control. We even carried Deneen's own precinct. There never has been, before or since, such a sweeping aside of the professional politicians in Chicago as there was on that primary day in 1911. It was all due to the work of a hastily recruited but hard-working volunteer organization, adequately financed but economically directed. We wasted no money manning the polls.

A day or two after the primary, I received a cable from Julius Rosenwald: "My hat is off to you. I am returning by the first steamer."

The election to come was going to be something else, and it was still my opinion, in spite of our remarkable primary success, that we were probably in for a defeat in the finals. The Republican regulars could be depended upon to do their daily dozen in that regard. Besides, Harrison had always been a great vote-getter. More than any other Democrat of his generation he appealed to the independent Republican voters, upon whom we had largely to rely if we were to win. But Merriam was young and attractive and besides, two things gave us hope. Dunne, who had been defeated by Harrison in the primaries, had a large liberal following which was anti-Harrison; the Sullivan-Hopkins-Brennan faction had been gaining rapidly in strength and was against Harrison. We had reason to believe that there would be a considerable shifting of party lines.

I decided to go to New York for a break of a few days. On the same train with me, by chance, was Frederick W. Upham, a close political friend of Busse's, as he was of everyone else. Upham, who was later to be treasurer of the Republican National Committee, was also a politico-businessman who sold coal to public institutions, public utilities, railroads, and so forth, and did very well at it, thank you! As treasurer of the Republican National Committee, he had the entree to the White House of Harding. He also had another key to the same door; he was a busy cupbearer to the "Sairey Gamp" from Ohio when Volstead was something to curse by.

My three old friends, Sullivan, Hopkins, and Brennan, also by chance, were additional fellow travelers. They soon had me in their drawing room, where they proceeded to tell me in detail just what should be done to defeat Harrison, the nominee of their own party. Roger Sullivan was the Democratic national committeeman at the time. He would start off something like this:

"I'm regular. Of course I'm for Harrison, but—" and then he would talk about what he would do in my place.

Whereupon, John Hopkins would turn on Sullivan and say: "Well, you goddamned fool, you're not, and why don't you say so? I'm not for Harrison." Whereupon he would tell me what *he* thought should be done.

Next the canny "peg-legged" Brennan: "I don't like your man Merriam. He's against my friends and my friends are against him. I know that if he is elected I will be opposed to everything he does, but I want to beat Harrison so bad I can taste it." And then he would give me the benefit of *his* experience and judgment.

Until late at night in that drawing room, opaque with heavy cigar smoke, the sole topic was how, expertly but completely, to dissect the political carcass of Carter Harrison so that it could never be articulated again. It seemed to do Roger Sullivan's "regular" soul some good to insist from time to time that as the party nominee "he was for Harrison." Never once did he blink an eye. Then Hopkins and Brennan would chorus: "You goddamned fool, of course you aren't for Harrison, and neither are we." Roger would reiterate that he was, but all of the time the trio kept searching their brains for political wisdom to put into my hands, knowing full well that it was my job to win with Merriam if I could.

These three big Irishmen interested me hugely. They were going off on a lark, as they often did, just their three selves. They would take luxurious quarters at the Waldorf Astoria Hotel and live off the fat of the land. They would go to the theater. They would spend long and late hours in their common sitting room "goddamning" each other through the smoke emitted from their own cigars. To hear them talk one would have thought that they were hereditary feudists. The fact was that they had so sentimental a feeling for each other that they felt called upon to shout insulting names and swear like pirates, in the belief that thus they could dissimulate their warm mutual affection. Any one of these men would have gone to the stake for either of the other two.

At the end, the consensus of opinion was that the Sullivan-Hopkins-Brennan crowd would make no open overtures of support of Merriam. It would make no contribution, directly or indirectly, to his campaign fund. The smartest of them all, George Brennan, said to me: "Harold, you go on in your own way and run your campaign. Pay no attention to us. We know who our friends are and we know how to reach them."

I was in New York for only two or three days. Before leaving Chicago, I had urged upon Merriam the running of his election campaign as he had his primary fight without reference to the regular Republican organization. There rarely has been a bitter intraorganization primary fight following which those who have supported the unsuccessful candidate have not gone over to the opposition and knifed savagely their own party nominee. I had tried to make him see that if we hewed to our own line, instead of delivering ourselves to the pay-roll boys, they would be facing us and therefore in no position to stab us in the back. The people would have them under observation.

However, Merriam decided, upon my return to Chicago, that we had better move in with the Republican organization, and I have always thought that he lost the election for sure then and there. I never have been able to see the consistency in denouncing a political group as knaves and crooks and then pretending to fraternize with them afterward. But Merriam was the nominee and there was nothing that I could do but accept his judgment with the best grace possible. And I did accept with good grace. As a matter of fact, I did not blame him for playing what he, and others too, regarded as "safe."

Accordingly, we moved over. I continued as manager. The principal factional leaders, Busse, Lorimer, and Deneen, made no pretense of taking an active part. Deneen had the excuse that he was busy at Springfield. But we knew that he was sore. Busse was sulking. He hated Merriam, and he knew that I knew how grossly he had betrayed John Harlan. Lorimer, discredited by the nature of his election to the United State Senate, wasn't showing his face any more than he had to. We wouldn't have liked the looks of it anyhow.

While none of these political gargoyles showed up at headquarters or spoke at a single meeting (Deneen had promised to speak and was actually scheduled but at the end found a pretext to justify a walkout), they saw to it that there was a constant stream of their henchmen through headquarters. We had set up a campaign committee on which all three were represented, with one or two rare exceptions, by as rare a lot of political pirates as ever scuttled a ship of state. There was one decent man in this outfit who had given me his word, which was good. He kept me fully informed of what moves were being made in the dark. Besides, I knew these men of old. I knew their records. So I watched them out of the tail of my eye, with one hand gripped in my money pocket and the other on my watch fob.

Roy O. West was of particular interest to me during this campaign. He had come back from Europe full of sweetness and light, perfectly delighted that Merriam (his candidate!) had won and oh, so eager, to help elect him. I pretended to accept West's proffers of aid at face value, but it has always been a favorite axiom of mine that "any man can fool me once, but I am a damn fool if I let the same man fool me a second time." And West had had his "once." He made himself quite at home in my private office, walking into it or through it without so much as "by your leave." He was completely "one of us." He was earnestly trying to create the impression that he and Merriam and I constituted a mutually trusting triumvirate that would win in April and make of Chicago a second Garden of Eden—without himself offering the apple. I have always wondered whether he thought that he was fooling anyone.

But Merriam at headquarters gave me the greatest kick of all. He knew a lot of these politicos himself and those that he did not know he could smell with that keen political sense of his. Every afternoon in my office he would sit hunched up in a chair with his legs crossed while the "faithful" came in for interviews. With his shoulders thrust forward and his hands in his lap, he looked as if he were prepared to fend off an expected blow. Usually there was a look of incredulity on his face, especially when some ward heeler became particularly unctuous. One day I was moved to say to him: "Merriam, I want to win this campaign if I can and so do you. Suspect everyone in the world, including your own wife, but for God's sake, when these highbinders come in, don't proclaim by your expression that you think they are crooks."

The election campaign was, generally speaking, a continuation of the primary fight. Rosenwald returned ready for total war. He had tasted blood and he liked it, and nothing but Merriam's election was going to satisfy him. I think that he would have given a big piece of his fortune for victory. He wanted to man the polls with paid workers. I was against it. Money given to the regulars would be used against us, I said, and our volunteers wanted no pay. Rosenwald insisted, however, and finally we agreed upon the modest sum of $10 a precinct. He even insisted that this amount be doubled for the heavily Democratic principality of Ernest J. Magerstadt. Smooth and dapper "Ernie" had told Rosenwald that with $20 a precinct he could carry "Bridgeport" for Merriam. I laughed out loud at this, because I knew Ernie of old and I knew how his crooked machine operated. I somewhat miffed Rosenwald. He said with dignity that Ernie was a friend of

his and that he believed in him. On one occasion he had
tipped it off to Magerstadt to buy some Sears Roebuck stock.
Magerstadt had followed this perfectly sound advice and had
made some money. So Ernie would not betray him.

When Rosenwald offered to make an additional contribution to take care of the extra $10 per precinct for Mager-
stadt, I could not very well hold out. I told Rosenwald that
Ernie would get his $20 a precinct, adding that he would un-
doubtedly put the extra $10 into his own pocket. Generally
speaking, I felt sure that practically all the money that was
paid to the Republican precinct workers for "delivering the
vote on election day" would be spent in behalf of Harrison.
After election I was told, on excellent authority, that the
Busse organization had not even pretended to employ Republican workers for Merriam. The money went into the
ward treasury and was used to pay some back debts.

I have always objected to undue sums of money being
spent in political campaigns and I have believed implicitly
that all receipts and expenditures should be publicly accounted for. I have also been opposed to paying workers at
the polls on election day. On more than one occasion I have
denounced this as "indirect bribery." Certainly it is a form
of vote-buying, if indulged in to the extent that it has come
to be in certain sections of this country. So, during the primary campaign I had sent a proposal to the managers of the
other candidates that we enter into a pledge not to pay
workers at the polls. This proposal was met either with silence or with heavy sarcasm. After the primaries I had made
the same suggestion to Carter Harrison's manager. He, too,
replied in a satiric vein and that ended the matter.

I also suggested to Harrison's manager that we make a full
and detailed statement of our campaign contributions and

expenditures. Again I met with an ill-mannered rebuff. I was charged with trying to "put something over." There was no law requiring the disclosure of campaign contributions, but just the same we did make ours known voluntarily, and despite the fact that the Harrison people had refused to meet us on this issue. We made one statement shortly before election day and a final and complete statement as soon after election as we could get our figures together.

My recollection is that in total we spent in Merriam's primary and general election campaigns about $150,000. Of this, approximately $50,000 were contributed by Charles R. Crane and a similar amount by Julius Rosenwald. The hypocritical horror with which these figures were met by the Harrison management was amusing. It pretended to make a complete statement, but no one ever believed that it was anywhere near accurate.

Of course $150,000 looked like big money in a day when the ordinary citizen had not the slightest conception of how much money was spent in campaigns. Some seemed to think that elections just grew on bushes and could be picked by the candidate who was the quickest on his feet. As a matter of fact, anyone with political experience knows that this sum of money spent on two elections in a city the size of Chicago is very modest indeed. Now that people have become accustomed to the known expenditure of large sums of money in elections it looks like chicken feed.

In considering the expenditure of money in campaigns it is only fair to take into account that one candidate may have a smoothly running, well-oiled political machine behind him, consisting of public employees paid out of the public treasury, while the opposing candidate has nothing of the sort. In the campaign in question, Harrison had already taken over the Democratic machine that had been built up in Chicago under Judge Dunne. Merriam, on the other hand, had no such machine. As a matter of fact, the Republican officeholders, as has been pointed out, had been working cheek by jowl with the Democratic precinct men.

The debated issues of the primary were those of the final election. But there were ugly mouth-to-ear issues, too. Religion was one of these. Harrison, in an autobiography that he has written recently, makes some very critical statements about "Merriam's manager" without mentioning me by name. He charges that Merriam raised the religious issue. This is not true. We raised no personal issue, religious or otherwise. We carried on no whispering campaign. We did not hit below the belt.

Both Mrs. Harrison and Mrs. Merriam were Roman Catholics. We did not question, openly or surreptitiously, whether Mrs. Harrison's children had been baptized in the Catholic Church. We were not interested. On the contrary, this issue was injected with respect to the Merriam children. In Protestant territory it was alleged that Merriam was a Catholic, as a result of his wife's influence, while in Catholic circles he was charged with being responsible for his wife's nonattendance at church and for his children not having been baptized. As a matter of fact, they had been baptized.

A Mrs. McMahon, afterward rewarded by Harrison with an appointment to the school board (was this purely coincidental?), was responsible for circulating, after mass on Sundays at various Catholic churches, an attack on Merriam charging that his children had never been baptized and that Mrs. Merriam was a backslider. That hurt, I know. Certainly it was not intended to help.

It was also whispered in anti-Jewish sections that Merriam

was a Jew, and attention was called to his dark complexion and wavy hair. Among the saloon element he was pictured as a bigoted dry, although I knew him as a man of temperate habits with a discriminating taste in wine. While in Berlin and Munich, both as a student and on many subsequent visits, he had acquired a real liking for good beer.

Harrison makes many statements in his book that are both untrue and unsportsmanlike. Without the saloon and the "flop," and their deliverable vote, Harrison would have been badly beaten, despite the stealthy efforts of the Republican bosses—big and little—in his behalf. Apparently he resented the defection of the better element to Merriam. These voters had been with Harrison on four previous occasions. To have them go to another in his last fight must have galled him. It wounded his pride. On no other theory am I able to account for some of his statements.

Looking back from this distance of more than thirty years, I am bound to say that we conducted as fair and honorable a fight as it is possible to conduct. Merriam has always been one of the most high-minded of men. He would have brooked no questionable practices, even if I had wanted to indulge in them. On the other hand, Harrison had always had the reputation of keeping his eyes closed and accepting results without asking embarrassing questions. How otherwise explain the faithful perennial support of "Hinky Dink" Kenna, "Bathhouse John" Coughlin, John Brennan, and a hundred lesser knights of the underworld?

We made a good fight and, on the whole, I think an intelligent one. We worked up to the usual climax with the whole city stirred as it had not been stirred for a long time. At the election Harrison polled 177,997 and Merriam 160,672. This was a remarkable showing for a freshman in politics, with an amateur manager, especially considering that the only sincere active support that he had came from a small group of volunteer workers and that he was opposed by practically his entire party organization.

If I had known then as much as I do now about the kind of arithmetic used by light-fingered judges and clerks of election who are selected by a certain type of party machine, we would have demanded a recount, and I am not at all sure that Harrison would have been found to be the winner. It shows what amateurs we really were. Merriam and I have talked about this a number of times since and we are in agreement on the point. It isn't unreasonable to believe that Merriam might have been counted out when one realizes that we did not have a single clerk or judge of election in a single precinct in the city. All of the election officials were the appointees of the regular party organizations.

I was, of course, bitterly disappointed, although not surprised. I had allowed myself to dream of victory, and assuredly I had worked for it.

Crane took the defeat philosophically. He was fighting for a cause, for the ultimate, not the immediate.

Rosenwald was sorely grieved by the result and I think that, without knowing why, he held it against me personally that we did not win. He was a successful man who expected his investments, even those in a political campaign, to turn out well. Perhaps, too, he did not relish the sly jokes of his friends and business associates. But he had his own little joke out of it at that. Throughout his life, if I were present, he referred to me as one of his *dearest* friends.

Merriam never said much about the whole business. He, too, accepted the result philosophically, but I have often wondered whether, like Rosenwald, he thought that he might have won if I had been less suspicious of the political crooks with whom I was perforce associated during the election campaign. In any event, we have remained fast, mutually respecting friends. We often refer to ourselves as the only surviving liberals of those rare days in Chicago.

(In 1933, when the President directed me to set up in the Public Works Administration, under myself as chairman, the National Resources Planning Board, he suggested his uncle, Frederic A. Delano, as vice-chairman. I proposed Charles E. Merriam as one of the members. Both have done a superb job during the intervening years.)

If a candidate wins, he gets the credit. If he loses, the manager gets hell. Shortly after the election we held a powwow of our volunteer workers at the Grand Pacific Hotel. There were a few men in the organization who had been selected by me but who were not unwilling to take advantage of his defeat to ingratiate themselves with Merriam by covert criticisms of me. Even in those days, I was a good deal of a lone wolf and ran on my own power. I did not much care whether people liked me or not.

I made a speech at that "get-together" and what I said exploded like an "egg" from a Focke-Wulf 190. I declared publicly that Merriam had not been defeated by Harrison, but by a Republican Governor, Deneen; a Republican Senator, Lorimer; and a Republican Mayor, Busse. The effect of the speech was to make some people shy away from me, but I had told them the truth whether they liked it or not. And it is still my opinion.

Deneen struck back, issuing a statement in which he accused me of "passing money for Merriam over the bar of 'Billy' Skidmore's saloon." Of course, this was a gross libel. It was libel per se. Merriam urged me to sue, and I have many times since regretted that I didn't. What a liar I would have made of Deneen!

In those incredible days when William Hale Thompson buffooned it in Chicago to the acclamations of people who seemed to have gone loony by the wholesale, the shriveled Deneen group offered the only oasis of political sanity in the Republican party. So, with the Progressive party silently moldering in its grave, my friends and I began to co-operate with Deneen. In this way we were able to elect occasional former Progressives to important public office in which, generally speaking, they acquitted themselves with credit. But I never acquired a personal attachment for Deneen, nor he for me.

In 1932, when we were caucusing on our primary ticket, I had a violent altercation with a political barnacle named William Busse (no relation to Fred). If I should be reincarnated a hundred years from now and go back to Cook County, I would expect to find William Busse rooting among the political garbage for choice morsels just as he has for so long as I can remember. Mrs. Ickes had served her constituency of the Seventh Senatorial District as a member of the State Assembly for two terms, creditably and intelligently. Busse, who lived in her district, did not want her nominated for a third term. He pretended that because Anna was a dry by conviction she would be a load on the ticket in such territory as his, where there was a heavy German American vote. I insisted that, as at the two previous elections, Anna would run way ahead of her ticket (as in fact she did).

Deneen, by now an ex-Senator as well as an ex-Governor, knew in his heart that I was right, but it irked him to have to cross Busse. He couldn't go against Anna, but he could give Busse some satisfaction. Apparently old festers, resulting from earlier political behavior on my part, had not completely healed. So with feeling he burst out: "Mr. Ickes, you have never been regular. Unless the candidate who is nominated suits your particular taste you won't support him," following which he read me a short, but stern, homily on the virtues of "regularity." My reply was: "Senator Deneen, I have never pretended to be regular. It has always been my policy to support the best candidate, regardless of party. The difference between you and me is that I openly oppose a candidate, even one of my own party, if I believe him to be unfit for office. On the other hand, you pretend to be regular, but stick a knife into the back of any candidate to whom you are personally opposed, whether he is a fit man or not."

It will be seen that I still regarded myself as a Republican —of a sort.

CHAPTER EIGHT

BIG STICK

Far better it is to dare mighty things, to win glorious tri-
umphs, even though checkered by failure, than to take rank
with those poor spirits who neither enjoy much nor suffer much,
because they live in the gray twilight that knows not victory
nor defeat.—THEODORE ROOSEVELT.

WILLIAM LORIMER was kicked out of the United States
Senate as unfit company. (I can think of at least one
present member of that club who is even less fit and of two
or three who, if they really loved their country, would lose
no time in checking out.) For the same reason, for years
some of us had been trying to kick him out of Chicago. His
friends had taken a hatful of money to Springfield and paid
for his election by the State Legislature. Those were the days
before Senators were chosen by a direct vote of the people.
Since there was a group of Republican members who opposed all that Lorimer stood for, it was necessary to have
some Democratic votes in order to get the filthy business
done. This was accomplished through a notorious bulldozer
from Ottawa, Lee O'Neill Browne, on the House side, after
a long-drawn-out fight in which public suspicions were
aroused when he and other Democrats moved across the aisle
to vote for a Republican with a record as moldy as the one
enjoyed by Lorimer.

When the scandal finally broke with all of its smell, it developed that the pay-off had occurred in a bathroom of the Leland Hotel in Springfield. On this occasion the *Chicago Tribune* did a fine and worth-while job—one greatly to its credit. Inasmuch as the public had been given the lurid details of the transaction, there was nothing for the United States Senate to do but to appoint a committee of its members to get the complete story. It was perfectly clear from the facts adduced that Lorimer had been corruptly elected. Accordingly, he was unseated and never again held public office.

Subsequently, with a man by the name of Mundy, Lorimer organized a national bank in Chicago. Charles G. Dawes, later a Vice-President of the United States, and at the time president of the Central Trust Company of Illinois, caused his bank to lend Lorimer a check for $1,000,000 in order to satisfy the State Auditor that the Lorimer bank had sufficient assets to open for business. There followed a scandalous failure, with large losses suffered by depositors. I know, because I represented some of these sufferers from "Dawesitis." Later, Dawes's bank was sued and recovery was had for the fraudulent misrepresentation to which it had been a party, although the Supreme Court toned down considerably the scathing language used by the Appellate Court, which had found Dawes and his bank guilty of misrepresentations and fraud. The Supreme Court also scaled down the damages assessed against the Dawes bank by the lower court.

Lorimer and others were indicted, but Lorimer escaped conviction. Later, he went into the lumber business in Central or South America and disappeared from Chicago for a number of years. Upon his return, he attached himself to the political fortunes of William Hale Thompson the Gross, but he never again became prominent, nor did he ever recover from his business crash. The last time I saw him he looked as he had always looked—undisturbed, innocent, apparently at ease with his conscience and at one with the world.

Before the Senate had gone through the formality of "scuffing" Lorimer out of his seat, Theodore Roosevelt, then President, went to Chicago to attend a banquet of the Hamilton Club. The Hamilton Club was always a hidebound Republican organization, consisting, in large part, of political mediocrities. All that was necessary to find favor in the eyes of its membership committee was to be a Republican. It was never interested in keeping its party clean. With little sense of the fitness of things, the club had invited Lorimer to share the honors with the President of the United States that night. When Roosevelt reached Chicago, some of the decent Republicans represented to him that he could not break bread with a man under grave suspicion of having bartered for his seat in the United States Senate.

The President sent word to the Hamilton Club that if Lorimer attended the banquet, he himself would have to be excused. The poor club couldn't do anything except to send word to Lorimer to stay at home. Roosevelt was loudly applauded by those of us who felt that he could not properly shed the light of his countenance upon Lorimer, even as a Republican and a fellow guest. On the other hand, he was bitterly criticized by Lorimer's friends on the technical ground that Lorimer had not yet been found guilty and that until he was, he was entitled to a place at the head table.

And while Roosevelt very properly refused to sit down with Lorimer because he was what he was, the following night he was the guest of honor at a banquet in Cincinnati which was presided over by George B. Cox, one of the most notorious bosses of a corrupt political machine in the country. Shall we say that's politics!—and let it go at that?

Following the Merriam defeat, we decided to set up a small executive committee, with a view to keeping our organization alive, and we made Fletcher Dobyns chairman. Dobyns was a good fellow—a lawyer who at one time had been Assistant State's Attorney under Deneen. He was a Harvard man who had both political and social ambitions. He wasn't very astute in politics, but he was honorable and wanted to do the right thing. And that was something.

I was married on September 16, 1911, to Anna Wilmarth Thompson. We went abroad, where we spent a little more than three months, returning to Chicago early the following January. That was a tough crossing. I can become seasick merely by thinking of it.

In the meantime, lines had begun to form for the 1912 national fight, which was to be one of the most interesting in American political history. During my absence, the group to which I belonged had decided to enter candidates on the Republican ballot for Governor and United States Senator, as well as for some lesser offices, in the 1912 primary election. Fences were being built or rebuilt and alliances formed with Republicans in different parts of the state.

The result of the winter's activities was the candidacy of State Senator Walter Clyde Jones of Chicago for the Republican nomination for Governor, and of State Senator Hugh S. Magill, representing downstate, for the nomination for United States Senator.

Jones was one of the leading patent lawyers of Chicago—a sincere and able man, but cold and distant. He could make a great speech that would leave his audience unmoved.

Magill was a schoolteacher in private life who also had rendered unusual service as a member of the State Senate. Magill, like Jones, was an intellectual, but with a somewhat warmer personality. Neither Jones nor Magill had any prospect of organization support except such as could be built up with the old Merriam group as a nucleus.

Although I had followed the movement uncertainly in such American newspapers as I was able to pick up in Paris and elsewhere, I felt no enthusiasm about getting in touch with my political cronies when I got back home. I had no hope for the success of this ticket.

Two or three new faces had appeared in the window during my absence. The most significant one belonged to Medill McCormick, brother of my brother-in-fists, Bertie. Both Medill and Bertie were actively connected with the *Tribune*. They used to alternate, month by month, as editor. Thus as to policy the paper was consistently inconsistent. One could always tell, by reading it, which genius was steering. It was either rolling in the trough under Bertie, or cutting across the waves under Medill. Their mother was still alive and she kept them pretty well in hand. However, Medill was beginning to lose favor with his mother as well as with his aunt, Mrs. Patterson, who had an equal financial interest, because he was less conservative than Bertie, and the property didn't seem to get along as well as it did under the cold-blooded, tight-fisted management of the man who later became Chicago's Morning Colonel.

William Hard, who was then one of the *Tribune's* editorial writers, stimulated political ambitions in Medill. Medill, who had married Ruth Hanna, the daughter of Mark Hanna, who had died eight years before, had thrown himself into the Jones-Magill movement. I met him for the first time at headquarters and I got at once a distinct impression of hostility. He was supercilious and snooty and left me in no doubt that he wasn't glad to meet me. I didn't fancy him, either. It was like biting deeply into a green persimmon.

John F. Bass was another of the newcomers in the insurgent movement. He was a much friendlier person than Medill McCormick. I had known him pleasantly for some time. He, too, had inherited wealth, and, as a brother of Robert P. Bass, then Governor of New Hampshire, had developed a liking for politics. He was an old newspaperman and had served as war correspondent for the *News*. He was brave and adventurous and had a charming wife who herself wasn't lacking in those qualities.

My interest in the campaign continued to lag. I considered it a mistake. I couldn't see the slightest chance of making even a respectable showing against the regular Republican organization, despite the fact that Jones and Magill would have made superior public officials. I was glad to be out of it all, watching from the sidelines.

I hadn't been home long before Walter Jones came to my office, where I was trying to ease myself into the practice of law. He was not impressed with the political skill or sagacity of either McCormick or Bass, and he wanted me to take over the direction of his campaign. I could put life into it and perhaps save it, he thought. I told him that no one could do that, and I declined as emphatically as I could without being uncivil. I even undertook to persuade him that it would be a mistake, not only from my own point of view but from his, if I should yield to his urging. I said to Jones that I was well aware that I was being blamed because Merriam hadn't been elected Mayor, and that if I should take over the management of his political campaign, it would be seized upon as an excuse on the part of some of his supporters to fall away from him on the theory that he was foredoomed to defeat. I felt that I had some political usefulness left and I didn't wish to destroy it by getting mixed up with Jones or anyone else for the time being. He persisted, but so did I.

I did not get into the campaign, which dragged on to an inglorious end. Jones and Magill were overwhelmingly defeated. I thanked my stars that for once I had refused to be a Don Quixote in a good cause. After this debacle, my old associates weren't so sure that I was responsible for Merriam's failure. In fact, they began to think that I might be all right as a campaign manager. By contrast with what had happened to Jones and Magill, Merriam had achieved a glorious victory.

When the liberal underground swell for the nomination of Theodore Roosevelt for President in 1912 came along I had, in large measure, lived down the Merriam reverse and had regained my former prestige. The Roosevelt movement was coincident to, but not coterminous with the Jones-Magill campaign. After Taft's inauguration in 1908, Roosevelt had gone to equatorial Africa to hunt big game. His plans for this trip had been made long before his term of office had ended and Taft had scarcely been sworn in as his successor before Roosevelt was sailing out of New York Harbor. I have never doubted that it was his honorable intention to give Taft an entirely free hand and a fair field. He had nominated Taft and his influence had been largely responsible for that gentleman's election in 1907.

Years afterward, in one of a number of private chats that I was privileged to have with Colonel Roosevelt, I asked him how he had happened to support Taft for the Presidency with so much enthusiasm—or even at all. I confessed to him that I had been so doubtful of Taft's liberalism that I had not been for him; that Charles Evans Hughes had been my choice for the nomination. I had not even voted for Taft on election day, although knowing that he would be elected, but had thrown away my vote on Bryan. I do not pretend to quote the Colonel verbatim, but this was, in effect, his answer and substantially his language:

"I thought that Taft was the most progressive member of my Administration. Whenever I proposed a measure in the public interest, Taft always wanted me to go a little further than I thought wise. He supported me in every detail. I believed that he would carry out my policies. My only fear was that he would try to go too fast or too far. I never was so deceived in a man in my life."

Roosevelt told me, on another occasion, that, shortly after the election, the question of his Cabinet had been brought up by Taft, who said to him: "Theodore, I want to keep all of the members of your Cabinet." Roosevelt told him that he shouldn't do that; that he ought to have a Cabinet of his own choosing. To which Taft replied: "Well, at any rate I am going to keep Jim Garfield."

James R. Garfield was Secretary of the Interior and as such had made an excellent record. Roosevelt spoke approvingly of Taft's choice. Taft then asked Roosevelt to inform Garfield of his intentions. Roosevelt did so and, on the strength of this assurance, Garfield renewed the lease on his home in Washington. That was the last that Garfield heard about a Cabinet post under Taft. Later he was to pack up his household goods and quietly go back to his home in Cleveland.

The Taft Administration, from the beginning, was a tremendous disappointment to Roosevelt and his friends. In the early days of it the Ballinger scandal broke. On the recommendation of Garfield, Richard A. Ballinger had become Commissioner of the General Land Office on March 4, 1907, under Roosevelt. A year later to the day he resigned to return to his private practice in Seattle, after having introduced desirable administrative reforms. He went home with the warm encomiums of Secretary Garfield ringing in his ears, and with a cordial letter over the signature of Theodore Roosevelt in appreciation of his patriotic services.

Exactly a year later, again to the day, Ballinger found himself in the Taft Cabinet as Secretary of the Interior. Ballinger did not, so far as I know, seek the office. In fact. he was not easily persuaded to accept it.

When I came to Washington in 1933, I shared the practically universal opinion that Ballinger had personally benefited from fraudulent practices, or at least had been so indifferent as to the public welfare that he was unfit to hold office. I was convinced that he was guilty of maladministration and a lot of other things, among them conspiracy to defraud the United States of valuable public lands. In due course (after I had full access to the records of the Department of the Interior), my associates and I, to our utter amazement, were forced, as the result of a thorough study by us, to the conclusion that Ballinger had been persecuted and unjustly driven from office as the result of a conspiracy, the center of which was Gifford Pinchot, at the time Chief Forester. The record convinced us that even though he had died a broken man, Ballinger was in fact an honorable and patriotic public servant.[1]

---

[1] I made every effort to give the facts in the Ballinger case the widest possible circulation, including an article in the *Saturday Evening Post* under date of May 25, 1940.

Continuously since this affair, Pinchot has persistently made mischievous use of wholly false accusations against a guiltless man in an attempt to discredit the Department of the Interior. Not only has he never overlooked an opportunity to traduce the Department, he has smeared vindictively the memory of a man who, whatever his faults and shortcomings, was nonetheless a decent human being and an honorable public servant. Moreover Pinchot, whom I used to honor as a public man and cherish as a friend, conspired against Ballinger from the basest of motives—to aggrandize his own political power and enhance his personal prestige.

I was never an admirer of William Howard Taft, but I honor him for the stand that he took when a carefully stimulated public clamor demanded Ballinger's scalp. Taft wrote: "If I were to turn Ballinger out, in view of his innocence, and in view of the conspiracy against him, I should be a white-livered skunk. I don't care how it affects the Administration and how it affects the Administration before the people; if the people are so unjust as this I don't propose to be one of them. Mr. Ballinger has done nothing of any kind that should subject him to criticism. He has been made the object of a despicable conspiracy, in which unscrupulous methods have been used that ought to bring shame to the faces of everyone connected with it. . . . Life is not worth living and office is not worth having if, for the purpose of acquiring public support, we have to either do a cruel injustice or acquiesce in it."

So much for Pinchot. On January 7, 1910, he was dismissed by President Taft for insubordination. Later, on one occasion, Theodore Roosevelt referred to him impatiently as one of the "lunatic fringe."

There were other unhappy breaks during the Taft regime. Taft made a very unfortunate speech on reciprocity with Canada which alienated, to a large extent, the farmers of the country. There was also the incident of the famous "Norton letter." Charles D. Norton, whom I had known well in Chicago and for whom I had worked for a year in his insurance business, had gone to Washington as the private secretary of Franklin MacVeagh, whom Taft had appointed Secretary of the Treasury. Norton was also a friend of John Harlan's, through whom I had met him. He was highly intelligent and energetic and he had original ideas. It was he who had given birth to the catchy name "Straphangers' League" that we had used to great effect in one of Harlan's campaigns.

As MacVeagh's secretary, Norton came into personal contact with President Taft, and he so impressed the President that the latter wanted him for his own private secretary. Of course MacVeagh had to consent.

There had been growing up in the United States Senate a small group of insurgent Republicans, consisting of such men as La Follette of Wisconsin and Clapp of Minnesota. George W. Norris of Nebraska, who had always been independent in the finest sense of that term, was "insurging" valiantly and to good purpose in the House. Moreover, Taft's administration early developed such tendencies that some of the more regular Republican Senators had broken with it. The most prominent of these was Dolliver of Iowa.

After Dolliver had become one of the most active and most able anti-Taft Republicans in the Senate, he wrote to the President about an appointment in which he was interested. Norton replied over his own signature in effect that of course a Republican Senator who didn't go along with the President could not expect any favors; that the way to get them was to be with the Administration. Dolliver made the letter public, and a tremendous outcry went up from all parts of the country. Even though people knew that this was the general rule in politics, this callous exhibition of the cloven hoof disgusted them.

Shortly afterward I met Norton in Chicago at his telegraphic request. He was in a disturbed state of mind about the public reaction to this letter. It must have been quite a shock to one who had never had to stand much punishment. He remarked plaintively that he knew nothing about politics and that no one else on the White House staff did. This was preliminary to asking me to accept an appointment on Taft's immediate staff. I thanked him for the compliment but declined. I was still determined to be a lawyer and I still was not enamored of the President.

Sentiment against Taft continued to grow in the Republican party, especially in the West. Roosevelt was still in Africa. Some of Roosevelt's friends began to confer and to correspond. They were of the opinion that Roosevelt should oppose Taft for the nomination in 1912.

After Roosevelt had finished a successful hunt in Africa, he made his grand tour of the European capitals, where he was received as though he were of high royal rank. Roosevelt told me later of his visit to Berlin. Mrs. Roosevelt had joined him after he came out of Africa. The Kaiser had invited Roosevelt to be his guest at the Imperial Palace, but no invitation had come for Mrs. Roosevelt. Apparently she was to go to a hotel. Whereupon Roosevelt, in characteristic fashion, caused word to be conveyed to the Kaiser that while he appreciated "the Most High's" offer of hospitality, he would find accommodations in a hotel with Mrs. Roosevelt. I doubt if anyone else could have got away with it. After all, the German Kaiser was next to God, or thought so, and who was Theodore Roosevelt? An invitation was promptly issued to Mrs. Roosevelt also to be the guest of their Imperial Highnesses.

I do not want it understood that I was consulted in the plottings that went on to bring Roosevelt out as a candidate against Taft for the Republican nomination. I was only one of the thousands who wanted him. When the time came for Roosevelt's return to America there had developed a general and widespread sentiment for him as the next Republican President. Unfortunately, when he was elected President in 1904 he had voluntarily expressed the view that he regarded that as his second term and that he would not be a candidate for a third term. This was the chief stumbling block that confronted both him and his partisans when they began to consider the possibilities for 1912.

There can be no doubt that when Roosevelt stepped onto the wharf in New York, he was definitely opposed to Taft. He felt that not only had Taft broken faith with him, he had turned the party and the Administration over to the big interests. Organizations, newspapers, and individuals continued to importune him to announce himself a candidate. Senator Jonathan Bourne, Jr., of Oregon, took the position that Roosevelt had referred to an "elective" period when he had barred himself from a third term. But the people were not interested in the third-term banter. (They showed how little this myth meant to them in 1940.) They wanted Roosevelt and they didn't want Taft.

Finally, Republican Governors of seven states called on Roosevelt and demanded that he become the party's candidate. Undoubtedly this pilgrimage had been carefully prearranged. Undoubtedly, also, Roosevelt had already made up his mind to be a candidate, for soon after the visit of the seven came his announcement that his "hat was in the ring."

Volumes already have been written about the preconvention fight between Taft and Roosevelt. I shall therefore cut this reference short. While I was an intensely interested spectator of the cat-and-dog fight, I was not a part of it. The convention was held in Chicago, and although I had hoped to be able to attend it, a pending "blessed event" in the Ickes household made it unwise for me to lose myself in the crowd, where I could not possibly be reached.

Even so, I had a small part in that memorable battle. Under the pressure of public opinion, Governor Deneen had called a special session of the State Legislature which passed a Presidential primary law. This took a lot of hammering, because Deneen was not a Roosevelt man and he wasn't easily swayed by public opinion. However, the *Tribune* (right again, for a wonder) and other newspapers kept clamoring at him until he yielded. The law had been passed with an emergency clause, making it available for the selection of delegates to the 1912 convention. Roosevelt's friends at once entered him in the Illinois primary and plans were made for him to come to Chicago for a great meeting at the Auditorium, to be held just before the election in May.

As I have said, the terrible beating that Magill and Jones had taken earlier in the same year had suggested to the old Merriam crowd that perhaps I wasn't a bust after all. Antagonism to me began to disappear and I again shared with Merriam control of the organization that I had built for him. It was small but virile, and it had principles.

I was delegated to go to New York and travel West with Roosevelt for the purpose of filling him full of our story— how we had made the fight for Merriam; the kind of people composing the Merriam forces; and what our political objectives were. As a matter of fact, we wanted him to say a word for Merriam in his Auditorium speech, but he objected that if he did this for Merriam he might have to mention other people in the same speech; and if he gave personal endorsements in Chicago he might have to do so elsewhere. I could see the force of his argument and I did not press him.

En route to Chicago I was invited to have breakfast with Roosevelt. All through the meal he talked politics in his vivacious and eager way. It was a great occasion for me. I was reminded, when his breakfast was served, of the rumors of excessive drinking on his part. Fruit, a large order of oatmeal, an extra allotment of specially cooked whitefish, a man's portion of bacon and fried potatoes, large quantities of toast, and two cups of coffee—I reflected that no heavy drinker could stow away a breakfast like that.

In dismissing finally the subject of Roosevelt's alleged intemperance, let me say that, by and large, I spent many hours with him. At luncheon at Oyster Bay when he had guests he would drink a small glass of sherry. When he lunched with me in Chicago, he would have sherry or some other light wine. I never saw him drink a cocktail or distilled liquor. When I gave him a large luncheon at Winnetka in 1916, I served no cocktails, but I did offer a favorite wine of the Colonel's, Château d'Yquem, of which he drank a couple of glasses. I have never met anyone who ever saw Colonel Roosevelt under the influence of liquor. And when he was given a chance to bring the question out into the daylight in open court, he was able to scotch the story which had plagued him for so many years and which had been spread by word of mouth until an unfortunate Michigan editor crawled too far out on a limb and found it sawed off between himself and the tree.

When we reached Chicago there was a great crowd at the station. A mob thronged the streets on the way to the Congress Hotel. Medill McCormick and John Bass had given out a hundred thousand "admission tickets" to the meeting at the Auditorium. They avowed later that they had resorted to this trick because they didn't want to fail to have a big turnout. There wasn't merely a crowd—there was a crush. It was almost impossible for people with box tickets to get inside the place at all. A disappointed throng milled in Congress Street and Wabash and Michigan avenues, while the Auditorium itself was packed to suffocation. And McCormick and Bass had been fearful that we wouldn't fill the place!

It was a great meeting, with the Colonel at his best, denouncing the political bosses and the big interests that were seeking to deny the rank and file of the Republican party the chance to nominate their own choice for President. I listened with enthusiasm. This meeting determined the result in Illinois. At the primary election Roosevelt carried virtually every district in the state, and this gave great impetus to sentiment in other states of the Union.

I was, of course, tremendously eager to attend the sessions of the Republican National Convention and to go to Roosevelt's headquarters, but with a baby expected at our home almost any minute I simply would not even attempt it. The radio was still a thing of the future, so that I had no recourse except to sit out in Evanston and wait for the next edition of the paper. When Taft was finally declared the nominee and the Roosevelt people marched out of the Coliseum and down to Orchestra Hall, where they held an impromptu rump convention at midnight on June 23, I was thrilled and wished that I might be taking part in it. However, Raymond was born late the morning of June 24, and by that time most of the fun was over for the time being.

The moment that it was decided to hold a Progressive National Convention at the Coliseum in August, I became active. Medill McCormick and Bass had grabbed the leadership of the Roosevelt movement in Illinois. They were young and ambitious and they both had money. They too had modified their views as to my political ineptitude in the light of their own that had been so convincingly demonstrated. They were willing to have me tag along, but they were going to see that I was kept in my proper place.

McCormick assumed responsibility for organizing the state and Bass was to take care of Cook County. Irregular catch-as-catch-can meetings were held to organize by congressional districts. I was living in the Tenth Congressional District. McCormick and Bass had determined that an inexperienced young schoolteacher by the name of Harry F. Nightingale was to be selected as the representative of that district on the State Central Committee.

Nightingale not only did not know anything about politics, he was lacking generally in political capacity. But he would have stood hitched. Just to let them know that I couldn't be kicked about, I stepped out and got myself elected instead. It hasn't been often that I have gone out for an election to anything. It was easily enough done. It was setback No. 1 for the two peripatetic statesmen, and more were to come.

Bass opened himself an office and let the whole world know that he was waiting for volunteers to come in and organize the county and set up a county committee. We told our people to stay away until further notice. John was having a lonely time of it. In the end we got together and elected

Chauncey Dewey chairman of the state committee. I became its treasurer. We elected Bass county chairman, but at least 90 per cent of the members had been chosen by Merriam and me.

I took hold of the county convention and ran it in plain sight of all. It was *our* county ticket—Merriam's and mine— that was nominated, and we wrote the platform. We also dominated the subsequent state convention at Urbana. Mc-Cormick didn't want to nominate a candidate against Governor Deneen, but as Merriam and I were waiting to pay our respects to that gentleman for having helped to knock us out in the mayoralty election of the year before, we served notice that if the Progressive party endorsed Deneen, or even failed to nominate a candidate against him, we would invent a procedure for Al Smith to follow later and "take a walk." So Frank H. Funk, a Republican State Senator from Bloomington, became the new party's nominee for governor.

I was treasurer of the State Committee, but once again I had nothing to treasure. Our state chairman, Chauncey Dewey, was a seasoned politician—one of the few regulars who had joined the new party. In Illinois, campaigns open earlier downstate than in Cook County. In the latter, a hard-driven intensive canvass is put on for the fortnight preceding election day.

When it was time to turn our attention to Cook County, we found that Dewey had spent or obligated all of our meager funds for his downstate campaign. With fifteen days to go, I went to headquarters one morning and found that we did not have enough money to buy postage stamps for that day's mail. I yelled for help in the direction of La Verne Noyes and he heard me. I estimated expenses at about $15,000. Noyes gave me his personal check for this amount on the condition that no one else was to know about it. I was to handle the money through my personal account. When the campaign was over, I returned $7,000 to him.

It was shortly before this that McCormick had sought me out and led me, affectionately, arm in arm, into his office where we could talk privately. He began to pace up and down agitatedly, leaving behind him a trail of hair. He said that it was absolutely necessary that John Bass be demoted as county chairman and that I take his place. Then he made me this remarkable speech:

"Harold, figuratively, I am down on my knees to you, and if anyone had ever told me that I would one day be down on my knees to Harold Ickes I would have said that he was crazy. John Bass and I went into this campaign with only one plank to our platform and this was that in no circumstances would we ever let you inside the breastworks. We were determined to run this show ourselves. But John hasn't got what it takes. He is a total failure. If we don't get him out as county chairman right away we will lose Cook County. You are the only man who can do the job. For God's sake let bygones be bygones and take it. I will see to it that John resigns and asks you to take over." And he did.

This from a McCormick! (I hope that it blisters Brother Bertie to learn that his own flesh and blood had "crawled" in front of Harold Ickes!)

We lost the state, although we elected scattered candidates for various offices, but we carried Cook County for Theodore Roosevelt and Hiram Johnson. We elected Charles M. Thomson to Congress from my district, five members of the County Board of Cook County to hold the balance of power there, and enough of the legislature to give us the balance of power in the State Assembly.

History will tell with what enthusiasm and almost religious fervor we Progressives worked. It has been seen how little money we had—barely enough to put on a decent campaign and far from enough to man the polls, even if we had wanted to. In our hearts there was still great resentment at the ruthless manner in which Roosevelt had been denied the Republican nomination in June. But there was more than hatred of political gangsterism at the base of the Progressive movement. The new party expressed the hope and aspiration of the American people for a "square deal for all." The Progressive movement was a middle-class movement; it was the "new-deal" march of 1912. Generally speaking, those who went into it wanted those less favorably conditioned than themselves to share prosperity and happiness with all. I have always believed that this aspiration was the heart and soul of the Progressive party movement, within which developed the distinctively crusading spirit which distinguished the Progressive campaign of 1912 from all other campaigns that I have known anything about in this country.

Our greatest triumph was the carrying of Cook County for Funk over Deneen. It was by a small vote, but it was enough to defeat Deneen and elect the former Mayor of Chicago, Edward F. Dunne—a victory that did my curmudgeonly soul no end of good. It was all the more remarkable because Deneen was a resident of Cook County and had lived there for many years, while Funk was from McLean County and was virtually unknown in the Chicago area.

I won't pretend that we didn't awaken the day after election with a bad headache. Roosevelt himself was very much taken aback by his defeat. Shortly after, he prepared to go to Brazil to explore the upper reaches of the "River of Doubt" and to determine its course. This was to lead him into wild

I enjoyed an interesting correspondence with Colonel Theodore Roosevelt. I have chosen to reproduce his letter to me of December 21, 1915, because it shows that I, the curmudgeon, was a "comfort" to someone more than a quarter of a century ago. And observe also, if you will, that as far back as 1917 the pro-German leanings of the *Chicago Tribune* did not escape the notice of the former President. The Knox referred to in the letter dated December 29, 1915, is Philander C. Knox.

Private   OYSTER BAY   December 21st, 1915.
                           LONG ISLAND N Y

Dear Ickes:

         You are always a comfort to me! I think that it would be a capital idea to use those posts as you suggest in order to get the great number of extra officers this country will require; but I do not want to be drawn into advocating any details at present. I want to keep myself down to the main issue. Moreover I absolutely agree with you that this main issue must be Americanism, with the two-fold expression of insistence on preparedness to hold our own in the face of the rest of the world and, as a pre-requisite, insistence upon national solidarity, including the elimination of the hyphen within our own ranks. Like you, I am a radical. I stand for every particle of our platform in 1912; but overwhelmingly my chief interest at present is in the relationship of the United States to the present European situation and also to Mexico and affairs in the Pacific. I am ashamed of America at this moment; and that is a feeling that it is mighty uncomfortable to have. Like you, I do not believe in a large standing army and do believe in a large navy and efficient universal military training.

                         Faithfully yours,

                         Theodore Roosevelt

Harold L. Ickes, Esq.,
    Harris Trust Building,
       Chicago, Illinois.

December 29th, 1915.

Dear Ickes:

I am glad you have told me just what you did
tell me. What is more, since that article appeared, I
have had the most emphatic protests from two United
States Senators who stated that Knox as Secretary of State
under Taft was just as bad in his handling of the Mexican
policy as Wilson himself.

Faithfully yours,

Theodore Roosevelt

Harold L. Ickes, Esq.,
    Harris Trust Building,
        Chicago, Ill.

METROPOLITAN
432 FOURTH AVENUE NEW YORK

Office of
Theodore Roosevelt

October 25, 1917.

Dear Ickes:

I am very glad to get that report.
I hope I needn't tell you how thoroughly I enjoyed
both the lunch and the dinner at Chicago.   As
for the Tribune clipping: - the tribune has usually
been against me and at least half the time has been
pro-German.

Faithfully yours,

Theodore Roosevelt

Mr. Harold L. Ickes,
Harris Trust Bldg.,
Chicago, Ill.

I have long treasured this letter from the former Chief Justice. Although the loss of the election in 1916 was a great disappointment to him, Mr. Hughes took his licking like a good sport.

~~Bridgehampton, New York~~

Lakewood, New Jersey,
December 4, 1916.

Hon. Harold L. Ickes,
   1818 Harris Trust Building,
     Chicago,
       Illinois.

Dear Mr. Ickes:-

    Your letter of November 24th has been received and I appreciate most deeply your very kind words. I know the earnest and effective efforts that you put forth and I am very grateful for your strong support. I wish that we could have had more of the sort of work that you put into the campaign in those places where the result shows it was lacking.

    With assurance of my high esteem, I am,

      Faithfully yours,

Charles E. Hughes

and dangerous sections of Brazil that had never been penetrated by a white man. It would also mean his absence from the United States for many months, during which time the political situation would have an opportunity to simmer and thus make it easier to determine what the future might hold for the young party that had burgeoned so fast.

Roosevelt welcomed this opportunity to escape from incessant political importunings. He couldn't look into the political future four years off and so determine upon present moves. He must take bearings, get a perspective. How many voters had already fallen away? How many would desert in the months to come? Anyhow, he was no man to lead a losing cause. Yet, he could not easily turn his back on the millions of voters who had followed him over the great political divide. Neither could he show the white feather to the enemy.

A large farewell banquet was held in New York prior to Roosevelt's departure for Brazil, at which the speakers declared that although we had been defeated, the Republican party had run such a bad third, with only Vermont and Utah to its credit, that the Progressive party must and would go on to establish itself as one of the two major parties of the country. In saying his good-by, Roosevelt gave off a lot of steam and spirit that seemed to satisfy his followers. With enthusiasm running high, he pledged himself to carry on the fight. He had enlisted for the war, of which only one battle had been fought. He exhorted Progressives everywhere to remain true to their principles, to close their ranks, and to proceed to build up for the engagements that lay ahead.

After the November election, many members of the Progressive party, especially those who had political ambitions, had hurried back to the Republican party like rats leaving a sinking ship. I never doubted that I would stick to the end. After all, guts and an appetite for punishment are implicit in a curmudgeonish character. Dewey had had more than he wanted and I became state chairman, in addition to continuing as county chairman.

Medill McCormick had been elected a member of the State Assembly. He proceeded to assume the leadership of the group of Progressives who held the balance of power and who therefore were in a strong position. Not one of these Progressives had been a politician or had ever held political office. They constituted an oasis in the State Assembly. Medill promptly aspired to the United States Senate. There were two vacancies to fill, a long term and a short one. He tried to make a deal with the Democrats. The outstanding, and later the successful, Democratic candidate was James Hamilton Lewis. Lewis had sent a mutual friend to me to suggest that he would support me for the short term if I would throw our Progressives to him for the long term. I did not aspire. Subsequently, Lawrence Y. Sherman was elected for the short term. I thought that this was only fair, since he was really the choice of the people.

Medill always had to be watched in politics. He had a good deal of ability and so did his wife. And they both rolled in arrogance as they rolled in wealth. Generally, however, they could be countered, because, in their disregarding selfishness, they tried to move too fast. And then we would clip them. John Bass was on our side by this time. He too had come to size Medill up for what he was and to regret his former alliance.

Medill proceeded to run things with a high hand at Springfield. He had called a meeting of the State Central Committee there, planning to control it. We all went and tied him up good and tight. No longer could he assume that he was the sole Progressive leader in Illinois. We had the organization by a large margin. After we had operated upon Medill (and Mrs. Medill, too, be it said) he asked if he might go back to Chicago with me on the train. It was a mournful procession. Shut up in a compartment, he licked his wounds and deplored the humiliation to which we had subjected him. He professed great personal friendship for me. As a matter of fact, I had come to like him a lot myself. I even loved him as Damon loved Pythias when I thought of Bilious Bertie, the bingy bully. I was frank with him. I told him that if he would go along with the crowd we would be very happy to have him. But he had to get over the notion that he was a Mark Hanna or even a Mark Hanna son-in-law. The organization was in our hands and we intended to use it for the good of the party. That we were not using it for personal ends was testified to by the fact that neither Merriam nor I was ever a candidate for office on the Progressive ticket.

Medill ran again for the State Assembly in 1914. He was the only one to be elected. He had Republican organization help on the side and he had the real support of the *Chicago Tribune* and other newspapers. Although elected as a Progressive, true to form he scrambled clamorously back to the "party of his fathers" without calling in the Progressive leaders to tell them that he was going to run out. He even forgot a promise to me, on which the ink was not yet dry, that he wouldn't desert without another personal conference with me. I had insisted that he and I, as leaders, must stick so long as there was anyone to stick to. So I also took over the job of Progressive national committeeman which Medill had hastened to cast aside, preparatory to surrendering to the Republicans. In addition, I held the permanent proxy of Jane

Addams as a member of the national executive committee, which was the top boss of the party. The real politicos in the Progressive movement were busily preparing a line of safe retreat, and they were all cheerfully willing that I should hold what they distinctly regarded as the bag. I served out Medill's term and in my turn was unanimously re-elected to the office at the Progressive National Convention in 1916.

Perhaps it was then that I got the training for holding at one time the thirteen (or is it fourteen?) jobs that I do at present.

I wanted to keep the party going, regardless, and to that end I was willing to undertake all of the chores that no one else wanted. I believed that we held the balance of power in the country and that if we continued to click our knitting needles, we could lick the Republican party in 1916 as we had in 1912. And it couldn't survive the second beating. But treachery was at work. George W. Perkins hadn't deserted, but he was getting ready to betray the party that he had helped to found.

CHAPTER NINE

THE LAST SAD RITES

At last they came to where Reflection sits—that strange old woman, who had always one elbow on her knee, and her chin in her hand, and who steals light out of the past to shed it on the future.—OLIVE SCHREINER.

THEODORE ROOSEVELT had returned from Brazil, where he had undergone hardships that no man of his age and sedentary habits should have risked. He had been in such straits that on two or three occasions he had begged his son Kermit to press on with the party and leave him behind. He believed that he had seen civilization for the last time. Death faced him close up, without seeing a flicker of fear.

With true Rooseveltian fortitude, he fought his way through and reached home. Soon after his return to Oyster Bay, I saw him for the first time since the election of 1912. A group of Progressives called on him and what we saw saddened us. There was no doubt that the Brazilian jungles had left an indelible mark upon the man. He was slow and sluggish; his reactions were hesitant; he seemed to have lost his decisiveness. As he slumped in his chair on the broad portico of his home, he resembled anything but the vigorous candidate we had so recently pressed closely from behind.

The purpose of our visit was to discuss with him the

future of the party and to plan for the 1914 campaign. Raymond Robins in Illinois, and Gifford Pinchot in Pennsylvania, were our two outstanding candidates, both of them seeking seats in the United States Senate. We had other important stakes in the campaign, and we felt that without Roosevelt's powerful and far-reaching voice there was no hope of success anywhere or chance of anything short of ignominious defeat.

Roosevelt was reluctant to climb back into his armor and, considering his physical condition, none of us blamed him. But before it was over he made a circumscribed tour of Illinois and spoke his piece in New York and Pennsylvania. Our only hope in Illinois, as we knew, was that the Democrats behind Roger Sullivan and the Republicans behind Lawrence Y. Sherman would beat each other to death. But they didn't. Sherman was re-elected, much to the disappointment of Sullivan, who had been depending on the Republicans and the Progressives to exterminate each other.

As I have said, Medill McCormick was returned to the Illinois Legislature as the only Progressive to survive, and he promptly decamped to the Republicans. We elected no State Senator. Our candidates for Congress were defeated to a man.

What happened in Illinois happened elsewhere. Pinchot in Pennsylvania and all of the Progressive candidates in New York were beaten to a pulp. It was a staggering blow for the party. We were plainly on our way back whence we had come, provided we could get back. The disintegration of the party became accelerated after this miserable showing, and even some of the leaders, who had sworn that they would go down with the ship, were not slow to strap on their water wings and jump overboard with McCormick.

I have written elsewhere and in detail of the last days of the Progressive party.[1] I have told who killed it—George W. Perkins—and I have tried to analyze his motives. I don't intend to repeat here the gruesome story of his perfidy. It is long, complicated, and by now merely a historical incident.

After 1914 I was called upon to play what I often described as "political poker." More than once it seemed to me more like solitaire. Everyone knew that the Progressive party was disintegrating, but no one in Illinois knew so well as I how numerous and widespread our defections were. I realized that only the skeleton remained of what once had been a vigorous political body. It was up to me to put on as cheerful a face as I could, to keep a stiff upper lip and get out of the situation all that I could for the men and women who faithfully had gone down the line. It was a job that called for the talents and the finesse of a crusty curmudgeon. What an experience for one who had already collected so many cherished souvenirs of personal selfishness, questionable maneuvers, and political treachery! But what a priceless schooling for one who was generally looked upon as being on the way to be regarded as the best-hated man in America!

Although at the Progressive National Convention of 1916 we gave Brother Perkins a farewell boot in the pants by taking control of the convention away from him and nominating Theodore Roosevelt again as our candidate, with John M. Parker of Louisiana as his running mate, we were really performing the last sad rites over what had shown the promise of becoming a great political movement. Many of us had had our premonitions of a moldy future. Roosevelt quit

---

[1] "Who Killed the Progressive Party?" by Harold L. Ickes, *American Historical Review*, Vol. XLVI, No. 2 (January 1941).

us cold. He gave the impression that he didn't want to waste any more time on us.

Deneen had never cared for me. Nor I for him. We had highly offended each other during the 1911 Merriam campaign and he knew that I had had a good deal to do with insisting upon a Progressive candidate against him in order to bring about his defeat for the governorship in 1912. He knew also that I had helped to prevail upon Theodore Roosevelt to blast him to high heaven during that same 1912 campaign. With the Progressive party about to expire, Deneen was planning on clubbing his way back to political position.

In the spring of 1915, he had sent his man Friday, Roy O. West, to ask me whether I would be willing to select five Progressives, including myself, to confer with a group of five Republicans, headed by Deneen, to see if we could agree on a city ticket. William Hale Thompson had announced himself a candidate, and Deneen was against him. And was I! Thompson was the playboy son of a father who had left him enough money so that he didn't have to think of working. He didn't even have to think. He had gone to Yale in a desultory fashion and had managed to hang on there for a brief spell. Then he played at cowboy in Nebraska, where he at least had learned that a head can be used to model a broad-brimmed Stetson hat. Finally he wound up in Chicago again for a whirl at politics. He was elected alderman from the Second Ward and later County Commissioner. In neither office did he distinguish himself. He knew how to vote from the way that the man ahead of him had voted.

Somewhere along the line, Thompson fell into the hands of a very clever politician—Fred Lundin, of Swedish birth —who was later to become a real power in Republican machine politics in Illinois. Lundin had been a patent-medicine hawker. He looked the country bumpkin, or raw immigrant, but anyone who mistook him for a fool was in grievous error and due for trouble. Lundin took hold of Thompson and became Svengali to an amenable Trilby. In the great hulk of a man that was Thompson he built up political ambition. Lundin made out of him one of the most accomplished demagogues of the day. Whereas as a member of the City Council and County Board Thompson had sat as dumb and as docile as a bashful boy, he now started making speeches. Years later when I dropped in with Raymond Robins at one of his noonday meetings to hear him croon to the people, I was compelled to confess to myself that as a platform performer Bill Thompson had developed great ability. He had acquired ease and fluency and the ability to hand out persiflage impressively and with eloquent conviction. He was the Huey Long of his time and locale—without Huey's brains, however.

The thought of Thompson's being elected Mayor of Chicago in 1915 amused me. I had been amused before and had lived to laugh ruefully out of the other side of my mouth. But in Thompson's case I didn't believe that it could be done. Nevertheless he soon picked up considerable momentum. I agreed to Deneen's proposal that Roy West had brought to me, and at our first conference I urged upon him the need for haste. And how he hated to hurry! It soon was revealed to me that Deneen's candidate was Bernard A. Eckhart. Eckhart was a very rich man, a miller, a banker, and, for all that I know, a candlestick-maker. He had been a partisan of Deneen's for many years, and a substantial contributor to his various campaigns.

On my part, the real motive that had actuated me in joining up with Deneen was the possibility that I might be able to slide Merriam into the mayor's chair. I still believed that he was the strongest possibility, in view of the wonderful showing that he had made in 1911. I knew that there was no one so well qualified for the office.

Deneen and I jockeyed for what seemed interminable days. With Thompson in the field, we were wastrels of valuable time. I kept shoving Merriam at him and he continued to tell me that Merriam wouldn't do. As we tried to outpoint each other, our tempers became shorter and shorter. We at last locked horns—Deneen charging that I couldn't be regular in any case, and I replying that I had never pretended to be. His rejoinder was that I did not belong in a caucus that was trying to set up a Chicago city ticket, because I lived in Evanston. Apparently he had forgotten that it had been he who had suggested the caucus and my presence therein.

Thereupon I withdrew from the meeting. The other four Progressives whom I had taken with me soon followed, after telling Deneen that he was out of order and that they would not go along without me. Unable to get the ball rolling, Deneen ate crow and sent West to apologize for his shortness of temper. By this time I knew that there was no hope for Merriam. He was definitely out of the question. Merriam and I had agreed on the side that we could support Judge Harry Olson, Chief Justice of the Municipal Court, with whom we had had a quiet talk and who had said that he would be a candidate if we would all get behind him. Then I went to meet Deneen again. He was still for Eckhart. I told him it was Olson or nobody. And Olson it was.

The fight was on—Olson against Thompson. Meanwhile, Deneen let me name the candidates for City Treasurer and City Clerk—Charles H. Sergel and John Siman respectively. Both of these men were out of the Progressive ranks. They were loyal and straight. Sergel was a bit pompous and wore whiskers, but nothing worse could be said of him. Siman was one of the most unselfish men that I have ever met in politics—a simple, sincere, fine citizen, a credit to his native country, Bohemia, and to his adopted one.

Deneen thought that it would be easy to nominate Olson over Thompson. I thought so, too. It was plain to see that Deneen didn't want me to have anything to do with the campaign, so I gulped down a runout powder and went to Excelsior Springs, Missouri, for a vacation. After all, I did live in Evanston. Primary election day found me still there, and to my amazement Thompson pulled up the winner. It was a crushing defeat for Deneen, particularly since both Sergel and Siman had won easily. Subsequently, Olson insisted to me that bad management had lost the fight for him, and deplored my absence in Missouri. So here we were in the anomalous position of having two Progressives on a city ticket that was headed by the ineffable William Hale Thompson.

It soon dawned on me that, with very few exceptions, all of our so-called Progressives in Chicago were for Thompson. My disgust was unbounded to think of men and women who had voted for principle since 1912 being attracted to this political *symplocarpus foetidus* in the mistaken belief that a flickering and sickly flame was a real beacon of civic righteousness. But the Progressives were hungry for victory. Many were looking for a bandwagon.

Personally I took no hand in it. I set about to make good on Deneen's characterization of me. I told Sergel and Siman that I couldn't be for Thompson even to help them. I refused to confer with him when it was suggested that I might get some commitments out of Thompson in the public interest. I did not trust him. I encouraged Marion Drake, who had been a member of the Progressive County Committee, to give vent to her feelings against Thompson by organizing a "We-Can't-Stand-for-Thompson-Club." It was a paper organization—and thin paper at that—but it annoyed Thompson and that suited me.

Thompson was elected by nearly 140,000 votes over Sweitzer, the Democratic nominee. Sergel and Siman were elected, too. Siman finished with a bigger plurality than Thompson, much to my delight.

During those years I saw Theodore Roosevelt frequently. Each time that I talked with him it was on the tip of my tongue to ask about his possible candidacy in 1916 on the Progressive-party ticket—knowing all of the time that the Progressive party was a pretty rickety vehicle. It was not until the time was getting very short that I became convinced that he was out of it. He did not say that he wouldn't be our candidate, but his reluctance was clear. He continually offered countersuggestions. On one occasion it was Senator Philander C. Knox of Pennsylvania. I was against Knox. I especially objected to his "dollar diplomacy." Later the Colonel agreed with me on this point. I said that Elihu Root would be better than Knox if we had to support a Republican, to which Roosevelt replied: "He's pretty old." I retorted that that was the reason that I had suggested him.

Roosevelt was getting deep down into the doldrums. Once when I caught him in a mood of depression at Oyster Bay, he told me that he didn't think that he would ever again be a candidate for office. He believed that his role in the future, and I quote him literally, would be to "raise the black flag and fight evil whenever it appears." But while he did not want to be our candidate, he was not unwilling to keep us in suspense and use the party for whatever nuisance value it might have.

In April of 1916 Roosevelt was invited to speak before the Chicago Bar Association on "Preparedness." I had told him that I would be happy to give a luncheon in his honor at any time that he might wish. His secretary sent me word that, if agreeable to me, I could give a luncheon for the Colonel on the occasion of this visit of his to Chicago. I was given a general idea of the sort of men whom he would like to meet.

Those who were my guests at our recently finished home in Winnetka were: La Verne Noyes, Julius Rosenwald, John V. Farwell, Jr., Walter L. Fisher, Bernard A. Eckhart, Benjamin Carpenter, John C. Shaffer, George F. Porter, Alexander H. Revell, Theodore W. Robinson, James B. Blake, Conrad H. Poppenhusen, Donald R. Richberg, Otto C. Butz, Dwight H. Perkins, Murry Nelson, Nelson N. Lampert, Charles E. Merriam, Judge Thomas Taylor, Jr., Alexander A. McCormick, Alfred L. Baker, Edgar A. Bancroft, Nathan W. MacChesney, Judge Orrin N. Carter, Judge Stephen A. Foster, and Judge Charles M. Thomson.

The luncheon was a great success. One of my most important guests, Julius Rosenwald, had never met Roosevelt and he was delighted to know him in this intimate way. We sat at a large round table and halfway through the luncheon I changed places with the Colonel. This gave more people a real chance at him. I saw to it that Rosenwald sat next to him during one of these periods. There was no doubt that Roosevelt made a great impression. He was in rare form. We had a great wood fire burning in the living room, and after luncheon we all gathered in front of it and gave the former President such an audience as he delighted to talk to. I had not asked Medill McCormick to the party but he came anyway. Just like conferring a distinction.

One incident of the luncheon deserves recounting. One of my guests took on the self-appointed job of escorting the Colonel to the Fourth Presbyterian Church for morning services and then bringing him to my home. He insisted upon driving the Colonel past his own house just to show him the plush palace in which he lived. Roosevelt curtly refused to be taken in and shown the interior decorations. As though the Colonel gave a damn! Anyway, the result was that he got separated from his police escort and was late in arriving. He was quite put out.

At once I took him upstairs to let him cool off before luncheon and give him a moment's privacy. My son Raymond, who was then not quite four years old, called out: "Mother, where is Colonel Roosevelt? Ick (as he called himself as a baby) wants to show off."

Colonel Roosevelt's show of temper disappeared instantly. His love for children was one of the best things about him. Turning with a broad grin to Mrs. Ickes, he said: "Mrs. Ickes, I admire the perfect frankness of your child. There are people downstairs who feel just as he does, but they aren't so open about it."

The Progressive party was tottering to its deathbed, although its ghost was to walk for some little time. Clever politician that he always has been, except for an occasional lapse, Charles Evans Hughes so managed it that the 1916 Republican nomination was handed to him on a platter, and the Progressive party endorsement as well.[1] The Republican

---

[1] We are asked to believe that members of the Supreme Court, above all other courts, keep their eyes on the stars across illimitable space and never allow a vagrant political thought to taint their thinking. But do we believe this? In any event, there can be no doubt that Hughes played a consummate

bosses didn't want Hughes, and neither did Roosevelt. The doughty Colonel hated Hughes, perhaps because he too had great ability and was his nearest rival in public esteem.

Hughes had been my real choice for President in 1908, so after Roosevelt declined to lead what he regarded as a forlorn hope in 1916, it was possible for me to adhere to Hughes with a clear conscience. After his nomination, Hughes decided that if he wanted to be elected he couldn't trust the exclusive management of his campaign to the Republican National Committee that was controlled by Crane, Penrose, and Smoot. Accordingly, he set up a campaign committee of his own, consisting of nine Republicans and six Progressives. Hughes chose me as one of the half-dozen Progressives over the bitter and explosive opposition of Senator Lawrence Y. Sherman, of Illinois, and William Hale Thompson, by now Illinois national committeeman, as well as the wearer of motley in the mayor's office.

Thompson always turned my stomach politically. I had never fallen for his blundering blandishments. In this respect my record is better than that of the *Tribune,* which, however, to its credit be it said, did come to give all that it had toward the undoing of Thompson. The trouble then was that it gave too much. It was Thompson who discovered that *Tribune* opposition was a political asset. So long as the *Tribune* openly opposed him, Thompson was successful. It was only after someone put Misanthropic Mac wise to the fact that his vehemently expressed dislike was like a cup of cold water to a weary politician's parched throat, and

---

hand of politics, the prize for which was a nomination for President, although at the time he was a member of the Supreme Court of the United States. Later he contrived not only to work his way back by customary political methods to the Supreme Court, but into the Chief Justiceship itself. Later still, he was to perform an even greater political feat when he thwarted the President in his effort to change the structure of the Court.

stopped printing Thompson's name, that Thompson was finally run out of office. That was a great day for Chicago.

Senator Sherman and Bill Thompson flattered me by making a special trip to New York to protest to Justice Hughes his selection of me. Hughes received them courteously but coldly—as he well could—and told them that I was on the committee to stay. The regular Republicans in Illinois fairly choked over my appointment, but there wasn't anything that they could do about it.

The Republicans on the committee were: John T. Adams of Iowa; William H. Crocker of California; F. W. Estabrook of New Hampshire; James A. Hemenway of Indiana; Alvin T. Hert of Kentucky; Robert B. Howell of Nebraska; Alvah H. Martin of Virginia; Herbert Parsons of New York; S. Albert Perkins of Washington; Charles B. Warren of Michigan; and Ralph E. Williams of Oregon.

The Progressives were: Everett Colby of New Jersey; James R. Garfield of Ohio; George W. Perkins of New York; Chester H. Rowell of California; Oscar S. Straus of New York; and myself.

Two major blunders were made in the campaign. Eastern headquarters was responsible for one, Hughes himself for the other.

It was conceived in the East to be good politics to send a special trainload of rich society women into the West to beat the sagebrush for Hughes votes. When we learned of this plan at Western headquarters we swooned, but recovered in time to protest vigorously. But the East would have it so, and the "millionairess special," as it came to be known, swung out to the Pacific coast and back, losing votes for Hughes all along the way.

Then Hughes, with Mrs. Hughes, started off on a trip to

the West. Again there were protests from the West. Again they were overruled. Especially, we did not want Hughes to go into California before the Republican primary election had been held in that state. Hughes was in a difficult position. Having decided to make the trip, he couldn't keep out of California without being on one goring horn of the dilemma. If he went into California he would be spitted on the other. He accepted the second horn and that was the one that did him to death in the end.

Hiram W. Johnson had gone back from the Progressive convention at Chicago and had entered the Republican primaries as a candidate for the United States Senate. He was just finishing his second term as Governor and I think that it is conservative to say that he had made as notable a record as any Governor of any state, either before or since.

In his two state campaigns, Johnson had thrown down the gage to the Southern Pacific and other great corporations. They hated him as the Devil is said to hate holy water. Elected Governor the first time as a Republican, he had been re-elected as a Progressive. In 1912 he had run as a candidate for Vice-President on the Progressive ticket. Now he was running in the Republican primary for the Senate. It was not to be wondered at that the regular Republicans of the state had to be put in strait jackets before his name could be safely mentioned. In no other state did such bitterness exist between Republicans and Progressives.

Hughes knew or should have known of this situation. He was warned that if he ventured into California he was not to let either group monopolize him. But evidently Hughes was pretty sure of himself and his political sagacity. Either that or his credulity was imposed upon. I suspect that some trickery may have been employed.

Before the train bearing Hughes and his party reached the state line, it was "swarmed" by a herd of "hoof-and-mouth" Republicans. Chester H. Rowell, our Progressive national committeeman, as well as a member of the Hughes campaign committee selected by Hughes himself, also climbed aboard, only to find Hughes completely surrounded by his and Johnson's bitterest enemies. Rowell was made to feel so unwelcome that he effaced himself as quickly as possible.

The Republicans continued to surround the candidate completely with an impenetrable cordon of Johnson-haters. Hughes was taken to the roof of the San Francisco Chronicle building and there photographed with Mike DeYoung, the notorious publisher of that paper, and other Republican crustaceans. He breakfasted with Republicans; he lunched with Republicans; he dined with Republicans. He may have slept with them for all that I know. He paraded with Republicans; his meetings were overflowing with Republicans; he was introduced by Republicans. And in the end he was escorted to the political graveyard by Republicans.

To cap the climax, he was deliberately jobbed by Republican tricksters. He actually spent several hours in the same hotel in a small city where Johnson was also a guest. Information that Johnson was in the building was carefully kept from him, but Johnson knew of Hughes' presence and he also knew that Hughes sent him no message and apparently made no attempt to see him. How could he even be sure that Hughes was not deliberately snubbing him? After Hughes had left the city he was told that he had been under the same roof with Johnson. He at once sent a cordial message of apology to Johnson and Johnson responded in kind. But the damage had been done. The news was already on all of the wires. Wilson carried California by less than 4,000 votes out of nearly 1,000,000 cast. Johnson won by his usual landslide majority. If Hughes had carried California, he would have been President in 1913.[1]

Much as Roosevelt disliked Hughes, he took the stump for him. I recall with what bitterness he told me that there wasn't any difference between Wilson and Hughes except a set of whiskers.

---

[1] It has been said, probably with some basis in fact, that if Hughes had carried California in 1916, Wilson would have contested the result in Minnesota, where Hughes won by less than 400 votes out of more than 360,000 cast. (A likely story!) It has been said also, and no doubt again with some basis in fact, that the St. Louis County (Minnesota) returns were held up until it was determined how many votes Hughes had to have to carry. When his requirements were known, the necessary number for Hughes was certified to the state canvassing board.

CHAPTER TEN

GUNS ABROAD

And blood in torrents pour
In vain—always in vain,
For war breeds war again.
—JOHN DAVIDSON.

W HEN THE KAISER succumbed to the disease of which Hitler is the most virulent example, and the extent of his ambitions began to be understood over here, I early became of the opinion that we ought to jump in and help Great Britain and France. Every democratic nation in the world was in danger—or so I thought. I would have supported Woodrow Wilson for President in 1912 if Theodore Roosevelt hadn't "thrown his hat into the ring"; again, I would have been for Wilson in 1916 if I had not been persuaded that his re-election would mean that England and France and all that they had meant in our civilization might go to the dogs for all that we might do. Nor was I any too sure about Hughes on this issue.

Time proved me wrong as to Wilson. Hughes had no record on the subject. To this day I don't know what he would have done. The Republican party during that 1916 campaign pussyfooted on the issue as only expert pussyfooters can pussyfoot when they really want to walk on eggs without

184

breaking a single shell. I doubt if any Republican leader ever whispered to another, or so much as confided in his own wife—if indeed he knew—what his own views were about getting into the war.

Roosevelt felt about Germany as I did. Personally he disliked the Kaiser, and everybody, including the Kaiser, knew it. The Republican pussyfooting management was therefore nervous lest the Colonel, who had taken the stump for Hughes, say something that would drive the German vote in this country to what it might consider the lesser of two evils —Wilson.

As I have stated, I was on the Hughes campaign committee consisting of nine Republicans and six Progressives. Another Progressive on it was James R. Garfield. Both of us were attached to Western headquarters in Chicago and we occupied adjoining offices. As fellow Progressives there was a special bond between us, and every day we were in close communion with each other—consulting, speculating, inquiring.

Chicago was a hotbed of pro-Germanism, which was concentrated in large colonies of German Americans and Scandinavians. Outside of these, generally speaking, sentiment in Chicago was distinctly pro-Ally. The issue raised by the Kaiser wasn't as clear as the one of today in relation to Hitler. Nor was the German *Kultur* of 1914 the Hitlerian *Kultur* of bestiality. So the Germans in Chicago, of both the first and second generations, were pretty generally pro-German in their sympathies, although many of them disapproved of the Kaiser's wanton ambitions. The same thing was true in other sections of the country where there were concentrations of German Americans. Feeling ran high.

William Hale Thompson, still making a blatant ass of

himself in the mayor's office, was openly and disloyally cultivating pro-German sentiment. Almost daily he dared King George of England to come to Chicago to have his nose tweaked by "Hizzoner." He hated England. As in the present war, so in the First World War there were men of his type who were willing to play politics even at the expense of their country's safety and welfare. Chicago wasn't considered to be any too healthy a spot for a pronounced interventionist.

During the Hughes-Wilson campaign of 1916 there was held in Chicago a secret meeting of German Lutheran ministers from all parts of the country. Only a few individuals at Republican headquarters knew of it. The party was playing with dynamite, but the high command wanted the German vote for Hughes.

After rumors of such a meeting had reached my ears, I poked about a bit and satisfied myself that all of the expenses of each one in attendance had been paid out of the Republican war chest. The preachers had arrived unostentatiously, met "off the record," and dispersed quietly, with scarcely anyone in the know. This disturbed me. Here I was, supporting Hughes because Wilson had set his face so solemnly against intervention, confronted with the fact that the German ministers of the country were perfectly satisfied with some assurance that had been made, either by Hughes, or by his high command with or without his authority—which, to this day I do not know, although I have always suspected that this strictly undercover assembly was without the knowledge or consent of the candidate. Had I cast my lot with the man who would permit the Kaiser to overrun Belgium and France and England and do nothing to stop him?

Colonel Roosevelt was on a speaking tour in the West for the Republican ticket and was scheduled for a big meeting

in Chicago. Republican leaders must have had their finger-
nails chewed down to the wrist by that time.

One day when I reached headquarters I discovered that
Jim Garfield had left the city. I couldn't understand why he
would do that without saying something to me about it. We
had had no secrets from each other. No one seemed to know
where he was. As the mystery deepened, my curiosity got the
better of me. Finally, I went into the office of "Tobe" Hert,
the Western manager, and asked him point-blank where Garfield was.

In a whisper, Hert told me that Jim was on his way to
meet Roosevelt. He had been detailed to try to prevail upon
Teddy not to say anything in his Chicago speech that would
in any way miff the Germans. At once I telephoned my law
partner, Donald R. Richberg, asking him to come to headquarters. On his father's side, Richberg was a second-genera-
tion German who had no pro-German leaning; quite the
contrary, in fact. I asked him to go West at my expense and
catch up with Roosevelt's train wherever he could. So he departed from Chicago even more mysteriously than had Garfield, because only he and I knew of his mission. He was to
tell the Colonel for me that I didn't like the way in which
the Republican managers were wooing the disloyal German
vote; that I suspected that this was a give-and-take affair that
would be to the interest of Germany and that I hoped that
instead of laying off of the disloyal Germans in his Chicago
speech, as the GOP high command wanted him to do, he
would lay on vigorously.

Hert and I, and a number of others from headquarters,
met Roosevelt's train about fifty miles out of Chicago. It
was a mad Teddy that greeted us. He looked black. After a
biting "Hello" he showed me into his sleeping compartment

and closed the door. Richberg had given him my message.
The Colonel had also talked with Garfield. He snapped at
me that he wasn't going to be muzzled. He didn't like the
secret pastoral meeting. The thought that there might be
some understanding between the pro-Germans and the Republican management made him see red.

Roosevelt's main speech was to be at the Coliseum that
night. But he was also to address a women's meeting in the
Auditorium theater in the afternoon. The Auditorium was
packed to suffocation. And Roosevelt was still mad. The
Republican bigwigs were as nervous as kittens, and when
Roosevelt let go with both barrels against German disloyal-
ists, they almost fell down en masse in a swoon. Roosevelt
did a thorough job of overturning that particular fat into
the fire. He came out of the meeting with gleaming teeth
and snapping eyes. I suspect that he had derived a double
pleasure out of it—the pleasure of probing into disloyalty in
high places and that of messing up a sinister plan that might
have had Hughes's approval.

A fortnight before the election, I warned National Chairman William R. Willcox and George Perkins and "Tobe"
Hert that in my opinion Wilson could be elected. I had
caused a careful survey to be made of all of the states west
of the Mississippi River where the Progressive vote had been
strong, and the information that I had received convinced
me that Wilson was in the lead. In state after state the regulars had made no real effort to conciliate the Progressives.
Neither Hert, Willcox, nor Perkins was disturbed. They
believed that we were sure to carry New York, Illinois, and
Indiana—as I also believed; and that, therefore, we were
unbeatable—a conclusion that I doubted. If I had been a
porcupine instead of merely a curmudgeon I would have

started to shoot darts from my tail (if that is the way of porcupines, which I doubt!) in all directions, and especially toward the Republican managers. Hughes, of course, was defeated.

The future Chief Justice was a good sport about his defeat. To this day I cherish the letter that he wrote me while the mourners gloomily brooded over the result. As I read it—or perhaps misread it—I wondered if he intended to say between the lines that all of those active in his support had not done as good a job as they might have done. I still believe that Hughes would have been elected, in spite of all, if his managers had heeded the pleas that were made to them to do something about the Progressive vote.

The Republican National Committee picked itself up and called a meeting of its members to be held in St. Louis the following February. There it elected Will Hays chairman, chiefly on the strength of Indiana's great majority for Hughes. Considering the dollars that were poured into Indiana when Progressive organizations in other states were being denied nickels, the campaign paraphernalia and the man power that were literally dumped into the Hoosier campaign, any second-rate precinct committeeman could have delivered it to Dopey the Dwarf. Not that I would disparage Will Hays. He was a very clever politician, although I don't agree with some that he ever had the makings of a President.

We went into the war the following April, a few weeks after Woodrow Wilson had been sworn in for a second term. I was restless to get in, too, in some capacity.

I was forty-three years old; I had been married in 1911 and I was the father of a four-and-a-half-year-old son. A mastoidectomy had left me almost without hearing in my left ear. Governor Lowden was setting up a State Council of Defense. I hoped to be made a member of it, as I did not see much chance of getting to Europe. The chairman of the council was Samuel Insull. Although I had the active support of Roger Sullivan, John P. Hopkins, and George Brennan, as well as of John Oglesby, Lieutenant Governor, and David E. Shanahan, Speaker of the Illinois House, I was not appointed. Later, under pressure, Insull put me in charge of patriotic propaganda.

Insull and I got to know each other quite well during our association on the State Council of Defense. At that time my partner, Don Richberg, was representing the city as special counsel in an intensive legal fight against the People's Gas Light and Coke Company, which Insull had just tucked under his all-embracing wing. Insull acquired the habit of coming into my office when he had nothing else to do, especially on Saturday afternoons, and there ripping into Don Richberg in vituperative and picturesque language, much to my own and to Don's subsequent amusement.

George Creel next recognized me on behalf of his Committee of Public Information. My salary was $1 a month. But then the cost of living wasn't so high in those days, either. I never got but one salary check and that one I framed, thus throwing Uncle Sam's ledgers out of balance and keeping them out. What trouble a man can make if only he keeps his mind on it!

I came down to Washington on official business on one occasion and went to call on Creel, whom I had never met. Without consulting his engagement pad, he invited me to lunch and discovered too late that he already had a date with Herbert Hoover. When he remembered it, he asked me to go with him anyhow. I did, and that was the only time—I say it without a trace of regret—that I ever met Hoover.

Hoover monopolized the conversation and I forget what it was all about. Turning sideways and facing Creel, he never once looked in my direction or addressed a remark to me, after telling me, mechanically, what a great pleasure it was to meet me. It wasn't a pleasure at all; it was a bore. And so was he. It became perfectly clear to me that I never cared to meet Hoover again. It gave me "great pleasure" to vote against him when he ran for President in 1928 and greater pleasure still to fight him openly in 1932. Talk about *me* being a curmudgeon. I at least have some manners— That is, occasionally.

I wasn't happy in my job with the State Council of Defense. It wasn't the $1 a month salary from Uncle Sam that made me unhappy, either. We seemed so far removed from the seat of trouble. Arranging meetings and signing up speakers was a dull chore that I had grown tired of from too much repetition. The only real fun that I had was when a handsome French captain by the name of Paul Périgord came over to tell us of his country's trials and of its will to win the war. I escorted him to several meetings that I had arranged for him in Chicago and took him home with me one evening. He is now a professor at the University of California at Los Angeles. When the war stopped, Périgord came back to become an American citizen and took unto himself an American wife. Now too old for active service, he is chafing to do something for France just as I chafed twenty-five years ago.

A letter reached me from Washington suggesting the scarcity of commissioned men in the Quartermaster General's Corps. Would I accept a commission with the probability that I would be stationed in Washington? This didn't appeal to me at all. I wanted to cross the Atlantic. Someone suggested that I might persuade the Y.M.C.A. to take me on for its foreign service. I had never been a member of the organization, although I recognized the fine work that the Y.M.C.A. had done for many years in helping young men to improve themselves mentally and physically. But then I have never been much of a "jiner." I hooked up with it on this occasion because it gave me my only chance to get abroad.

One day, shortly after arriving in Paris, I was walking in the almost deserted Rue de la Paix in the direction of the Opéra when ahead of me loomed a big husky fellow in an American uniform that bore the insignia of a colonel. I recognized my to-be "admirer and friend," Robert R. McCormick. We stopped for an amicable greeting, during which I made the natural inquiry as to what he was doing in Paris. He told me that he was suffering from a "slight case of shell shock." I was to learn later that the "Morning Colonel" of Chicago kept a fine big private automobile of his own conveniently near his field headquarters and spent a good deal of time in Paris. But not so his cousin, Captain Joseph Medill Patterson, who was with the same artillery regiment. He stayed with his troops, with whom he was very popular.

The Paris of 1918 was a far cry indeed from the Paris I had become somewhat acquainted with and had come to love during the fall and winter of 1911. So many people had fled before the German threat that the city seemed almost deserted as to civilians, although there were always many uniforms in evidence—not only French, but American, British, Canadian, Australian, Belgian, and Colonial. Especially during moonlight nights, there was much bombing, and Big Bertha, from somewhere way off, kept dropping shells by day at frequent intervals.

There was one Sunday, when the German thrust had projected itself to the point nearest Paris that it was ever to reach, that I was given the opportunity of appraising the real quality of French citizens. From all directions, hour after hour, French men and women and children tramped to the railway stations that offered a gateway into the south of France. There were practically no automobiles or other vehicles available. They had to walk and as they walked they carried valises, and even paper bundles, containing their most precious and most portable possessions. Paris might fall again to the Germans. The possibility was in the air. I had been able to get no comfort even at General Dawes' headquarters. Notwithstanding all of which, and although they were leaving behind them the bulk of their possessions which might become loot for marauding German soldiers, there was no hysteria or quivering excitement evident in any direction. Fate was being accepted because it was fate.

I had hardly reached Paris before I regretted my decision. I had gone over with a letter of introduction to E. C. Carter, who was in charge of all of the fieldmen with headquarters in Paris. Don Richberg had been acquainted with Carter at Harvard and when I came to know him ever so slightly I agreed with Richberg that he was genuine. It was some brother from Philadelphia, a professional "Ymcaer," who gave me a sharp pain in the neck. He was the exhorting type. He had never been near a battlefield himself, but he knew all of the answers. His idea was that our first duty when we met a wandering soldier was to bring him down to his knees and join in prayer. One day he said to a room full of recruits: "If any time you talk to a soldier and fail to mention 'sweetheart,' 'mother,' and 'God,' you will have failed in the performance of your duty. You will not be worthy of your uniforms."

Thus equipped spiritually for my job as a field man in the

Y.M.C.A., I went to Mr. Carter's office, he having returned from London, where he was when I reached Paris. I told him of the sentimental drivel that was being dished out to us and frankly avowed that if that were the official concept of my duties I was in the wrong pew. I was ready to get out. Carter reassured me and suggested that I ought to get a firsthand view of what the Y.M.C.A. was doing in France. With that in mind, he sent me to Brest, a picturesque and impressive-looking city, even if it did have open sewers. Oh! what a smell was there, my countrymen! But the Y.M.C.A. performance was good. Later I was sent out to the Forty-second Division, which was then engaged in Alsace. I was admitted to an officers' mess. The Y.M.C.A. canteen there was badly run. It stank almost as badly as Brest.

I struck up an acquaintance with a captain in the Signal Corps of an Alabama regiment. I told him that I would like to have a look at the trenches. He was on rest leave and was going back in a few days. I induced him to let me trail along without seeking permission from the commanding officer, which I was afraid I couldn't get.

I was supposed to have been drilled in the use of my gas mask before I left Paris. The drill consisted in my being told briefly, by someone who probably had never done it himself, how to put one on.

The Alabama regiment was to be brought back, with another one replacing it. Apparently the Boches had discovered this, because for three nights the shell fire from German batteries was too intense to permit an orderly or safe withdrawal. Then one day my captain friend told me that he would be going up to his outfit after supper. Without my taking anything with me except my warlike paraphernalia—

gas mask and steel helmet—we set off at a brisk walk over the fields. It would take about an hour for the trip.

Dusk was falling as we drew near what had been a happy little French village, the ruins of which were now occupied by American soldiers. Firing began to be heard. Shells were hitting the ground about us. It wasn't bad, not bad enough to scare even me—yet. I asked about the possibility of gas shells. I was assured that there had been none. So I continued to trudge forward. Then a smell assailed my nostrils that I identified as chlorine. After all, I had worked in a drugstore. After two or three sniffs, my companion's smeller corroborated mine and without a word he began climbing into his gas mask. Awkwardly, I proceeded to do the same thing, but I had my glasses to cope with, in addition to a steel helmet that kept getting in the way. After some difficulty, I got myself untangled and found myself inside of my mask. By this time we were not far from the village. Also, by this time the Germans were demonstrating that they were not fooling.

We decided that it would not be undignified to run, and so broke into a dogtrot. It was getting dark. Of course no lights were permitted. Finally, my escort dashed into what was left of a stone house that had been badly battered by German artillery. He didn't stop on the first floor, either. Opening a door quickly so that the light that was behind it would show only momentarily, he hurried down into a well-barricaded basement. I lost no time in following. As soon as he got there my captain went to work. Here was part of his Signal Corps—soldiers lying about, especially in an excavation extending beyond the basement of the house, listening, transmitting messages, and testing to see if communications were open. They didn't know who I was and didn't care. I was just another man in a gas mask who might have been the Prince of Wales or Mike de Pike for all that they could tell.

We had barely reached shelter before the Germans really began to get busy. I have never pretended that I enjoyed my position, but I confess that I was more worried as to whether my gas mask was on straight and in working order than I was about the barrage of German shells overhead. My suspicion that the mask was not on right began to grow as I salivated more and more and became more moistily uncomfortable. I was sure that the damn thing was no good and that I was about to have a good case of gas poisoning. With difficulty, I restrained myself from tearing it off. Then at least I would be able to breathe until I died. I don't know how the gas masks of today are, but I hope they are more comfortable than the one I had on twenty-five years ago.

The alert began to sound and ambulances could be heard dashing to field hospitals with casualties. That wasn't a comfortable suggestion, either. The barrage had broken communications, and my captain started out with a few of his men to discover and repair the breaks. I asked if I might go along and permission was granted. Anything was better than sitting in that cellar with nothing to do except worry about my gas protector. It was a positive relief to get out and be on my feet even if I still had to hang onto my mask. Outdoors we discovered that there was also mustard gas about, but apparently, and also fortunately, only in small amounts.

The break repaired, we returned to our quarters. A number of cots had been set up on the main floor, and here officers and men had thrown their dog-tired bodies down for a few hours of rest. A cot was assigned to me and I fell onto it, after having managed to jimmy my head out of the gas mask. The soldiers were soon heavily asleep. I was still lying there, much later, with my eyes wide open when some heavy artillery opened up. I hopefully supposed that it was American guns blowing hell out of the Huns. I wasn't sure and I would have liked to find my way down to the basement again, but I wouldn't show the white feather.

I continued to lie there, scared, but afraid to show that I was afraid. Finally, one of the officers near me was awakened and came out from under his blanket. In a voice that was not too bold I asked him, hopefully, whether the guns were American. He listened and then said: "No, they're German 155's," and promptly ducked under the cover to sleep again. I did not close an eye all that night. I suspect that I was the only one in the building to lie awake.

Finally all firing ceased, and then the ambulances did begin to go back and forth in earnest with their burdens of hurt humanity. At daybreak I went outdoors. I could still smell chlorine gas but it didn't seem too bad. I didn't want to climb back into my gas mask. Tied near what was left of a stone barn, were horses laboring heavily under the gas that had been their lot during the attack. One or two of them looked pretty badly off. The day wore on. A heavy mist lay over the ground. One venturesome bird from a branch of a dead tree twittered a note of hope for a world that would be different (I have often wondered where that bird ever went); of a world where men would not maim and destroy each other because of a madman or two.

I looked in all directions. Except for the horses that belonged to the Army, there wasn't a domestic animal in sight. There wasn't a chicken. There wasn't any sign even of wild life, excepting the one little bird twittering his song of a better world to come. There wasn't a human being in sight until later, and then they were in uniform. Wandering out, I saw that the main road was literally pitted with shell marks. There was no doubt at all that the Germans had the range of the road down which our troops would have to march.

It was a tired bunch of soldiers who shared their rations with me that morning. The captain told me that his men might be relieved that night. It would depend upon how the Germans felt about it. But they might not go back for several nights. So I decided to return by the road. It was a plain highway even if it was within easy range of the Germans.

After I had taken a look at the trenches that I had heard so much about, and marveled that a human being could make his way through the barbed-wire entanglements that lay in every direction, I started off alone down the road. It was a lonely walk and a nervous one. I didn't know what minute some German might decide to take a pot shot at me just to test his aim. My fancy was as good as that of the next one in conjuring up unpleasant possibilities. I didn't see a sign of life of any kind during that walk of several miles until I neared headquarters, when I saw an automobile approaching. The officer in it was Lieutenant Colonel Noble B. Judah, Jr., of Chicago, a young lawyer who was with the Army Intelligence. He suggested that I try for the same service, but I knew no German and my French was of the feeblest.

I returned to Paris with my mind made up to resign from the Y.M.C.A. and join up with the Red Cross, if I could. There were several friends of mine at Red Cross headquarters, among them Henry J. Allen, who had been active in the Bull Moose campaign. I sought him out and told him my story.

"Why, Harold," said he, "I am just transferring to the Y.M.C.A. Stay where you are and we'll hook up together."

I couldn't resist the temptation to chide him a bit.

"Don't you remember, Henry, when I first saw you over here you expressed your distaste for my uniform and suggested that I get into Red Cross livery?"

He admitted it with a grin and then explained why he was switching. Our common friend William Allen White had uncovered a plot which was being hatched in America with a view to getting Henry Allen dismissed from the Red Cross in a manner that would do him no good if, as it was anticipated, he should decide to become a candidate for Governor of Kansas at the coming election. It was one of those discreditable things that slimy politicians will do even when a war is on.

Henry did switch, and we went arm in arm to the Y.M.C.A. headquarters at 12 Rue d'Aguesseau to suggest to Carter that we would like to be assigned together. Carter had had the business managership in London in mind for me, but I wanted to stay in France. Soon Henry and I found ourselves together in a Ford car, en route to join the Thirty-fifth Division, which was composed of Kansas and Missouri troops. Henry was to be head of the outfit with me second in command as business manager.

We found our division in a section of France which neither of us had ever seen before and to which we were to become very much attached. The division was occupying a quiet sector in the area of the lovely Vosges Mountains, with divisional headquarters in the town of Saulxures, where the civilian population was leading as normal a life as was possible during a time of war when the community was overrun with soldiers. While the sector was an inactive one, Germany was just beyond and it was therefore part of the front line, so that trenches had to be manned, even although sorties, or even bursts of artillery fire, were a rare event. Here Henry and I were to have a comparatively long stay, but we were comfortably established in the two best rooms in the "best" hotel, where, if dirt was plentiful and the plumbing of the most primitive, we nevertheless found good food and I discovered as fine a variety of rich red Burgundy as I have ever drunk.

Personnel soon began to come to us from Paris and we were exceedingly lucky, as to both the men and the two or three women who were assigned to us. We established a canteen in a large building beautifully adapted for that purpose, and when Paris headquarters turned a cold ear to our insistent demands that we have a piano, we went into a larger neighboring town and bought one, lawlessly, with Y.M.C.A. money. However, we virtuously entered the purchase in our books. That piano meant a lot to the men in our division and I hope that the money spent for it has long ago ceased to worry the auditing department of the Association.

Our Missouri regiment was a "chewing" one, and one of my jobs was to find enough plug tobacco to keep the men's jaws lubricated. This was not an easy task in France. I had to go back to Paris frequently, because supplies were not sent on in sufficient amounts or they were the wrong kind. Sometimes, even if they were shipped they would be purloined by other Y.M.C.A. outfits nearer to Paris, whose ungodliness would have shocked the pious gentleman from Philadelphia, but which I would have emulated if I had had the chance.

After a long and unexciting, but very pleasant, sojourn at Saulxures, orders came to move to Gérardmer, an attractive, but practically deserted, summer resort. Here, with the help of a sharply bargaining French notary I closed a lease for a large hotel for our headquarters. We were established and ready for business even before the division settled itself into its new billet. As I remember it, this was our location when the American Army did such a good job at St. Mihiel in September of 1918. The Thirty-fifth Division was not in that action, although there was a feeling that we were approaching active service.

One day we awoke to the fact that the whole division had vanished. Virtually everyone was gone, from the general to the lowliest private. Henry and I had taken advantage of what seemed to be an extremely quiet time to slip away for a day or two of scouting against the immediate future. From our point of view, it was a poor time for the division to advance over the horizon.

When we sought to discover where the troops had gone, we got the surprising reply that this information was not to be given out. At once we surmised that they were on their way into action. We were marooned at the very time when we most wanted to be with the soldiers. Locating an officer with whom we had been on especially friendly terms, we put the mental screws on him until, forcing us to swear that we would not give him away, he told us where we would find our regiments. We jumped into our indispensable Ford and, setting off at our best speed, were soon back with the division, listening to Major-General Peter E. Traub, a sputtery individual who wanted to know what the hell we were doing there! We had beaten him to his own headquarters. Our absence was a damn sight more welcome than our presence!

Henry Allen had a rare gift of gab that was second to none, and when he had finished, the General was bubbling over with good nature, all apologetic about having tried to get away from two men without whom it was not going to be possible to win the war.

It was here that I saw my first—and only—fight in the air. A German plane came over to poke its nose into our affairs. It was flying low. Soon a Frenchman went up to engage it. The lone airman lost no time in attacking. Guns flashed as the planes twisted this way and that, suddenly shooting up and even more quickly dropping. Soon the main street was lined with American soldiers gaping, open-mouthed, at an exhibition that none of them probably had ever seen. To be sure, we were all under strict orders to take to cover in the event of a sky fight, or even of a hostile plane. But the fight was over before the order could be enforced. The German plane was downed. It landed safely and the two Germans who had manned it were marched into headquarters as prisoners.

One day, from a different headquarters, I went to get supplies and was told that a new order had gone through to the effect that the Army was not to furnish us anything more. I went to see G1. We had the money to buy, but there was no one to sell to us. We were in terrain that had been swept clean by the Huns. There were no stores; no farmhouses, even, where so much as an egg could be bought. And our larder was completely bare. G1 couldn't help us. He didn't even know the reason for the abrupt and unexpected order.

So I went back to the quartermaster. There was a long warehouse literally bulging with food, because the American Army in France was well fed. The captain in charge said that he was sorry but he couldn't do anything about it. However, in response to my hungry despair, he added, with a significant gleam in his eye, that he was about to go to the far end of the warehouse on important business that might keep him half an hour. He had no sooner turned his back than my Y.M.C.A. driver and I began loading canned beans and meat and bread and butter into our car. I do not mind admitting, now that the statute of limitations has run, that I did, then and there, commit larceny. The food-craving brethren thought that it was *grand* larceny.

Our next move (unhindered this time) was to Nancy, where, following our custom, Henry Allen and I provided ourselves with as comfortable hotel quarters as we could find. It was a pretty busy town and my room was on the top floor of a seven- or eight-story building. Nancy had been raided from the air repeatedly by the Germans and during the nights that we spent there, there was not a single one when we were not routed out at least once by the alert. One night I scampered down those eight flights of stairs into the abri five weary times. No bombs fell on any of these occasions. Our guess was that the airplanes that worried the soldiers defending the town were on their way back and forth to the lines. But by this time I had decided not to run any unnecessary chances. Exploding bombs do not discriminate and we had come to respect them.

The reason for this dated back to an experience that I had had one night in Paris on one of the occasions when I was trying to pry loose some supplies. Anna's adopted daughter had been assigned as a Red Cross nurse's aide to a field hospital at the Auteuil race track just the other side of the Bois de Boulogne. When I planned a Paris trip, I always wrote to her in advance so that she could engage rooms at the Hotel Castille in the Rue Cambon, a quiet retreat that I always sought out when I was in Paris during the war. There Frances would come when she had finished her day's work. We would go to one of the better restaurants and do ourselves the honors implicit in the best meal that money could buy. Even as that time, the food in the Paris restaurants was not to be excelled, although there might be occasions when it was difficult to obtain some particular thing.

One night there was an unusual to-do. It was dark as a pocket. Every light was out. Fire engines were coursing through the streets hell-bent, screeching the warning that the Boches were again approaching Paris. I had been through a number of air raids and Frances had been through more. She had reached Paris earlier than I, and the house where she lived at St. Cloud with family friends was right on the bank of the Seine, which was a perfect guide for airplanes on a moonlit night.

Soon we heard the unmistakable sound of what appeared to be a number of airplanes. I went into Frances' room, which adjoined mine. She had always maintained that she could distinguish a French from a German airplane by the sound. They all sounded the same to me—unpleasant. We could tell that this outfit was flying low. The antiaircraft guns were barking, but antiaircraft guns were not worth much in those days. Frances gave it as her opinion that the planes were hostile ones. And so they proved themselves to be.

The two big French windows in Frances' room were wide open. I stepped to one of them to stick my neck out (as usual) to see what I could see. What I saw, or at first heard rather, was something dropping rapidly through the air, and instantly there was such a noise as I had never listened to before. It was horrendous, frightening. There appeared to be a great ball of molten metal hurtling through the air at incredible speed. It might have been a flaming red moon. Then came a great crash. That thing which I had seen falling had hit something. And simultaneously I found myself surrounded by pieces of broken glass. Every pane in every window in that hotel and for a considerable distance on either side of the street was smashed to bits. It was only by the greatest good luck that neither Frances nor I was scratched. Sensibly, she had pulled the covers up over her head, but I was as close to the window as I could get.

The thing that had flamed through the air with a great down-rushing noise fell squarely on the roof of the house of the Minister of Justice, which opens into the Place Vendôme. It was not easy to get authentic news of what were the casualties inflicted by German raids in Paris those days, but it was rumored that two of the servants in this house were killed that night. Fortunately for themselves, the Minister of Justice and his family were not in the building.

We were glad to be in Nancy, because Walther's Restaurant there was famous for the food and drink that were regarded by many as equal to the best in Paris. The weather was cold and rainy, and Henry and I had to range far and wide every day, because our division had been broken up, with segments of the troops stationed here and there. It was not always easy to keep in touch with our personnel, which was scattered with the troops, or to get out supplies, but we did our best. This meant that we were on the road from early until late. The days were short. We would not get back to Nancy until nine o'clock or later, so that when we finally found ourselves behind the tightly drawn shutters at Walther's we were ready for good food and lots of it. One of those dinners, sluiced down by a bottle of excellent vintage wine, made the hard cold day that had preceded it a real pleasure in retrospect.

From Nancy, our division moved right up into the Argonne, where it was sent in as shock troops. We could not pretend to open and operate a canteen in the Argonne. There was no possible location and the troops were all well up ahead of us anyhow. It was difficult to find billets for our headquarters staff. The first night of this tour, my personal driver and I finally tucked ourselves away in a cow barn. I don't know how many hundreds of years that well-built stone cow barn had sheltered gentle bossies from the weather, but it must have been a long time because, whatever else we might find to complain of, we could not say that the bed on which we lay was not soft—almost too soft. It was also odoriferous. Later, Henry and I and the few people who were not up at the front shared with the MP company the hayloft of an enormous barn farther toward the front, at Autrecourt. There, at night, after we had come back from visiting our various groups and carrying them supplies, we would stand in the open and watch and listen to the intense bombardment that went on without cessation at the front. Never was the sky dark, even for a minute, and never was the air free from tortured sounds.

General Traub and his staff were about ten miles ahead of us, north, beyond Varennes, where Louis XVI and Marie Antoinette had been captured in their attempted escape to Austria. The Germans had already been driven back far enough so that American troops could occupy some of their concrete-lined dugouts. Our soldiers complained bitterly of the filthy condition in which the departing Huns had left these habitations. They were full of dirt and harbored countless lice.

So crowded was the narrow road that led to the front that on one occasion it took us ten hours to cover the ten miles back to our barn. A snail could have beaten us. Our little car was wedged in between moving troops and cannon and great camions and caterpillar guns, which on this occasion I saw for the first time. Here and there, detours were necessary to avoid plunging into huge shell holes. It did not make us any too comfortable to reflect that we were in range of the German guns or that the Germans knew all about the road, having themselves used it only recently.

We were not permitted to strike a match or to smoke a cigarette. We literally felt our way along in that moist Stygian darkness, almost touching the vehicle in front while being touched by the one behind. Sweating and swearing MP's did their best to control the traffic. Then, through our mirror, we saw the reflection of automobile lights from the rear. All of us who had the proper vocabulary began to swear, and that included everyone. The lights indicated that the automobile was weaving its way in and out along that crowded road at a rate much faster than we in front of it were able to proceed. In time the car reached us, pushed us out of the way, and hurried on. None of us knew who was in the car. But whoever it was, we consigned to the nethermost hell. No one had the right to run the risk of attracting German fire which might blow all of us to bits.

As I lay, fully clothed except as to boots, on my ration of straw in the haymow that night about eleven o'clock, a highly vocal MP came in. And was he swearing! And was he mad! He announced in unflattering language that it was General Pershing himself who had come down the road behind undimmed headlights. This MP had stopped the car and was about to raise hell when he saw who the occupant was. He was wondering whether he would be arrested.

After our division had played its part in the Battle of the Argonne, we were sent to a rest area. There, Henry came down with diphtheria and I took over his job, in addition to my own. The doctor established him in a pup tent in a field way off by himself. Here they sluiced large doses of antitoxin into his back every day. He had one attendant, but much of the time he was alone. I drove out every day to see him, in spite of the fact that I had never had diphtheria. When he was permitted to rejoin us he insisted upon undertaking activities for which he was not yet physically fit. And the one thing that would make him mad was a suggestion that he take things easy. On more than one occasion when I was walking with him his knees would buckle under him, and, good-natured man though he always was, he would almost strike at me when I tried to help him to his feet. The only thanks that I got was a growl.

Allen would not admit that he was not able to carry on, but one of the ranking Army doctors, who was his friend, took me aside privately one day and told me that we had to get Henry out of there if we wanted to avoid possible serious consequences to him. Henry had already been elected Governor of Kansas *in absentia.* It was to prevent this, if possible, that the plot had been hatched to have him dismissed from the Red Cross. It was to circumvent this plot that he had transferred to the Y.M.C.A.

I went to work on Henry, telling him that, since he was going back to Kansas anyhow, he might as well get away soon. Our division was in a rest area and no one knew when it might get into action again. This was the time to go. I would meet his counterarguments with such statements as: "You had no business running for Governor of Kansas if you did not intend to take over the office if elected." "You wanted to be Governor of Kansas, and you won't be faithful to your trust if you do not take it."

Finally, Henry agreed to go back to Paris. He wanted to

stay there for a short while and then sail for New York. I
knew that I did not want to stay with the Y.M.C.A., especially now that Henry was going. The Thirty-fifth Division
needed officers in the quartermaster corps. General Traub
and Gl had said to me on more than one occasion that they
wished that I were available. So I decided that I would return to Paris with Henry—he was anxious that I should—go
down to GHQ at Chaumont, ask for waivers of my physical
disabilities, and get a commission if I could. I carried with
me to Paris cordial letters from both General Traub and
Gl, supporting my wish that I be granted the necessary
waivers, asking that I be granted a commission and be assigned to the Thirty-fifth Division, where I would be put to
work helping the overtaxed staff of the quartermaster corps.

We decided to make a little trip of it back to Paris. First
we drove to Verdun. There we found a shattered city of silence, except when the Huns gratuitously threw in still another shell just to prove—as if that were necessary—that they
were still Huns. We stood in the shell-battered cathedral, of
which little was left except some of the walls. The floor was
covered with broken glass, splintered wood, and smashed
images. As far as we could see in all directions, not a human
being—not even a sign of animal life—was visible. I cursed
the terrorists from across the Rhine and expressed the fer-
vent hope that in their turn the Boches would be caused to
experience what modern warfare meant, by having their
towns and cities smashed as they had ruthlessly destroyed
French towns and cities. Perhaps such a lesson would have
made them less eager for war this time.

We drove up to take a look at the great fortress of Verdun,
but we saw little beyond the entrance. Here the French had
held out, as they were not able to hold out when the Ger-

mans struck again, more cunningly and in greater force and with far more ferocity, in 1940. Some of the officers who were with American troops near Verdun described to us the vast city that lay underground, impregnable to the enemy. As we walked back along the road that was deserted except for us, the Germans sent a couple of small-caliber shells popping at us. They were gas, as I could detect from the smell of chlorine. As we had stood near the fortress the Germans had also fired some shells. No one of the group of American soldiers wanted to be the first to seek shelter, which I thought was silly. At least I had learned one thing since reaching France, and that was that there could be no personal satisfaction nor any gain to the country in needlessly exposing one's life.

On the way to Rheims after Verdun, we sought for and found Quentin Roosevelt's grave. As Henry and I stood there with uncovered heads, we commented upon what a loss this had been to an especially devoted father and mother. It has been said that Quentin was his father's favorite. Someone in the neighborhood must have realized this as we did, because there was a little Mason jar of fresh flowers at the head of the grave. There were no other graves near. This gallant son of a great American President had been brought down from the air by a wild enemy shot and he was buried in the wide field where his body had been found. I have always thought that Colonel and Mrs. Roosevelt did well when they decided against reburying their son.

We stood before the glorious cathedral at Rheims and beheld the devastation that the Huns had wrought. And again we hated war and those who made war, either for loot or for transitory glory.

Then on to Paris, through the area where the First Division of the American Army and the American Marines had demonstrated to the world that American soldiers know how to fight. This was the nearest approach of the Huns to Paris in that First World War.

Henry wanted to go to the Hôtel Continental. He was entitled to some ease and comfort. I could do with a little soft living myself. It was a lucky chance that took us there, where we had adjoining rooms looking out over the Rue de Rivoli and the Tuileries Gardens. There was a small balcony on which we could stand. Looking out casually on November 11, I was curious to see people pouring from the near-by subway station. I called Henry's attention to the activity which neither of us could understand. A trickle became a steady stream and the steady stream swelled into a torrent. From every direction we could see hundreds and then thousands of joyous Frenchmen converging upon the empty spaces that lay beneath our eyes. Then the report reached us that the contending armies had signed an Armistice.

The war was over.

We had no Roy Howard in Paris, so we had no false Armistice. This was the real thing. All that day and all that night, or at least until the small hours of the morning, the people of Paris indulged in a spontaneous but at the same time the most genuine celebration that I have ever seen. For awhile, vehicles could proceed at a snail's pace, but shortly they were blocked altogether from the Tuileries Gardens, the Rue de Rivoli, the Place de la Concorde, the Rue de la Paix, and most of the boulevards. On one occasion I saw General Pershing's big car insist upon pushing forward through the dense crowd past the hotel. Again, I could distinguish Thomas G. Masaryk, who was to become the founder and first President of Czechoslovakia. Other figures appeared, and there was cheering. But, in general, the people were just busy being happy. They would sing snatches from the "Marseillaise." They would sing other characteristic French songs. They would sway in and out in long hand-holding ropes of people. They would form rings and dance, singing around the people caught inside the rings—impromptu and ever changing rings around the "roses." The ring could be broken only by a kiss—a friendly kiss.

For hours I wandered about without meeting a soul that I knew. But this made no difference. We were all friends together. We were neither Americans nor Frenchmen. As I was walking up the Rue de la Paix toward the Trafalgar monument I felt a hand within my elbow. I glanced down to see a French woman. She was probably in her early forties, pleasant-looking, apparently of the lower middle class. She was at the end of a line of people who, arm in arm, were swinging up the avenue. I was happy to join the group, and soon I found someone else on my left, similarly attached. We would form circles or be caught in one, and we knew the key that would open the circles. And so it went hour after hour. No horseplay after the American fashion, no drunkenness after the American fashion, no over-self-stimulation nor stimulation of others after the American fashion. It was just true feeling, expressing itself normally and genuinely.

Then the kings began to come to Paris, as recently they have been flocking to Washington. When we were in Cologne in the fall of 1911, the King of Denmark had a suite in our hotel. Later he was joined by his two sons, the King of Greece and the King of Norway. But I was interested to see the kings of some of the countries that had just come through a successful war. And I did see them as, in their turn, they were driven in triumph up the Bois de Boulogne, which on each occasion was packed on both sides with crowds that demonstrated in the self-contained French manner that I have described.

I do not now remember the order of their coming, but from my vantage point in the Bois, I saw the King and Queen of Italy, the King and Queen of the Belgians, and King George and Queen Mary of Great Britain. So it will be seen that long before Washington became the mecca of the aristocratic and royal houses of Nazi-overrun Europe, kings and queens had ceased to be a novelty to me.

Of the lot, the King of the Belgians really looked the part. He and his wife would have been a regal-appearing couple even if they had been the merest commoners. The pocket edition of a king from Italy, Victor Emmanuel III, was perched on a high seat so that his deficiency in stature, as compared with that of the Queen, would not make him appear at a physical disadvantage. Quite aside from his Lilliputianism, he was an insignificant-looking specimen. Little wonder that the braggadocio Mussolini took him in his stride and has kept him virtually a prisoner ever since. Queen Mary, of the inseparable umbrella, and King George V looked normal enough and were able to pass for authentic royalty, even if they suffered somewhat by comparison with the King and Queen of the Belgians.

But the greatest of all to come was the last—Woodrow Wilson, President of the United States, accompanied by Mrs. Wilson. When he was driven up the Bois he was greeted by a wild torrent of enthusiasm. No cheer-leaders were needed on this occasion, even if such had been in character with French crowds. Shouting jargonized words in unison would have sounded false, anyhow. The French threw their hearts in front of Wilson's carriage. He was their hope of the future. Important avenues had already been named for him in every Allied capital. All of Europe, excepting only Germany and Austria, was at his feet. What a tragedy the power politicians of Europe wrote at Versailles when they might have inscribed a peace treaty that would have made impossible the cataclysm of two decades later.

When I heard that Wilson was coming to Paris I was apprehensive. I said in conversations with my friends that I feared that he would be sent home in a barrel. The germ of the tragedy of Versailles lay dormant in the error of judgment when Wilson decided to participate personally in the writing of the treaty. From the perspective of Washington, with sound American public opinion expressing itself, he could have seen, and insisted upon the avoidance of, mistakes that were the seeds of the present war.

After the Armistice, there was no point in my applying to GHQ for a commission. I did not want to be an officer in the Army when the Army would be disestablished as fast as possible. My life had been lived along civilian lines and I had family and other obligations that could not be disregarded. So I kept my letters in my pocket. The Y.M.C.A. felt that I ought to continue in the active service until the American troops really had made a job of going home. I could not see it that way. The Y.M.C.A. was not my bent either. A certain gentleman from Philadelphia was inclined to become insistent. I resented it strongly and threw at him some of the unjustly critical remarks that he made about another. I told him flatly that I was going home after I had spent two or three weeks in Paris. And home I went, sailing on the *Rochambeau,* which disgorged me in New York on January 1, 1919.

After seventeen years in the front-line trenches of Chicago politics, the First World War had seemed almost tame. But I was glad that I had gone to France.

CHAPTER ELEVEN

"NO!"

These Macedonians, said he, are a rude and clownish people, that call a spade a spade.—PLUTARCH.

AFTER 1916 I was more than ever a political waif and/or stray. I didn't want to go back to the Republican party and it, mistakenly, thought that it was well rid of me. I was unhappy. Theodore Roosevelt had been tremendously interested in the war. If he could have had his way the United States would have gone in much sooner than it did. He wanted with all of his heart to go abroad as a soldier. He offered to raise a regiment of fighters, an offer which Wilson promptly scorned. In many ways Roosevelt was the greatest war asset that America had, but Wilson would have none of him. Wilson not only would not send him to France; he would not send him anywhere. I have always believed that the Rough Rider should have been put at the head of the mission that went to Russia at that time. But the President was adamant in his hostility to the ex-President. Perhaps Wilson would have agreed to let him knit socks and sweaters if the proper pressure had been applied by way of a Gallup poll.

All of this burned Roosevelt up, as it did us few die-hard

Progressives. He was bitter in his feelings toward Wilson as the result. One day he and I were driving in Chicago on the North Side. It was a Sunday morning. On the sidewalk, apparently headed for the Fourth Presbyterian Church, was a tall, slender man with a Wilsonian cast to his features. Roosevelt glared as though the man had personally affronted him.

"That man looks like that damned Presbyterian hypocrite Wilson," he said, with feeling.

Failure to get into the war was one of the great disappointments in Colonel Roosevelt's life. He not only wanted to go to France, he was ready and willing to die there, so keenly did he feel about the issues involved. I am not guessing at this. I know it of my own knowledge. I know it from what he said to me more than once. He wanted to be at the front where the fighting was the hottest. That he was thinking of a campaign in France as a steppingstone to further political preferment I do not believe, but he might have thought of it in time. He was an American who disliked the German system and who wanted to do his part in keeping it from contaminating his own beloved country. He sent four sons to France, and all of them made fine records. He told me one day that he did not expect all of them to come back. One of them, the favorite one, did not come back.

As I have previously recorded, I got back to New York from France on January 1, 1919. Theodore Roosevelt was in a hospital and I could not see him, a circumstance that distressed me. And then when I stepped from the train in Chicago a few days later, I was met with the announcement that the Colonel had died during the night. I don't mind saying that something went out of my life that has never been replaced.

For the time being at least, the death of Colonel Roosevelt dashed the hopes not only of liberal Republicans, but of decent conservatives. Who was left to cope with the Crane-Penrose-Smoot gang? It hardly seemed worth attempting. Only such mavericks as I happened to be even cared about keeping the flag flying. And the sum total of our efforts was bound to be mighty small. A wave of deep reaction had set in. If such a wave sweeps in after this war, then, indeed, may God help America!

It is difficult to pick up threads that have been so completely dropped as mine had been, but I resumed as nearly as I could where I had left off as a practicing lawyer—as much practice as I wanted, but not enough to absorb all of my time.

I had lost much of my interest in local and state politics. Why try to reform a world that had set its iniquities to jazz? I followed closely the doings in Washington. Woodrow Wilson broke under the strain and national power slipped from his enfeebled grasp. Republican irreconcilables were in the saddle. Aside from the Democratic regulars, some of whom were not too dependable, there seemed to be only one man of national stature who was standing by Wilson, and this man was Herbert Hoover, who had appealed to the country for a Democratic Congress in 1918. And even if Hoover had been the man for the occasion, he had kept himself too busy moistening his forefinger and holding it aloft to determine from which direction the political wind might be blowing to do anything about it. He couldn't make up his mind whether he was a Republican, a Democrat, or an Independent and it was to be some time before he could decide. He did know that he wanted to be President, by whatever route.

However, I wasn't through with local politics, as I had

thought and hoped that I was going to be. Like an old fire horse, I smelled something burning and I began to paw the floor of my stall. In the spring following my return from France I began to look about for someone—anyone—who might beat "Bluffing Bill" Thompson, who had skewered Chicago for one term as Mayor. It did not seem possible to me that Merriam could make the grade.

I bethought myself of Kenesaw Mountain Landis, then of the United States District Court. Landis was one of the most picturesque figures in the country, as he still is. Having just slapped a fine of $30,000,000 or $40,000,000 onto the Standard Oil Company for violation of the antitrust laws, he was much in the limelight.

With Landis in mind, I went to call upon Victor Lawson in his new big mansion in the Lake Shore Drive. Lawson remarked that he could always tell that there was an election in the offing from the fact that I had come to see him. Lawson and Edgar A. Bancroft had been considering Alexander A. McCormick, once Sixth Ward alderman and then president of the County Board, as a possibility, but it was conceded that Landis would be much the stronger of the two.

Then I went to see Landis, with authority to tell him that the *News* would be in his corner if he would make the fight. The Judge was trying a case, but he left the bench and talked with me in his chambers. He could always hold the eye, what with his shock of prematurely gray hair waving at the top of a lean, Lincolnesque face and his lithe, quick body. We sat down at his desk, around three sides of which stood, on edge, thin plugs of black chewing tobacco. He explained that he put them thus in order to dry thoroughly. Taking one of them and offering it to me, he said: "Ickes, this is the sweetest tobacco that you have ever put in your mouth." I declined

as he did when he staged his "Prosperity Parade"—but he couldn't fool a majority of the voters. They saw through his hypocrisies and his buffooneries and, on a straight issue with only one opposing candidate, he would have been whipped to a frazzle. As Tony Galento would have put it, Landis would have "moidered de bum."

Then came the Presidential campaigns. Into the race there entered none other than Hiram W. Johnson of California. We had been personal and political friends since 1912. Upon my return from Europe early in 1919, I had written to him to tell him that I thought that he was all wet in his isolationist views. He came back with a letter that disturbed me. I went to Washington to convert him. He converted me. I returned to Chicago to arrange a mass meeting in the Auditorium at which both Johnson and Borah spoke. It was to be a long time before I reached the conclusion that I had been persuaded too easily.

In swinging over to the isolationist side, even for a time, I realize now how wrong I was, and I hereby do penance for that temporary aberration. Behold me in sackcloth and ashes —now a confirmed believer in the principle that we live in the world, that we are of the world, and that we can't play ostrich and safely bet that some rangy (or is "mangy" the word?) beast named Hitler won't sneak up on us and pull out our tail feathers.

Governor Frank O. Lowden of Illinois arranged through a common friend, Thomas J. Knight, for me to have breakfast with him in the Governor's mansion at Springfield. Lowden was shopping for support for the Republican nomination for President. Much to my surprise, Lowden had made a first-rate Governor and, at the moment, I could see nothing in the offing remotely resembling Illinois delegates for Hiram Johnson. So I adhered to Lowden with the distinct understanding that if he failed of nomination, he would make no attempt to deliver me to another. I told him frankly that Johnson was my real choice. Lowden, in turn, assured me that he would rather throw his strength to Johnson than to any of the reactionary candidates. So I went along.

While the Republican National Committee was laying plans for the convention, William Allen White looked me up one day as he was passing through Chicago. He thought that someone ought to get busy at once considering planks for the platform. The Progressives would have little to say about the nominee, but the Republicans might let us have something to do with framing the platform. After all, we were interested in principles rather than in men. White was on his way to New York. Would I join him there and call, with him, on Will Hays, Republican National Chairman, with a view to getting clearance for a group of former Progressive party members to get together and formulate planks that we would want to have considered? I thought that the idea was a good one.

Hays had already opened headquarters in New York. He had blossomed into a statesman. He bore himself as a man of great affairs. He had discarded the none-too-well-fitting business suit of the man from way back home in Sullivan, Indiana, and was clothed in the habiliments of power and prestige. Nobby, to say the least! He went about his daily tasks clothed in a well-tailored cutaway. I'll bet that he has long since got over that flight of fancy and has more or less reverted to type.

Will White and I told Hays what was on our minds. He was afraid of it. Of course, we had expected that he would be. He did not want anything done that might give rise to even a suspicion that the old Republican-Progressive split might recur. Sensing that he did not really care so much whether we should get together and talk each other to death as that he was afraid of unfavorable publicity, I told him that I would guarantee to pull off a meeting no word of which would leak to the newspapers. Hays was highly skeptical, but I pressed my plans—highly confidential letters would be sent to a small, select group; the meeting would be held at my home in Winnetka; I would have each man who accepted met at the station and driven direct to my home; none would register at a hotel, and there would be no conference in the heart of Chicago, even of two or three; at the conclusion of our meeting the conferees would be driven to their trains and so would be able to leave Chicago as unobtrusively as they had entered it.

The meeting came off as advertised. Ogden L. Mills attended as Will Hays' personal observer. No dangerous radical, he! Will White, of course, was there and, at my suggestion, was made chairman of the conference. Others present were Jim Garfield, Gifford Pinchot, Chester H. Rowell, Raymond Robins, Governor Robert D. Carey of Wyoming, Donald R. Richberg, Albert D. Lasker, and Harriet E. Vittum. There were a few others whose names have now passed from my memory.

We went into session about ten o'clock in the morning and adjourned at the same hour in the evening. We had expected to serve luncheon, and dinner in addition was a severe strain upon the Ickes ménage. However, we accomplished it. I must say that the meeting was a flop, aside from the pleasure of seeing each other. Even White didn't seem to have much idea as to what we should discuss (perhaps Mills "discombobulated" even him) and everyone talked, most of the time several at once, all around and around Robin Hood's barn in a regular eight-day marathon. The total and net result of the meeting was nothing. Our deliberations, so far as I could judge, had not the slightest effect upon the platform that was later adopted at the Chicago convention.

Many months before the election, it was clear that whomever the Republicans nominated would be elected. The country had repudiated, so far as repudiation is possible under our system while a President is still in office, Woodrow Wilson and the Versailles Treaty. There had followed a severe nervous breakdown of Wilson. How serious this was no one outside of Mrs. Wilson and of course his personal physician, Admiral Carey Grayson, knew, and to this day the extent of Wilson's collapse at that point has never been clarified. But, according to report, the Cabinet considered gravely just what ought to be done in view of Wilson's inability to transact public business. There was some talk of the Vice-President and members of the Cabinet joining in a statement to the country to the effect that the President was incapacitated, following which the Vice-President would take over. But nothing was done. Wilson was kept virtually incommunicado and, so far as anyone knew, the Executive branch of the Government was running itself or was being run by Mrs. Wilson and Admiral Grayson. Accordingly, the Republican nomination was a prize worth striving for, and there were many eager aspirants.

Lowden and Johnson were two of these, as I have said. General Leonard Wood was a third. Wood had gone into the army as a doctor, and had come out a real soldier. He had been Theodore Roosevelt's colonel at San Juan Hill, although Roosevelt got most of the glory out of that battle of beanbags. When I called upon him at his Army headquarters (neither Lowden nor Johnson had announced his candidacy as yet), to size him up for myself, I found a big, well-set-up man, approachable and with a fine presence. The thing that impressed me at once was that he talked so much. One would have thought that he had known me all of his life. He talked of Roosevelt and about Wilson. Here was a general in the Army openly and severely criticizing his Commander in Chief for not having sent either Roosevelt or himself abroad. He seemed to have no reticences at all. And the more he talked, the less inclined I was to commit myself to his candidacy. I wouldn't have done so, anyhow, at that stage of the proceedings.

Following that meeting, General Wood stopped two or three times at my home at night, on his way to Fort Sheridan, where his living quarters were. He had expressed a wish to meet Raymond Robins. I brought them together. And Wood continued to talk. It seemed impossible to stem his flow of language. Word was carried to him by a common friend who admired him that I thought that he talked too much. He hurriedly explained to me that he was voluble in my presence because I had been a friend of his friend Theodore, and so he knew that he could trust me. Even this explanation did not convince me.

Colonel William Procter of Cincinnati, the rich president of the Procter & Gamble Company, was finally brought to Chicago as Wood's manager. He apparently was willing to contribute much Ivory Soap to the campaign. He certainly had not been selected on the basis of his political knowledge or experience. The first Presidential primary would be in South Dakota, as usual. By this time Lowden was also in the fight and the contest in South Dakota was between him and

Wood. Both had ample campaign funds—too ample for their own good, as it developed later, when Senator Borah began to draw beads on them for an excessive spending of money. It was reasonably believed that the winner in South Dakota would have a big psychological advantage in the other primary states.

One of the men active in the Wood campaign was William H. Malone, who had got his start politically as a member of the Progressive party, where his record had not been good. Malone, never lacking in nerve, and a facile speaker, had been firing his heaviest oratorical guns at Lowden. He accused the Pullman Company, in which Mrs. Lowden (née Pullman) owned a great deal of stock, of being an evader of its just taxes. Malone didn't stop to explain why, as a member of the State Board of Equalization, he had permitted the Pullman Company to dodge its obligations to the state.

I wasn't slow to make known my low opinion of Malone. Colonel Procter hunted me up to say that pressure was being brought to bear upon him to send Malone into South Dakota as the spearhead of the Wood campaign. In spite of my suggestion that Malone was no credit to General Wood, or to anyone else, Procter let him go into South Dakota, where he ranged all over the state, making what seemed to me to be a particularly unfair and blatherskitish attack on Governor Lowden. But then I may have been prejudiced.

Years later, Malone was indicted for failure to make an honest income-tax return and he was also sued civilly. Just about the time of his indictment he went to Germany "to collect some money that was due," and he stayed there for several years. In 1937 he came back and was tried. As a witness in his own behalf, he testified that when he had come back after "carrying" South Dakota for Wood, Colonel Procter, who had since died, insisted upon giving him a lot of money for his services in that one state. Much to Malone's surprise and disgust, the jury found him guilty.

The time came when I told Wood that while I was friendly to him in a personal way, I couldn't support him; that I was going to be for Lowden from my own state. Lowden had been one of our best governors. He had lived down the fact that when he was national committeeman he had given his proxy to Lorimer. At my meeting with him he had impressed me with his sincerity and straightforwardness. He convinced me that he had a real understanding of the Progressive point of view. He assured me that if elected, he would not run for a second term, thus causing me to daydream that Hiram Johnson or some other former Bull Mooser might be his successor. As I started for home, I told him that although I preferred Johnson, I didn't think that there was a chance to nominate a Progressive at that time and that, in the circumstances, I would support him as the best candidate in sight. Not very flattering, but I was trying to be honest with him.

To our surprise, we learned that the Thompson machine in Chicago was not going to be for Lowden, proving once again that nothing can be taken for granted in politics. Accordingly I advised Lowden to put up a delegate ticket in every Cook County district. My theory in politics has always been to capitalize the opposition, and here was a wonderful chance for real dividends. Thompson was the most unpopular man in the Republican party nationally. He was thoroughly distrusted, even despised. He was regarded as having been disloyal during the war. I advised Lowden to issue a statement that he not only did not want, he would not accept, Thompson's support. I also suggested that Louis L.

Ickes Still No. 1 Choice for Alaskans' Blacklist

By JULIUS C. EDELSTEIN

Intense friction in Alaska between the military services and the Interior Department's game commission shows no signs of lessening, this correspondent found on a recent tour of the territory's defenses.

Army and Navy officers and men bitterly object to a recent department ruling preventing them from qualifying for resident hunting licenses.

And civilian leaders who a year ago branded Secretary of Interior Ickes the most unpopular man in the nation, haven't changed their attitude.

as they likely to.

Object of the military leaders' ire is the ruling that Army and Navy men are ineligible for resident hunting licenses regardless of how long they have been in the territory, whereas civilians qualify after one year's residence.

Many commissioned and non-commissioned officers now claim Alaska

as their permanent residence, having built homes, and bought land. They are demanding their "rights." Commanding Gen. Simon Buckner actually has started a court case.

Recently Assistant Secretary of War Robert Lovett asked Mr. Ickes to clarify the situation. The Interior Department promised to "study" it.

The civilians hold different grudge

In Washington
With
GEORGE MORRIS

'Old Ick' Shows Off

WASHINGTON, July 2. — There was more to the incident of Secretary Ickes' picking up a rubber mat at the entrance to the executive offices of the White House and ordering his chauffeur to put it in his car and deliver it to a rubber scrap pile than the usual display of violent temper and vitriolic language.

Mr. Ickes had just emerged from a conference with the President at which he reported the collection of scrap rubber was disappointing and extended the drive another 10 days. The purpose of the ill-mannered exhibition put on the presence of White House reporters with an eye to publicity was to let the country know that he had authority to invade the White House and se...

Ickes Most Unpopular Man In Capital
But He's Classed as A-1 Administrator

And Even Those Who Hate Him Admit Secretary Is Honest.

By EVERETT C. WATKINS,
Indianapolis Star Bureau,
1201 National Press Building.

Washington, Oct. 25. — Harold LaClair Ickes — just "Ickes" or "Honest Harold" to Washington— is the most personally unpopular person of the Roosevelt dynasty, yet he may be classified as the best administrator among the New Dealers.

In a personal popularity contest, even with "Mme." Perkins, Ickes would lose by about 1,000 to 1. Ickes knows he isn't popular— he doesn't care much.

Take...

kick much because he works equally hard and also because, even though he may criticize them sharply, he is sure to defend them if outsiders jump on them.

Making an analysis of himself, Ickes recently admitted being short-tempered and arbitrary and knowing nothing whatever about the art of backslapping. He added he didn't want any yes men around him.

And then Ickes heard himself described as "onery, unreasonable, arbitrary, hard-headed."

Came From Mike Strauss.

The description came from Big Mike Strauss, brown-eyed, kindly voiced, intelligent press relations chief of the Interior Department and easily Ickes's best friend. Mike is indeed no yes man—he is Ickes's honest friend because he is Ickes's

"Honest Harold" Has Few Friends, but Likes Lot of Enemies.

Mr. Krock sent a note to the Baltimore Sun; the Krock note was printed in a box on page one. It was as follows:

"To the editor of the Baltimore Sun: In your report of Ickes' speech, your dispatch quotes him as calling me, the sly Communist of the New York Times.' It was an obvious misprint, but I hope you will correct it. If I were a Communist, sly or otherwise, I would not be denounced by Ickes at any time for any reason."

The newspaper clippings, reproduced here, will give you an idea of what drives public officials to drink. Me? I don't mind. However, if you will read the second line of the editorial written "by Harry Newman, Editor," you will note that it contains the genial assurance that "we aren't very mad at anybody." Then read the last line and you will quickly conclude that Harold L. Ickes is the only man in the world that Harry Newman doesn't like. Oh, well! I'll manage somehow. Perhaps he was just trying to be funny.

by
Harry Newman, Editor

We undertake, today, the conduct of the Journal in what we hope to be the best traditions of this 88-year-old newspaper.

We have no ax to grind—we are conducting no crusade—and we aren't very mad at anybody.

We are looking for no fights, but, being Irish, we have never had to, since fights have had a way of sneaking up on us unannounced.

We sincerely like Kansas City and the country around and about. If we didn't we wouldn't be here.

We like the traditions of this country and admire the spirit which has made this a great city. We even like and admire the Kansas City Star for being a great newspaper and for its contribution to the greatness of its environment. We remember, with no little pleasure, our personal association with the men who have made it.

So here we are—protecting an investment as wisely as we may and yet another while discovering the justification for that protection.

We like the opportunity that has been given us and we shall make the most of it.

We do not like the weather we have been having, nor Harold Ickes.

Emmerson, who was Secretary of State of Illinois, wasn't a good manager for Lowden. I nominated Hert of Kentucky, who later became Lowden's floor manager at the convention and—but that will come later. Emmerson didn't know national politics or any of its leaders. Lowden agreed with me on both propositions. Then he permitted Emmerson to back him down on Thompson and my whole plan of strategy fell flat. It was Emmerson who, in the end, was more responsible than any one else for Lowden's failure to be nominated. He was just a back-country cracker-box politician with neither aptitude for such a job, nor imagination. I am convinced that a smashing attack on Thompson would more than have recovered the ground lost by the discovery that Emmerson had handed over several thousand dollars in cash to each of two Missouri delegates, for some undisclosed purpose.

Later Hiram Johnson took off his wraps and started to warm up. I had not anticipated this when I committed myself to Lowden, but as I didn't think there was a chance for Johnson in Illinois anyway, as first choice, it didn't weigh on my conscience, although it bothered me on account of our personal relations. In this size-up of the Illinois situation, I was proved later to be mistaken. I did not want Johnson to misunderstand my position, so I made a trip to Washington to explain it to him. I do not think that he was quite satisfied, and I am quite sure that Mrs. Johnson was not. When we all closed in on Chicago for the convention, the Johnsons made it plainly apparent that so far as they were concerned I was on the outside looking in. Nevertheless, I was at heart for Johnson and continued to be.

Then came Harding, with the backing of the Old Guard. He was a typical small-bone Ohio politician. However much his façade might proclaim the President, he was distinctly lacking in character and in essential integrity. It was a clear case of "a Queen Ann front and a Mary Ann rear."

Johnson could not hope to win by organization support, and so confined his efforts to the primary-election states. His principal backers were Albert D. Lasker and William Wrigley, Jr., both old friends. Wrigley had a unique record. He ran as a Lowden delegate, he contributed to both Wood and Johnson, and he was one of the first to climb onto the Harding bandwagon.

Before Johnson was through, he had won more votes in the strong Republican states than any rival. Had rules of fair play and equity instead of the law of the jungle obtained, Hiram Johnson would have been nominated and elected. Looking through the rear-view mirror, we can see now that his foreign policies might not have been good for the country, but one certain thing is that he would never have scuttled the American Navy. Moreover, Johnson would have given us, especially on domestic issues, a wise, sound, and public-spirited administration which would have been helpful to the common man. His record as Governor of California showed him to be a great and humane administrator.

The miserable machinations that went on in that Chicago convention were stomach-turning. They made me feel as if I had a mouth full of alum. They gripe me still when I think of them. They were poison ivy even to a curmudgeon. Medill McCormick, thumbing his nose at the people, was happily hopping hither and yon, as one of the inside group determined upon carrying out the will of the notorious machine which he and I both had fought, sincerely as I thought, and with conviction, in the good old days. Boies Penrose lay on his deathbed in Philadelphia, while his safety-deposit box was bursting with banknotes of large denominations—dying but not yet ready to be shriven before delivering himself up to judgment. Penrose joined by telephone in the conspiracy that was being brewed in the "small smoke-filled room" where an evil candidate was to emerge from the witch's caldron.

Two sons of Theodore Roosevelt—Theodore, Jr., and Archibald—were in Chicago, and a day or two before the nomination was to be made they sought me out. They foresaw the nomination of Harding, who four years before had denounced their father in unmeasured terms and had held him up as an international criminal in the matter of the Panama Canal. Could anything be done to prevent his nomination?

I suggested that they—sons of Roosevelt—appeal to the thousands of Republicans throughout America who had loved their father; that they denounce Harding, and declare that no true Rooseveltian would support him, either in the convention or thereafter.

The twain backed away from my proposal. I didn't blame Archie, because he wasn't active in politics as was his brother, nor did he crave a public career. Even at that time, it was the policy of virtually all of the members of that particular branch of the Roosevelt family to make everything else secondary to the proud political career that young Theodore clearly hoped that he could eventually carve out for himself.

So what did I do, when the Roosevelt clan held back, although it had much at stake? I, the curmudgeon? Ickes the battle-scarred and not yet turned fifty years? As a former warrior under the banner of Theodore Roosevelt, I ran my neck out and wrote my own defiance of Harding. I signed it and threw it at the delegates.

Too late, Johnson, Lowden, and Wood got together. Here

were three men, any one of whom would have been a better candidate or President than Harding, who between them had held, at least in the early days of the convention, an overwhelming majority of the delegates. On that fateful Thursday night they decided to ask their delegates to vote to carry the convention over Sunday, and agreed that in the interval they would converge upon some candidate other than Harding. But the adroit Harry Daugherty, the realistic Crane and Smoot, and the dying Penrose had done their work. No one knew better than they how to stir up suspicions, how to capitalize on ambitions, and how to use money where it would count. Or, for that matter, how to get money to use.

The next morning, uneasy delegates flocked early into the hot and stinking Coliseum. Something was in the air besides foul smells. Many had forebodings, some others were hopeful. Were they really riding the bandwagon that would drop them off at the gravy bowl?

Our former Western manager of the Hughes campaign, "Tobe" Hert of Kentucky, was Lowden's floor manager. He had been told that it was Lowden's wish that the convention should adjourn over Sunday, but others had reached Hert, too. Arrogantly, he swept Lowden and his political hopes into the dustpan. It was he who helped to stampede the convention and to deliver its prize to the ineffable Harding. It was alleged at the time that the piece of silver offered him was the promise of a place in Harding's Cabinet. Hert delivered, but Harding did not. Hert received no consideration at all, which convinced me all over again that it is better to be a bushwhacker, harassing the flanks of the enemy, than to go meekly into camp on any terms. I have observed, on more than one occasion, that even the beneficiary of political treachery does not—nor should he—trust the traitor.

And so Harding was nominated with his Ohio gang hanging onto his shirt tails. But not with my help. The Lord forbid! If a curmudgeon is not true to himself, to whom can he be loyal? When the Lowden delegates, of whom I was one, broke all over the lot and Hert had gone to the enemy, I voted on the last ballot for Johnson. I voted, too, for my old friend Henry J. Allen for Vice-President. The political medicine man from Northampton, Massachusetts, did not appeal to me any more than did the Ali Baba from Ohio, although I must say that Coolidge was never capable of the skulduggery of Harding. Coolidge might have been quite a man at that if he hadn't been "weaned on a pickle." (Note to Alice Longworth: I have my faults but I am not a plagiarist.)

The last ballot showed that Harding was indisputably the nominee of those turbulent, grasping, selfish men who were thinking little of their country but much of postmasterships, district-attorneyships, and marshalships. The customary motion was offered to make the nomination unanimous. A voice vote was called for. And on that vote a delegate at large from Illinois—a contumelious curmudgeon by the name of Ickes, who had not been on a winner for President since 1904 and was beginning not to care if he never was again—yelled "No!" at the top of his lungs. Much good it did him!

When I record that I was a delegate to the convention, I want to have my status clearly understood. As a final compromise with Bill Thompson, and still hoping that he would graciously deliver his delegates to Lowden, Emmerson had agreed to more delegates at large than there were seats for. This was to take care of Sam Ettelson, the ambidextrous, who was Thompson's corporation counsel on the one hand and, between times, Sam Insull's lawyer on the other. There

were only enough seats to take care of the number of delegates to which Illinois was entitled. Thompson, as national
committeeman, had the distribution of both seats and
badges. When I got my ticket I found that it did not call for
a seat with the delegation at all, or even with the alternates,
but for a place way back under the gallery. When I protested
to Thompson personally, he said that he hadn't had anything
to do with it. Anyhow, it was not news to me how I stood in
the esteem of the City Hall and I was proud of it. However,
I did manage to be well down in front when the final vote
was taken.

* * * * * *

At the end of the convention some of the Progressives held
an informal meeting. There was the usual crowd—Robins,
Pinchot, Garfield, White, Allen, Richberg, and myself. We
were not happy over the result. We knew that Harding
would be elected. The Progressive party was sunk without
a trace. Progressive principles had been completely abandoned. From the moment of Harding's nomination I knew
that I would not support him. I was outraged and disgusted.
Here was reaction with a vengeance. The others thought
that we either had to go along or go dead. We just couldn't
get off of the reservation every four years. Someone suggested
that we ought to keep in touch with each other and meet
from time to time. I had the lists, I had always been the
"come-togetherer," and I silently resolved to call it a day. So
this was the last meeting of the remnants of the Progressive
rear guard that had fought so well in 1912, had faltered in
1914, had broken into full retreat in 1916, and was preparing
to follow the sutlers' wagons in 1920.

The second place on the ticket had been offered to Johnson. Remembering what Johnson had done to him at the primaries in his own state, Harding wanted him. Johnson could have had it unanimously and with acclaim, but he rejected it with scorn. Johnson would do just that, because he was Johnson. No second fiddle to a Harding for a first-rate man who, more than once, had run the gauntlet of painted politicians who had left many a scar upon his body. Certainly he would not accept second place on a ticket with a man for whom he had only contempt. When Harding's body had been taken to Marion for burial, the wily George Brennan remarked to me one day: "If Hiram Johnson had known, as we did, what Warren Harding's blood pressure was, he would have accepted the Vice-Presidency."

But Brennan did not know Hiram Johnson as I knew him.

Harding and his gang—as everyone who knew anything realized that they would—proceeded to give the country as corrupt and as disgraceful an administration as it had not had since the sordid days of Ulysses S. Grant. The worst of it was, no one in the country seemed to give a damn. Everyone was speculating financially. All that one cared anything about was $100 for margin in order to assure the fortune that was—just around the corner. With Mellon and Hoover and even tight-fisted Coolidge cheering them on to ever greater squanderings, elevator boys, waitresses, streetcar conductors, sweatshop workers, all of them, poured their savings, petty as to the individual but mighty in the bulk, into the nearest bucket shop, the while the big Wall Street sharks gorged on each other. What a holy show it was! No wonder that Hitler began to see things.

Republican Senators in Washington, and others, were beginning to look ahead to the 1924 campaign. Even the regulars realized that Harding was a foul ball that the catcher had muffed, and no one was giving serious thought to the little fellow sitting in the Vice-President's chair. He was busy building up a fictitious reputation—that of taciturnity—to add to the authentic one of Yankee frugality. It was recognized that the candidate had to be someone who was known to have ideals and who would be strong enough to make a good President. Strange as it may seem, eyes that had long looked askance at Hiram Johnson now began to turn his way approvingly. Moses of New Hampshire told him to set up his fences. He was profuse in his protestations of loyal support, and Johnson had already put the Indian sign upon Moses as his campaign manager.

And then Harding dramatically died on a trip that he was taking to Alaska. Why and how he died should not be mysteries, but they are.

Senators who were willing to plot Harding's overthrow were not willing to be irregular now that Coolidge had been promoted by a twist of fate. Moses was the first to run over to his side. He announced himself for Coolidge in 1924 without tarrying to tell Johnson that this was his purpose. Others followed quickly, with the result that virtually no one was left in the Johnson camp except a few political soldiers of fortune and the old Progressive following that had looked to him for leadership ever since the death of Theodore Roosevelt. I was one of these. As a curmudgeon, I was again on the march and reaching out, with malice aforethought, for the short end.

Postscript

Medill McCormick had not delivered the Progressives of Illinois when he went into the Republican caucus of the General Assembly in 1915. He wasn't even enough interested in his former comrades to attempt it. He was Medill-on-the-Make. What he had done was to climb up over our shoulders and kick us in the face as he dived headlong into the "party of his fathers." Nor was he any more averse to claiming the rich reward for his treachery than were the Republicans to giving it. Without consultation, probably even without thought, he had decided that any plum within reach of the Progressives of Illinois naturally belonged to him, on the basis of his "services" and "sacrifices."

In 1916 he was elected Congressman at large from Illinois on the Republican ticket. But his meteoric career did not stop there. Two years later he was elected to the Senate, defeating the same Charles S. Deneen whom he had wanted us to support for Governor in 1912 because of his good public record.

I always enjoyed Medill's company, even if he did remind me of Eliza skipping over thin and broken ice. He did not take life seriously; he did not have to. Not only had he inherited money; he had married it. He had never in his life had to work seriously at a job. After 1914 Medill and I saw less and less of each other. After he had announced for the Senate in 1916 he sent his friend, Elmer J. Schlesinger,[1] who was later to marry his cousin, Eleanor Patterson-Gizycki (to be sure, Cissie), to explain to me that he dearly hoped that, as one of his old "friends" and as man whom he "greatly admired," I would support him. He had not

[1] Schlesinger was a member of the strongly political law firm of Mayer, Meyer, Austrain & Platt of Chicago. He had a great and insatiable ambition to be identified with power, both political and financial. He was a social climber, too. Before he laid successful siege to the heart of the then Countess Gizycki (Eleanor "Cissie" Patterson) he had married and divorced the daughter of Joseph Schaffner of the famous clothing firm of Hart, Schaffner & Marx. I didn't grow up with any idea that I would ever be able to understand the ways of "these charming people."

broached the matter to me himself, he explained, because of his "diffidence." I told Schlesinger that if Medill wanted my support he knew where to find me; that I was not impressed by his pretended shyness. Then Medill did seek me out and I agreed to support him, although I had little stomach for it. Following this, he had his Cook County manager, an old political buzzard by the name of William H. Weber, whose appetite for public fodder was equaled only by that of William Busse, ask me to lunch to discuss what I might be able to do in the campaign. I told Weber that, beyond a public expression of my attitude, I was not prepared to do anything.

I have always been grateful to Medill for this opportunity to sit at table with Weber. I had heard of eating peas with one's knife but I had always imagined that this was the apocryphal invention of some clever wit. But Weber gave me an actual exhibition. And he never dropped a pea. Probably to him they were symbols of political jobs for the Weber family.

Medill defeated Deneen by a slight margin. I believe that virtually all the Progressives remembered Deneen's recalcitrance during the Merriam campaign of 1911 and they were willing to give Medill a chance. He had talked fair enough to me and I, of course, had reported to my friends what he had said. But from the day that Medill entered the United States Senate, he deliberately cut himself off from all his old Progressive associates in Illinois. I ran across him by chance once in the Senate Restaurant when I was lunching with Senator Johnson and Senator Borah, and I so excited his interest that I must, perforce, go to his office with him, there to listen to a long and unconvincing explanation of why he had turned over all of his patronage to the Republican machine. He had even turned down his close friend Fletcher Dobyns, who wanted to be United States Attorney, and he forgot his voluntary promises to Donald R. Richberg. This was our last political communion with each other.

Six years later he ran for renomination. This time he did not even go to the trouble to ask for the support of any of his old comrades-in-arms. To a man, we voted against him, even if Deneen were the alternative. Deneen won by a scant 5,000 votes, which was probably about the margin that the steadfast Progressives were able to give him. Thus what was doubtless anticipated to be a great career, ending possibly in the White House, came to a tragic end. And so did poor Medill, himself, come to a tragic end. He died shortly thereafter in mysterious circumstances.

Then Mrs. McCormick generously offered herself to the voters and was elected Congresswoman at large. She was never one to hide her light under a bushel, and so she essayed for the upper house when Senator James Hamilton Lewis was a candidate to succeed himself in 1936. But Lewis was too clever for her. I have never seen a campaign more adroitly run. His chivalry would not permit him to raise directly the issue of Mrs. McCormick's sex, but in no speech did he fail to make some such reference as "the charming lady who is opposing me," without mentioning her by name.

CHAPTER TWELVE

FROM ELEPHANT TO DONKEY

You have no enemies, you say?
  Alas! my friend, the boast is poor—
He who has mingled in the fray
  Of duty, that the brave endure,
Must have made foes! If you have none,
  Small is the work that you have done;
You've hit no traitor on the hip;
  You've dashed no cup from perjured lip;
You've never turned the wrong to right—
You've been a coward in the fight!
                    —CHARLES MACKAY.

I WENT TO SEE George Brennan—wily George Brennan. He was a Democrat; I was a greatly discouraged Republican whose sawdust was fast running out. But he was my friend. I suggested to him that when the Democrats met in San Francisco, which they were to do in a couple of weeks, they would do well by themselves if they should put Franklin D. Roosevelt on the ticket as the candidate for Vice-President. I didn't know Roosevelt, but my information about him was good. Harding had indulged in particularly savage attacks on Theodore Roosevelt in 1912. Theodore Roosevelt was dead, but his name was one that was both loved and revered in the West. Franklin Roosevelt had made a good record as State Senator in New York and as Assistant Secretary of the

Navy. The family name that he bore ought to be worth a good many Progressive votes, especially in the Western states. Thus I reasoned to Brennan.

Others must have had something of the same theory, because when the Democrats got together they put Franklin Roosevelt on the ticket with Governor Cox of Ohio, who was their choice for President. Again I called on Brennan. I told him that I felt like supporting Cox and Roosevelt and asked him if he would arrange for an interview with Cox. He called Cox and made a breakfast appointment for me for a day or two later at Cox's home at Dayton, Ohio.

Cox had made an excellent record as Governor. The impression that he made upon me, however, was more negative than positive. The impression that Harding had made was more positive than negative—positively bad. Cox didn't measure up to my conception of a Presidential candidate, but he greatly outpointed Harding. Besides, he shot straight. He did not regard public office as a private bust. Moreover, he seemed to be sound on Progressive issues, and he assured me that while he believed in Wilson's League of Nations, it was not his intention to make an issue of it during the campaign, or to push it if he should be elected. Before the end, however, Cox did make it his leading issue, as he had the right to do, and perhaps that was one reason why he didn't make more headway. But no Democrat could have won that year anyway, and recent history has proved that Cox was right in opposing isolationism.

After our talk, I told Cox that I was ready to announce myself for him. At his suggestion I went to his newspaper office and prepared, in longhand, a statement that was given to the press. Subsequently, it was printed and circulated as a campaign document, much to the distaste of most of my former Bull Moose friends, who were still trying to look into the mirror without blushing. Apparently, they got all the comfort that they needed out of the practical certainty that Harding would be elected, and this justified their support of anything on two legs. When I declared for Cox I knew in my heart that he hadn't a chance. But I sincerely believed that Cox was the better man of the two as to ability, and certainly as to character.

I did nothing more in the campaign except to have a few conferences with Senator Thomas J. Walsh of Montana, who was the campaign manager. Anna, who was less likely to stray from the Republican fold than I was, couldn't stand for Harding either, and so made some speeches for the Democratic ticket in South Dakota.

Harding conducted his campaign, à la McKinley, from his front porch in Marion. If you have an apple with a bad spot that you are trying to sell, your chances are enhanced if you keep the good side exposed to the public. The whole business was totally lacking in inspiration, although the Republicans spent a mint of money hiring bands and sending trainloads of men and women to Marion from all parts of the country to whoop it up with a simulated (or stimulated) enthusiasm that I suspect few of them really felt.

Cox made a good fight, but he was badly defeated and America stood committed to Harding and "normalcy"—to an outrage on the people and an outrage on the English language. Young Theodore Roosevelt, who had been so concerned when it appeared probable that Harding would be the nominee, was active in Harding's campaign, and as a reward was made Assistant Secretary of the Navy. The announcement of his appointment was almost simultaneous with Harding's proposal that the United States pay

$20,000,000 to the Republic of Colombia to balance the Panama affair. This was, in effect, an acknowledgment that the United States, and this meant Theodore Roosevelt the elder, had acted improperly in the matter, and squared with Harding's previously expounded opinion that President Roosevelt was an international criminal. On no other theory could a payment of any such sum to Colombia be justified. Thus Harding handed an eagerly coveted and gratefully accepted political plum to young Theodore with one hand while with the other he sullied the record of his father.

As Assistant Secretary of the Navy, young Roosevelt took part in the negotiations over the notorious Teapot Dome affair. There are those who insist that if he had not been the son of his distinguished father, Theodore, Jr., would not have escaped, as he did, practically scot-free of criticism. The fact is that Roosevelt, while personally innocent, played an important role in this murky drama. So far as the record shows, he raised no objection to the transfer of these rich Navy oil lands. He conferred both with Secretary Denby and Secretary Fall as to the manner and means by which Fall assumed control of the lands. It surely should have occurred to a responsible official to seek legal advice. He might even have thought it prudent to discuss the matter with the President himself. There is nothing to indicate that he ever did.

Young Theodore was subsequently appointed Governor of Puerto Rico. He spoke Spanish fluently and he made an acceptable official. He got along well with the Puerto Ricans, and I will admit that anyone who can do that is deserving of praise. Later he was sent to the Philippines as Governor General. This was his station when Franklin D. Roosevelt was elected President in 1932. Theodore was bitterly opposed to his remote cousin, as all other members of his branch seemed to be, and he made an ineffective speech over the air from Manila in support of Hoover. He might as well have tried to blow out a forest fire from the same distance.

Since his return to this country in 1933, he has been a perennial aspirant for office—some office—any office. Probably this itch of his is the principal reason for his jealous dislike of Franklin D. Roosevelt, a feeling that is obviously shared by all of his immediate kin except Kermit. Young Theodore once referred to the President as "a maverick Roosevelt," an ineffectual slur, weakly imitative of his sister, Alice Roosevelt Longworth, whose biting tongue has coined more than one reference to her distinguished relatives that would have been in better wit if they had been in better taste. In his consuming desire to get ahead, Theodore II even mimicked the expressions and aped the mannerisms of his illustrious father. He once ventured to run for Governor of New York against Al Smith, and Smith gave him a humiliating beating. That was in 1926. No doubt Junior saw a brilliant career ahead. He would start as Assistant Secretary of the Navy, just as his father had done. Then he would become Governor of New York, just as his father had done, and from there he would blossom into the Presidency—also as his father had done. But, even with Sister Alice's active and constant help, he has never been able to make a second start, the reasons being that he has never known how to chart a true course and he has been lacking in political principles. Fortunately, it frequently takes more than merely a desire for office to acquire one, especially if it is an elective office.

In the First World War, the four sons of President Roosevelt distinguished themselves. As has already been said, Quentin died gloriously in battle. Archibald still suffers from an arm disability that he brought back from France when he

I almost never wear a coat at my work. In this case my recollection is that the photographer insisted that I "dress" for the occasion.

Meetings, meetings, meetings!

Questions, questions, questions!

Faces, faces, faces!

And one lone curmudgeon!

was invalided home. Kermit also showed himself to be of a fighting breed. When Hitler began to course Europe like a mad dog, Kermit went to England as a volunteer in the English Army with the rank of major. He even gave up his American citizenship in order to accomplish this. Young Theodore's record in France a quarter of a century ago was also of the best. There was no doubt of either his bravery or his ability as a soldier. He came home as a colonel in the last war, and he is back again in this one with the rank of Brigadier General and, unhappily, his carefully cultivated mannerisms.

I will here draw the curtain of merciful silence over the scandals of the Harding Administration—Fall, Daugherty, Denby, et al. The glaring ones are too well known to require repetition. As evidence of the low moral state of the country that existed at the time, be it recorded that no member of Harding's Cabinet save Denby, Secretary of the Navy, and he was forced out by public sentiment, resigned rather than continue to associate with such a discreditable Administration, thus, by inference at least, subscribing to its record.

Hughes continued to sit as ranking member at the Cabinet table with his *savoir faire;* farther down the table was Hoover, his covetous eyes on the President's chair. He would endure any mephitic air if only he could in time occupy that seat. And with these two sat other men whose sense of honor, it seems to me, should have called for prompt resignations if they were fully aware, as they must have been, of the misfeasance in public office of certain of their associates. But Hughes hung on until he was sent to the Supreme Court again—this time as Chief Justice—and Hoover stuck like a leech until, having at last anguishously determined ("I love you, I love you not") that he was a Republican, he became the nominee of that party for President.

A moral revulsion was on its way throughout the land. The people might be complacent about an administration at Washington that merely marked time, if it were at least respectable. But they would not stand for actual scandals involving members of the Cabinet. They did not like the pervasive rumors of liquor flowing freely at the White House, and they liked even less the sex stories of which the "Little Green House" was the center. So, although he was still serving his first term, Harding was definitely on the way out. And the man whose name was uppermost in the mind of the public as a successor to Harding was, as I have said, none other than my old friend Hiram Johnson. Johnson and his wife had never been abroad, and so in 1922 they decided to cross the Atlantic. The League of Nations was still an important issue in American politics. Johnson thought, I imagine, that he could take a look at the Old World, come back, and be more of an isolationist than ever —perhaps a more convincing one because he had seen with his own eyes.

When the Johnsons returned, a banquet of welcome was given to him in New York. I was invited and went. Whose idea it was or who financed it I do not know, but I was introduced to Samuel Koenig, who was then the Republican leader in the Borough of Manhattan, from whose presence and that of others such I gathered that the regulars were not uninterested in Johnson. Johnson made a speech, which was a ringing declaration, of course, against any foreign entanglements, through the League of Nations or otherwise. He was in high feather. The banquet was a great success as banquets go, and Johnson certainly was justified in looking forward with pleasurable anticipation to the next Republican National Convention. And I was happy for him.

Meanwhile, Chicago had grown tired of Blustering Bill Thompson in the mayor's office. It was tired of hearing him snort that he was going to "poke King George in the snoot." Sensing that he was a dead pigeon, Thompson announced in 1923, after hopefully hesitating, that he would not be a candidate. If he expected the people of Chicago to storm the City Hall *en masse* and demand that he reconsider, he was disappointed. Everybody agreed that it was the best idea that had ever incubated in a mountebank's head.

Arthur C. Lueder, postmaster, was then trotted out. Dr. John Dill Robertson, Thompson's Commissioner of Public Health, whose published idea was that Americans bathed too often and who said that as for him, he took a bath a year, entered the Republican primary against Lueder. Lueder won. He had to keep in the lead or run the risk of being asphyxiated. Apparently, the people didn't cotton to the notion of having one of the great unwashed at the head of their government, especially one who had been so closely associated with Thompson, whom, incidentally, washing hadn't helped much.

On the Democratic side, George Brennan, who since the death of Roger Sullivan had strongly entrenched himself in power, was the undisputed boss. He had no particular candidate in mind out of the many "Barkises" who were "willin'" for the top job of the city, but he did want someone who would be a credit to Chicago in contrast to what we had been having for eight years. I suggested Judge William E. Dever, who was then serving on the Appellate Court. As a gauge of the cleverness and broad-mindedness of Brennan as a political boss, I put it down here that Dever, before going on the bench, had been one of the leaders of the Carter Harrison faction and therefore opposed to the Sullivan-Hopkins-Brennan trio. Of course, as a member of the bench he had not been active in politics. Brennan knew what kind of man he was and he realized that he would make an unusually strong candidate. Dever was able, square, and upstanding. His character was of the best, and, in the end, Brennan managed so cleverly that every other man with mayoralty ambitions in the Democratic party willingly yielded to Dever, who was unanimously nominated by a harmonious party. At the suggestion of both Brennan and Dever, I organized an active Independent Republican committee to get behind Dever, and with everyone pulling together, he won by more than 100,000 votes.

But people are queer—regard Louisiana and Texas and Ham Fish's district if you don't believe it! Four years later Thompson came back to beat Dever! Dever had given Chicago one of the best administrations that it has ever had, either before or since, but because his very capable Superintendent of Schools, William McAndrew, as stubborn as a stubborn Scotchman can be, got into a terrific row with the Teachers' Federation and expended as much energy on trivialities as on great principles, the subsequent bitter attack on Dever was centered on the public schools. And it was Dever who paid with his political life. We do funny things with the vote in this country, but the return of Bill Thompson, who was still talking about busting the royal snoot of England, was one of the funniest. Yet it was no laughing matter.

It was evident that Hiram Johnson still wanted to run for President, in spite of the fact that the party men had turned to Coolidge as the logical choice of the party. Johnson had an opinion of Coolidge no higher than my own. But where to get money for a campaign? Albert Lasker and William Wrigley, Jr., had been of the group that had intended to support Johnson against Harding. Whether they would go along now that there was no Harding was a question that Johnson wanted answered.

The Johnsons were in Chicago on their way to California, and I was called in. Apparently whatever adverse feeling they had had as to me had been dissipated. I know that I felt about them as I always had. Lasker had the Johnsons, the Wrigleys, and the Ickeses out to his summer home at Ravina for dinner. Johnson, Lasker, Wrigley, and I drove back to the station in one car. On the way down we went into the question whether Hiram should be a candidate.

Lasker said he did not think that Coolidge could be beaten. Johnson thought that he could and I backed him up. Johnson wanted to run and I wanted him to have his chance. It was clear that Lasker and Wrigley didn't want him to. However, they felt a moral obligation, and finally Lasker and Wrigley each promised to put in a round sum, making it clear, however, that there would be no more from either of them.

With the money question momentarily disposed of, Johnson told us that Frank Hitchcock had consented to manage his campaign. This surprised me very much. Hitchcock had run Roosevelt's campaign in 1904 and had been his Postmaster General. Since that time he had been a political soldier of fortune. He was supposed to know the secret of bringing in Southern delegates. It wasn't much of a secret. A combination of promises and free spending did the trick. I made no comment on Hitchcock's selection, but I had my own shocked ideas on the matter.

The campaign was a dud. I had wanted to help in Illinois, where I might be expected to do my most effective work. But I was willing to do anything. Hitchcock, however, didn't want me about. Time was slipping fast and no start had been made in Illinois, where Johnson had always had a very strong following. Hitchcock did not want to have anything to do with me but he could not find anyone else. Finally, Johnson sent for me and asked me if I would go in as manager of his Illinois campaign. I readily agreed, after he had told me that while he hoped that I could get along with Hitchcock, he would back me up in any case of disagreement. Hitchcock was to continue as national manager. The first thing that Hitchcock tried to do was to force two of his camp-follower friends on me, making a hydra-headed management, with a majority to rule. I declined to join a debating society. Said Hitchcock to me: "You know that I could order you to do this, Mr. Ickes?" Said I to him, looking him full in the eyes: "Are you ordering it, Mr. Hitchcock?" Looking in another direction, he replied: "No, I am not." And that ended Hitchcock. He left Chicago that night, without accounting to anybody. He did not communicate with Johnson, nor did he resign to anybody. No one heard of him during the campaign, though I strongly suspected that he was one of the termites burrowing under the Coolidge cabin.

My efforts in this campaign were pretty well confined to Illinois. With the aid of the long-distance telephone, by means of which I searched out Progressives of former campaigns, I succeeded in putting together a full delegate ticket and in obtaining the necessary number of signatures to assure it a place on the ballot. It was hard work, though. I asked Lasker to go on as a candidate for delegate at large. He declined on the perfectly understandable ground that while he was always willing to help behind the scenes, he had never stepped out in front, which was true. I also asked William Wrigley, Jr., who loved to sit in prominent places with the prominent. He declined. Then, true to form, he ran for delegate at large on the Coolidge ticket. Undoubtedly he had contributed money there, too; again true to form.

Needless to say, the money that Wrigley and Lasker had contributed to Johnson for his campaign needed to be spread pretty thin. I doubt whether he had many contributions from other sources. If he had, it could not have amounted to much. My allotment for Illinois was $15,000. We sowed and reaped all of the trouble for Coolidge that we could with this totally inadequate sum, and on primary day we put over six delegates in the state pledged to Johnson.

It soon became as clear as day that Johnson could not hope to win, or even to make much of a showing, against the New England "sphinx" who was always about to burst into distending conversation. Johnson kept up the fight with dogged determination, although early he had given up any hope of success. Toward the end of the campaign he was to make a speech in Chicago after a tour of the West. When he arrived, I handed him a blistering attack on Coolidge that I had written with an acid pen. Convinced that he had nothing to lose, he read my draft, laid it aside, and then proceeded to write, in longhand, a speech that used Coolidge as a punching bag. He tore Coolidge to shreds. This longhand draft I have cherished as one of the few rewards of the campaign.

Unlucky Hiram Johnson! The breaks were all against him. With any kind of good fortune he would have had his fling in the Presidency, and I do not hesitate to give it as my opinion that he would have made a great President. He had ambition; he was forward-looking; he was financially and intellectually honest; he was humane; he had brains as well as guts; and he had had valuable experience. Politics can be a cruel thing; and not easy to divorce *a mensa et vincula.*

That was the year that Senator Bob La Follette of Wisconsin decided that it was then or never for him. As usual, he sent a delegation to the convention, and, also as usual, a Wisconsin platform was presented only to be rejected, as usual, with derisive Bronx cheers. He had wanted the regular nomination in 1912, but a nervous breakdown put him out of that race and he had been reaching for the torch ever since. Personally, and with Johnson out of the campaign, I was for La Follette as soon as he became a candidate on the Progressive ticket. However, I couldn't conjure up any hope for him.

Donald R. Richberg was active for La Follette and kept urging me in. He brought young Bob and Basil Manly to Winnetka one night to try to sign me up. Then Congressman Nelson of Wisconsin, La Follette's manager, came to my office to solicit my active interest. He said that he was without experience wider than state politics and did not feel up to the job. He urged me to go in and run the campaign nationally, with him keeping merely the title of manager. After all, I couldn't spend myself without stint every time that there was a cause, no matter how much I believed in it, so I regretfully declined. Senator La Follette carried his own state, and that was all.

Coolidge had easy sailing, as who wouldn't have had with John W. Davis for an opponent? Davis was really the original "poor little barefoot Wall Street lawyer."

With 1928 came Al Smith. The religious issue raised its vicious head. On the Republican side the leaders had taken at face value the words of Coolidge that he did not choose to run when, all of the time, it was his eager desire to be re-nominated—by force, if in no other way. Enter Hoover, the "humanitarian," "the great engineer." Harding had put him into his Cabinet as Secretary of Commerce and Coolidge had retained him. He had been building himself up for President since 1916, when he had rated one nominating speech (a feminine one from a non-delegate) and one convention vote. It had cost him a lot of time and effort and money, and in 1928 he finally made a three-point landing.

To me Hoover has always been—well, Hoover. I took no active part in the Hoover-Smith campaign, although I did vote for Smith. As a matter of fact, I have voted against every Republican candidate for President since Hughes in 1916. Prior to that I had voted for Bryan against Taft. I tried everything possible to persuade Hiram Johnson to steam up to contest with Hoover for the Republican nomination in 1932, but without success. The late Senator Cutting—what a loss to the Republic was his tragic death!—Senator Gerald Nye, and a few others of us believed that Johnson could have won. I still believe so. And if he had, what a battle royal it would have been between him and Franklin D. Roosevelt! When Johnson had definitely turned thumbs down, Gifford Pinchot, of Pennsylvania, wanted to have a try. He came out to Chicago to ask me whether, if he supplied me with his lists and paid the costs, I would send out over my signature a letter that he had drafted in his own behalf. We were friends then and I was willing to undertake anything against Hoover, although I did not care for the letter and did not believe that Pinchot had a chance. I helped him to the extent of sending out $3500 worth of letters, including postage, suggesting his availability, but very few agreed with me.

I was becoming more and more weary of politics. I didn't mind so much being on the losing side—I had become used to that. Perhaps I even took some pride in it. It was something to boast of and to be kidded about. At the worst it left me free to follow my own bent. At the best it was like rubbing one's fingers firmly over a nutmeg-grater. I owed nobody an explanation when I continued to shift from party to party in search of the better candidate. I had been a delegate at large to the Progressive convention in 1916 and to the Republican ditto in 1920. I did not know then—in fact I would not have dreamed it—that I was to be a delegate at large to the Democratic conventions of 1936 and 1940.

If there is anyone in the United States who can come close to this record, let him say so now or forever hereafter hold his peace.

*   *   *   *   *   *

In 1931 "Bill the Builder" (he wasn't being sarcastic, either) again ran for the Republican nomination for Mayor of Chicago. He had already served three four-year terms, broken only by the Dever incident. George Brennan had died and there was a scramble for his scepter. I had known from Brennan's own lips that he wanted Mike Igoe to succeed him as leader of the party, but there were a number of strong men who were not willing to yield to Igoe. Brennan had carefully built up the Slavs and the Italians, but the real leadership had been retained by the Irish. With Brennan out of the way, the Irish found themselves opposed not only by strong Slavic leadership, but by overwhelming numbers. Anton J. Cermak, who had been president of the County Board, decided that he wanted to be Mayor. For years Cermak had represented the liquor interests as their open champion. He was nominated for the job and he beat Thompson by almost 200,000 votes. Merriam and I had known Cermak and we did not like his record. It was bad. But he had made his pile, and we believed him when he told us that he would give a straight administration. Even with our doubts we knew that he could not be so bad as Thompson.

After his election, Cermak proceeded to put the Irish strictly in their place. The one Irish leader who had influence with Cermak was Edward J. Kelly. Kelly had been close to Brennan, too. He was a clever person who had come up, through politics, from nothing into a position of wealth and influence. He had even achieved the extraordinary distinction of becoming the Chief Engineer of the Sanitary District without ever having taken a course in engineering.

Before he died, Brennan had regarded Kelly as a distinct possibility for Mayor. He said to me on more than one occasion: "Ed Kelly is smart. He will go far." Kelly was close to Frank Hague, the Democratic boss of New Jersey. He was also thick with Bert McCormick of the *Tribune*. They had been thrown together when McCormick, briefly, was head of the Sanitary District Board (hold onto your seats, but I voted for Bertie on that occasion!), where Ed Kelly also worked.

Ed was never anyone's fool and undoubtedly he decided that it would not do him any harm to do the playing up to "McComic" that the "Morning Colonel" dearly loves. A little deference does not cost anything and sometimes it yields rich dividends. It has in this case, as for instance when, not so very long ago, McCormick made a public speech (I do not know who drummed up the audience for him unless it was Kelly) in which he said that Ed Kelly was the best Mayor that Chicago had ever had. Shades of Fred Busse! Be that as it may, after McCormick, as a candidate for re-election to said position on said board, was soundly beaten by Peter Bartzen, former Building Commissioner from the North Side, to the permanent political undoing of Bertie, Ed continued to court him and they became fast political friends.

Because of the Kelly-Hague influence, the majority of the Illinois delegation, which was controlled by Cermak, went to the Chicago convention in 1932 against Franklin D. Roosevelt. Illinois was very slow in climbing onto the Roosevelt bandwagon, with the result that it was very nearly left behind. Realizing that he had put his worst foot foremost, Cermak set about to build himself up with Roosevelt after the latter's nomination. Cermak was then at the height of his power, and he had become arrogant. It was openly said that he would be a candidate for the United States Senate at the next election for that office.

In the spring of 1933, Roosevelt had gone down to the coast of Florida, on a fishing trip. On his return he was to land at Miami. Cermak was resorting there and decided to meet the President-elect. There was a great crowd. A shot was fired and the bullet penetrated Cermak's abdomen. The newspapers insisted that an attempt had been made on Roosevelt's life and that Cermak had heroically intercepted the bullet. From this wound Cermak died a "hero's" death.

I never believed that the assassin who shot Cermak was after Roosevelt. In Chicago there were many more "doubting Thomases" who knew Cermak's not quite savory reputation. He had undoubtedly made revenge-hungry enemies. Cermak was wearing a bulletproof vest on that occasion, which was some indication that he stood in fear of an attempt upon his life. After his death there should have been a special election to fill the vacancy. However, an emergency

law was passed by the Illinois Legislature giving the City
Council the right to select for the unexpired term. No sooner
done than the organization got together and put Kelly into
the place. It required some broken promises to achieve that
result. With the advantage thus gained, Kelly was renominated and re-elected at the next election, in 1935, by an
enormous majority. He was too smart not to take advantage
of his opportunity, and he had the ability to do it, too. Moreover, he had the canny advice and active help of Pat Nash,
who, in his own right, is as clever as the next one. The Republican candidate, Emil C. Wetten, an imposing figure
physically, had been selected and financed by the Democrats,
and the rest was easy.

And so here was Chicago, for which some of us had given
a good many quarts of blood, not only with virtually all
gains lost but with machine politics more firmly entrenched
than ever and with the prospect that it probably won't be
changed for a long, long time. Some day it may breed another John Maynard Harlan or Charles E. Merriam.

That's what makes curmudgeons—bigger and better ones.
But in the meantime, I had quit Chicago and gone East to
try curmudgeoning on a bigger scale.

CHAPTER THIRTEEN

A CHINAMAN'S CHANCE

Thanksgiving, like ambassadors, cabinet-officers, and others
smeared with political ointment,
Depends for its existence on Presidential appointment.
—OGDEN NASH.

WHEN 1932 ROLLED AROUND, I felt that I had seen nearly
everything in the way of politics that was worth seeing.
It turned out that it had been only a trial heat for a balky
horse. True, I had worked for, with, and, holding my nose,
against scores of candidates—some outstanding, some not so
good, and some terrible; but I had never been one myself.
My position was remindful of the frustrated female who has
often been a bridesmaid but never a bride. However, it was
definitely from choice. I had never hankered for public office.
I can say in all truth that I never entertained seriously a
suggestion that I seek an elective office, except once for
judge. In the first place, I was plainly not the vote-getting
kind. No one will argue with that statement. Moreover, I
had seen too much of candidates ever to want to look like one
or behave like one. I belonged to that exclusive group sometimes referred to, derisively, as "kingmakers." And let me
say here in all frankness that my production, as such, was

not good even for peacetime. If I had gone in for quantity instead of quality, my score might have been higher.

I have said that I "never hankered for public office." This needs to be clarified. What I really mean is public "elective" office. I have been, on a number of occasions, not only a candidate for, but a holder of, various party offices, notably when the Progressive party still thought that it was going somewhere, although it was not always sure of the direction. But even as a holder of party offices, I never submitted my candidacy to a vote of the people—party people in this instance—except once. I would have the world know that the public records show that I was on one occasion triumphantly elected Republican precinct committeeman in the sixth voting district of New Trier Township, County of Cook, and State of Illinois. The Republican organization that had flourished for many years in that local territory had been held firmly in the grip of one William Busse, to whom I have already aptly, if irreverently, referred. Some of us determined to overthrow Busse, and this we did in the first revolution that had ever taken place among the township Republican organizations of the county. In that commando raid it seemed expedient for me to do a little doorbell-ringing and try to capture my own voting district. I found that it was not any trouble at all. The water wasn't particularly cold when I at last stepped in myself after telling so many people for so many years how to get more votes than the other fellow.

At the time of which I write, I was all wrapped up in a couple of campaigns—one to elect, for the third time, Mrs. Ickes, a Republican, a member of the Illinois General Assembly, and the other to make a Democrat, Thomas J. Courtney, State's Attorney. I was watching my step, while keeping these two balls in the air at the same time, when I was invited to add a third to my juggling act.

I had been head over heels for the nomination of Franklin D. Roosevelt for President. I had followed his career and thought highly of him, although I had never met him personally. Basil Manly, now a member of the Federal Power Commission, again came to see me, this time from Democratic headquarters at New York. He wanted me to start a Western Independent Republican organization for Roosevelt. I told him that, what with having a Republican and a Democratic candidate as it was, I was finding it rather difficult to keep party lines from becoming so snarled that none of us would ever be able to get them unraveled again, besides which I had decided that I was through with politics, except for an occasional foray into a local campaign that would interest me, when I became too bored with myself. Gentleman that he was, Manly felt that I was well within my rights and I saw him no more.

A few days later, however, Roscoe Fertich, originally an Albert J. Beveridge man from Indiana, but for many years a Washington lawyer, also sent by Democratic national headquarters, sought me out, as he had on former occasions ever since 1912. He thought that I was overdue for precipitation into another political jamboree. I gave him a copy of the prescription that I had already written out for Manly. He told me that he was glad to have seen me again and departed. When I got to my office the next day, I found Fertich with his feet on a desk in the outside office. He would have been smoking his pipe if he had been a smoker. I asked him "What the hell?" He repeated his formula. Again I scorned it. But when I found him in my office every day for several days, on each of which occasion he solemnly assured me that he was not going back to New York except with my assent to his proposal, he broke me down.

My Presidential voting box score up to that point looked something like this:

	Republican	Progressive	Democrat
1896	McKinley		
	(After all, I was a callow Republican.)		
1900	McKinley		
	(Roosevelt was running for Vice-President.)		
1904	Roosevelt		
	(By all means)		
1908			Bryan
			(Not even for Roosevelt would I vote for Taft.)
1912		Roosevelt	
		(Again and gladly.)	
1916	Hughes		
	(I was afraid of Wilson on the war issue and Hughes was first-rate.)		
1920			Cox
			(I couldn't stomach Harding and Cox had qualities.)
1924			Davis
			(The only chance to beat Coolidge, although at heart I was for La Follette.)
1928			Smith
			(I didn't like either Hoover or religious prejudice.)

So having told both Manly and Fertich many times that while I was going to vote for Roosevelt, I hadn't any intention of getting myself all lathered up in another national campaign, I found that it was this precise thing that I was to do. I agreed to head up a Western Independent Republican Committee for Roosevelt. Before opening headquarters in the Auditorium Hotel, I went on to New York, at Fertich's suggestion, to meet the field generals there. Most of my brief time I spent with Arthur F. Mullen of Nebraska, whose advice on Western matters was usually taken. He was all for the plan; in fact, he had been consulted about it in advance. Knowing that it would take the Democratic management some time to act, he advanced $2,000 by his personal check to get things started. I was introduced to Frank C. Walker, treasurer of the committee, and, for the first time, I met James A. Farley, who had already built up something of a reputation on the basis of his adroitness in lining up delegates for Roosevelt and because he had so ably handled the delegates after they had all been herded together under the same roof. This was my only visit to national headquarters during the campaign. I knew what I was supposed to do, and I was never one to stand about headquarters in full view of the candidate and the high command so that they would appreciate what a heavy burden I was carrying and how busy I was making myself. We did our job on an appropriation of $10,000 made to us by the Democratic National Committee.

I was chairman of the committee that consisted of James L. Houghteling of Chicago, treasurer; Roscoe Fertich, secretary; Henry A. Wallace of Iowa; George N. Peek of Illinois; John Napier Dyer of Indiana; Ralph Snyder of Kansas; Henry M. Wallace of Michigan; Frank W. Murphy of Minnesota; John G. Maher of Nebraska; David B. Robertson of Ohio; W. R. Ronald of South Dakota; and Edward E. Browne of Wisconsin.

Before really going overboard, I had talked the whole thing over with Anna, who was, as I have said, by that time actively campaigning for re-election to the Illinois General

Assembly, where she had already acquired both influence and standing in her own right as a legislator. She hadn't been too keen about my political schizophrenia, as evidenced by dividing my support between her, a Republican, and Courtney, a Democrat. If I should now come out publicly for Roosevelt, I would be doing something for which even the latest dictionary would not have a word. She herself wasn't particularly interested in Hoover, but not only was she a Republican, she was a Republican candidate, and therefore disposed to conform to the principle of political regularity.

My first argument was that I was against Hoover. I had voted against him in 1928 and intended to vote against him again. I not only distrusted his public leadership, I disliked his personality. Mrs. Ickes demurred on the ground that it would put her in a most embarrassing position, to which I replied that I had always been as irregular as a rail-and-rider fence built without line or plummet. I wouldn't surprise anyone unless I suddenly decided to be regular. Besides, I had my principles, such as they were. I assured her that she was bound to be elected in spite of hell and high water. I must follow out with exactness the irregular political course that I had charted for myself. I had been a sort of wobbly Republican from the first and had become wobblier with the years.

As a solace to her I promised her that if Roosevelt were elected I would try to get myself appointed Commissioner of Indian Affairs. Both of us had long been interested in Indians, I from college days when I had specialized in anthropology, ethnology, and folk psychology—the last to tune me up, no doubt, for future political experiences. I had trouble convincing her that I wasn't just trying to feed her soothing syrup, but at last she believed me and accepted my decision.

Among other political notables, Senator Hiram W. Johnson had come out for Roosevelt. His open declaration may have been brought about by a group of "smart-aleck" Republican newspaper editors in California (leave it to editors to try to catch someone's tail in the gate) who had sent him a long telegram demanding that he declare for Hoover. They didn't know Johnson or they wouldn't have dared him like that. Even if he had been married to the press he would have been no John Thomson's man.

Along about October, a frantic long-distance telephone call came from New York headquarters. Farley had given out a statement that was supposed greatly to have offended Johnson. Judge Francis Heney had telephoned from Los Angeles to say that something had to be done about it at once. Would I hop onto the first airplane for the Pacific coast? Characteristically, I was willing to argue. I insisted that I wasn't familiar with the facts and that we ought to be able to handle the misunderstanding, whatever it was, over the telephone wires, anyway. So insistent was New York that I finally agreed to take to the air if Roosevelt himself would ask me to go as his representative. The request came from Roosevelt by telegraph and I started at once for San Francisco.

When I arrived, much bedraggled and airsick, Johnson wanted to know if I were crazy. I wasn't sure, so I left it to him to decide. He hadn't known that he was supposed to have been offended by Farley until I told him so. His nose wasn't even slightly out of joint. On the contrary, he was then in the act of mobilizing his Republican friends for a big mass meeting in San Francisco, at which, subsequently, he went all of the way out for Roosevelt. Later he repeated at Los Angeles. Anyhow, I got something out of this hysterical trip. I persuaded Johnson to make a speech in Chicago.

When he came later, we gave him one of the biggest and most enthusiastic meetings of the campaign, with me doing the introducing. The following night I took him to Rockford, Illinois, for another cheering rally.

And so the campaign progressed and came to a great and glorious end. Roosevelt, as must have been predetermined from the beginning (my Calvinism cropping out again), was elected. The Lord only knows what shape we would be in today if he hadn't been. Mrs. Ickes, Republican, was elected, too, as usual at the head of her ticket, and so was Courtney, the Democrat. It was my biggest year. Apparently, the worm had come to the well-known turning and had literally done a double back flip-flop.

Mr. and Mrs. Charles de Y. Elkus of San Francisco were in Chicago just after election. Elkus was a friend of John Collier's and was himself much interested in Indians. We discussed the Commissionership. This started the ball rolling. Elkus volunteered to communicate with Senator Hiram Johnson and subsequently Johnson and I had some correspondence on the subject. He assured me that he would gladly do all that he could for me, but he also took the position, which I regarded as proper, that he could not himself volunteer any recommendations for appointments. A good rule in the circumstances.

In the meantime, I had been thinking the matter over, and while I was still willing to be Commissioner of Indian Affairs, it didn't altogether appeal to me. The notion came to me that if, for the first time in my life, I should go out for anything, I might just as well try to become Secretary of the Interior. It would be no more painful or fatal to be hung for a secretary than for a commissioner.

Matters were in a state of flux when Newton D. Jenkins

came one day to my office and suggested that it was about time that I tried to do something for myself. I had always been expending myself for others, he argued. Quite on his own, he proposed me for the Interior Department and he offered to go to Washington and spy out the land. This he did, but he discovered no spot soft and yielding to the touch. Then John Collier wrote to me and I set out for Washington myself. There I talked with Collier, Lewis Meriam, and Nathan R. Margold, and, naturally, with Johnson. It was clear, however, that Collier himself would like to be Indian Commissioner, although he was perfectly genuine in his offer to me of support. The idea that Collier and Meriam and Margold had developed was that we couldn't do much for the Indians by way of the Commissionership alone, but if we should have, say, the First Assistant Secretaryship of the Interior besides, it would be all to the good for the red men. By this time I had definitely decided to shoot for the stars. I can't say that anyone thought that I had a Chinaman's chance, but here was one pseudo-Chinaman who was willing to make a try for it.

My difficulty was in having my name presented to the President-elect. I talked to Johnson, Senator Cutting, Senator Nye, and Senator La Follette. They all assured me that they would be glad to see me in the Cabinet, but that there wasn't much they could do about it, if anything. None of them was a Democrat. Then one day in the corridor of the S.O.B. (Senate Office Building) I encountered Senator Costigan of Colorado. He blew me off my feet by saying that he thought that I ought to be in the Cabinet as the representative of the independent Republicans who had supported Roosevelt. Moreover, he offered to do what he could to submit my name to Roosevelt. Now at last I had found someone willing to nominate me. I could be a candidate and at the same time manage my own campaign, but I couldn't electrify Roosevelt by sounding off voluntarily as to my many rare qualifications. Besides which I hadn't yet met him.

While I was still in Washington, Roosevelt came through en route to Warm Springs. He had sent word to Senators Johnson and Cutting that he would like to see them on his train. Johnson was the first to have his interview. Roosevelt offered to appoint him Secretary of the Interior. Johnson declined, but he couldn't suggest my name because the President-elect did not ask for suggestions. Later in the same day, Cutting had his meeting with the President-elect, and he was tendered the same post. Cutting also expressed his regret, but, under urging, finally agreed to give the offer further consideration. He told me that he did not see how he could take it, but in all sincerity I urged him to do so. I was fearful that if he too refused, there would be but a slim chance for any member of our group to occupy a seat at the first table. I reasoned that Roosevelt, with entire justification, could absolve himself of any further obligation to the Progressive Republicans, since he had already offered a Cabinet office to two of them and had been refused by both.

I returned to Chicago, believing in my own mind that my bolt had been shot. At any rate, there wasn't anything further that I could do until Cutting should make up his mind. I wasn't even interested in the Indian Commissionership any longer. At this stage, Raymond Moley, whom I had not met, called me up from New York to say that Roosevelt was getting together a group to discuss some economic matter. Would I come to New York for the meeting? Moley had asked George W. Norris, Hiram Johnson, Cutting, La Follette, and other Progressive Republicans to suggest a representative and they had named me. I said that I would answer the roll call. I wondered whether this was being offered as a consolation prize, but at any rate I would have a chance to meet Roosevelt.

On my way to New York I stopped off in Washington to pick up the latest news. The first thing that I learned was that Cutting had declined the appointment. Nor had he suggested my name to Roosevelt. He had not been asked for a nomination either, and his position, in the circumstances, was the same proper one as Johnson's.

The next day was a Monday, some time about the middle of February, and I was due to go up to New York that night. During the afternoon I ran into my friend Fertich, who had been working his head off for George Peek for Secretary of Agriculture. He stopped long enough to agree with me that I didn't have a chance to join the elect. However, as we were talking Fertich spied Arthur F. Mullen talking to Senator Thomas J. Walsh of Montana. Fertich told me that Mullen had wanted to be Attorney General but had been turned down. We butted in on the conversation and, as luck would have it, Mullen agreed to maneuver my name before the President-elect for me. Secretly I hoped, just to make sure, that he would spell it out carefully. Mullen had never met Johnson, and I took him into Hiram's office. He made an arrangement to call Roosevelt at seven o'clock that night while I would be on my way to New York.

I hadn't the least idea that anything would ever come of Mullen's telephone call; he might not get through, as a matter of fact. But at least I had the satisfaction of feeling that I had slung my last pebble and could do no more. I arrived at Governor Roosevelt's home at the appointed hour of 10:30 the following morning, and, along with a lot of other conso-

lation-prize winners, was ushered into the study on the second
floor. Shortly thereafter, Roosevelt appeared. Someone stood
up between the President-elect and me and started introducing those whom Roosevelt did not know. I wasn't included
in the introductions, because the introducer didn't know me
from Adam's overworked off ox, nor I him. When the introductions were finished, Roosevelt inquired "Is Mr. Ickes
here?" I made my presence known.

There followed a short conference, during which Roosevelt outlined his ideas to the group. I am not an economist
and didn't even at that time pretend to be one, so that much
of the discussion went over my head. I have always been smart
enough not to simulate wisdom in fields where I have none.
When the discussion was at an end we all filed out. I had
reached the head of the stairway when one of his staff caught
up with me and said that the Governor wished to see me as
soon as he had finished a brief talk with Mr. Baruch, whom
I was also seeing for the first time. I was kept waiting but a
few minutes. As I sat tête-à-tête with the President-elect, he
said:

"Mr. Ickes, you and I have been speaking the same language for the past twenty years, and we have the same out-
look. I am having difficulty finding a Secretary of the Interior.
I want a man who can stand on his own feet. I particularly
want a Western man. Above all things, I want a man who is
honest, and I have about come to the conclusion that the
man I want is Harold L. Ickes of Chicago."

I uttered a few conventional nothings without even pretending to be coy. I required no coaxing. After all, this was
the job that I wanted—miraculously falling into my lap.
Roosevelt went on to say that I wasn't to consider the matter
closed, as he wished to discuss it with Tom Walsh, who was

going to be his Attorney General, and with Cordell Hull, who was to be his Secretary of State, as well as with Senators Johnson, Norris, Cutting, La Follette, and others. He asked me where I would be at seven o'clock that night. I replied that, appropriately enough, I would be at the Hotel Roosevelt. He said that I would hear from him.

I was as nervous as a poor wretch waiting for his banker to warm up. I betook myself to a movie in the afternoon and had a celebrating dinner, with some good French wine, with my friend Charles E. Merriam at a speakeasy (one of the results of Hoover's "noble experiment") that he wot of. I was back at the hotel by seven o'clock. Shortly thereafter Moley called me to say that he was coming to pick me up. I met him downstairs and after we were settled in the car, he turned to me and said: "Did you have any idea that the Governor was going to make you that proposal this morning?" I told him that I hadn't. Moley said that he hadn't either, but that "the Governor sometimes does things that way." I still couldn't guess from the way Moley talked whether I was in or out, although I felt hopeful. His ambiguous language didn't serve to diminish my nervousness.

Soon after reaching the Governor's house I was ushered into his study. Frances Perkins was there. The President-elect then put on his best Santa Claus smile and said: "I would like to have the Secretary of the Interior meet the Secretary of Labor."

It was just like that. And it wouldn't happen again in a millennium. The newspapers were taken by surprise and so was everyone else, myself included. The press had to account for it somehow, and so, as if by common consent, they opined that my appointment was the pay-off to Hiram Johnson for his help in the campaign. Some newspapermen continue to insist upon this. Johnson cordially supported the suggestion when it was made to him, and the same was true of the others whom Roosevelt consulted, but that was as far as their efforts in my behalf went. In the circumstances, that was all that could be expected of them. They probably could have blocked my appointment, but only to the extent that they didn't were they responsible for my good fortune. I feel that I owe it to these men to protect them from the public wrath that might be visited upon them if they were known to be guilty of my appointment.

Some time later I was to read with interest Raymond Moley's account of "behind-the-scenes stuff" which appeared in the *Saturday Evening Post*. From it I was almost persuaded that if there were any glory to be had from my elevation, it was his. Sic him!

CHAPTER FOURTEEN

MR. I. GOES TO ████████████*

"I love my fellow-creatures—I do all the good I can—
Yet everybody says I'm such a disagreeable man!
And I can't think why!"
—WILLIAM S. GILBERT.

I HAD TO RUSH to my tailor for some new clothes. My ████ hat long had been used as a crèche for ████████ rabbits, although I had never been able to pull one of them out. And I was in need of a new "funeral" suit.

I took my family with ███ to Washington for the inauguration and incidentally to hear me sworn ███ on that momentous night of the fourth of March 1933, in the oval room on the second floor of the White House. I have always been proud of the fact that I was made official by that great jurist, the late Benjamin N. Cardozo.

The next morning ██ took over. I doubt if ever a man went into ████ Cabinet as ██████ as I was. I did not have to be told that Interior was the black sheep of the ████████ family. Besides which, ████████ ██████ ███████████ had raided it ████████ for bureaus to build up their own de-

---

* I am not able to write as freely as I might were I a private citizen. Burning questions will have to smolder until some other time. Some day, when I retire from office and can stretch out on my piazza and feed the doves of peace, I may do something about it.

272

partments way back in the █████████ ████████████ █████████.
The ████████████████ scandal was still fresh in the minds of
everyone; morale was at a low ebb; there was little fight left.
Come to think of it, why was the ████████████████████
spread so thickly over █████████████ when the ███████████
was *particeps criminis* even if it weren't *particeps pro* ██████?
Just preparing a bed of roses for me, I suppose.

I had been cautioned to watch out for ████████████████ who
would try to "do me dirt." This was pure ██████████████ in
view ███ my state of mind. Some had urged me to retain
█████████ █████████ ██████████ that others insisted ██████████
███ ██████, if I did not want to find myself in trouble. I knew
of █████████ █████████ who ought to "get the █████████" and I
lost no time in holding it open for them. ██████ among the
first things that I did was to persuade the ████████████████ to
appoint John Collier as Commissioner ███ █████████ Affairs,
a job that he has filled with distinction ever since. I had another good break when I appointed Nathan Margold ████
Solicitor. █████████ would not let me go wrong even if I
████████████. He is a great man on the law and ███ the utmost
intellectual integrity. A rare combination of qualities, ███████.

I could go on indefinitely reciting the names of industrious, able, and patriotic personnel in Interior but I do not
want to ████████████ even the idea ████████████████ the
"begat" chapter of ███████████████████. I believe that the
organization of my Department has been greatly strength-
ened during the past several years. Already largely under
Civil Service when I assumed office, I have supported and
even initiated, moves to extend the Civil Service to offices
that were not thereunder when I took ████████. There are
many scientific agencies in Interior, and when vacancies have
occurred, the endeavor has always been ███ fill them with

competent people, regardless ▆▆ politics. A great many of the questions, aside from scientific ones, that come to us for consideration and solution are legal ones, with the result that, next to the ▆▆▆▆▆▆▆▆▆▆▆▆▆▆▆, we are called upon to handle legal business more varied in character and more important in concept than ▆▆▆▆▆▆ other agency of the ▆▆▆▆▆▆▆. This has required an able legal staff, and Interior has ▆▆▆.

There is a constant ▆▆▆▆▆▆ against "bureaucrats" in Government—"bureaucrats" in many instances being those conscientious public servants who won't make a quick decision in favor of a private as against the ▆▆▆▆▆▆ interest. Once ▆▆▆▆▆ I offer myself as an ▆▆▆▆▆▆▆▆▆▆ for uttering the heresy that, without a reasonable-minded and smoothly functioning bureaucracy (yes, ▆▆▆▆▆▆▆▆▆▆), the Federal Government would be more of a milling ▆▆▆▆ than was the Tower ▆▆ Babel.

In ▆▆▆▆▆▆▆▆ I have occupied a favored seat for one interested in watching what ▆▆▆ Pearson and ▆▆▆ Allen have dubbed the "merry-▆▆-round." It is an apt description, except, in ▆▆ own case as to ▆▆▆▆▆▆▆. One may whirl around and around in ▆▆▆▆▆▆▆▆ circles while seated on top of a ▆▆▆▆, or an ▆▆▆▆▆▆▆, or a ▆▆▆▆▆▆, or a ▆▆▆▆▆, or even squatted in a ▆▆▆▆▆▆, and, though many are the grabs at ▆▆▆▆▆▆▆▆▆, few are the prehensile fingers that can securely clutch them.

When I came to ▆▆▆▆▆▆▆▆ in 1933 I had never been closer to the White ▆▆▆▆▆▆ than the iron fence. Once, during World War ▆, I did have a letter of introduction to ▆▆▆▆▆▆▆ Tumulty, secretary to ▆▆▆▆▆▆▆ ▆▆▆▆▆▆▆ Wilson, but I was never able to ▆▆▆▆▆▆ ▆▆ ▆▆ person. I

had been too active in politics and too friendly to Theodore
████████████ to suit ████████.

At the outset I adopted a very simple formula. It was this:
"I will so conduct my office that, at the end of any day, I can
put on my ████ and walk out for good and ████." Yet I have
managed to break all records for longevity among ████████████
of the Interior. I have been in office longer by approximately
two years (if I may guess at the probable date that this will
appear ████ print) than Secretary ████████ A. Hitchcock, who
owned the longest previous record.

Of course I have not been able to do all that I have wanted
to do. Much of this has been due to my own ████████████.
Being human, I have made ████████████. Being finite, I
have ████████████████████ for improvement. Other fail-
ures may have been due to ████████ and ████████████
and ████████████████ of which there is a plethoric abun-
dance in the ████████████████████. There have been
gangings ███ by men who preferred to see an enterprise, in
which they protested their interest, either ████████████████
or ████████████████████████, rather than to see
conferred on ████████████ which they themselves had
no chance either to ████████ or to ████.

I knew enough about politics to realize that if I should
"play" it in the ordinary acceptation of the word I would
████████; that the best politics is the ████████ politics—████ at
all, if possible—in an executive office. I would not need the
favor of the politicians if I could do a job that would satisfy
the ████████. This I set as ███ goal and I have had my ████
on it throughout the ████████ of my public service.

████ it hasn't been ████████ sailing. I have had my clashes
with the politicians. I have battled openly with some of the
most unabashed of them. Congressional attacks—silly self-

indulgences many of them—have left more than one ████████
on me, but I have never run away from an investigation or
████████ my knee to an unscrupulous political will. I have
never played ████████ politics. I have never played
████████ politics.

When my career in ████████ started I felt no antipathy
to████ the newspapers. I had enjoyed the newspaper game
and cherished the camaraderie that exists among newspaper
████. Although the ████████ ████████ had
never liked me—nor I, ███—it had not used me brutally before
I came to ████████. Occasionally we even found ourselves playing on the ████████ team. I was as bitterly opposed
to the ████████ gang as any ████████ man had ever
thought of being, and I had no circulation-building motive.
I had supported Theodore ████████ in 1912, a campaign
which gave the *Tribune* the opportunity to strengthen the
foundation of its present power which, I may say, it wields
like a cheap, ████████ bully.

I was well aware, from watching others, that a man in public life is expected to take a lot of punishment from newspapers, but no one realizes the extent or the brutal severity
of it until he ████████ becomes its target. No one who has
not been in the capital ████████ can conceive of the limits
to which newspapermen will go to ferret out scandals or to
involve a public man in reputation-destroying ████████.
Some will even play the role of *agent* ████████. Any
Daniel will do for these ████████.

The answer may be that competition in ████████ among
newspapermen is too keen. The cream of the profession is
sent ████ to get ████—to make it, if necessary. The result
is that ordinarily decent ████████, which the great
majority of newspapermen must have been ████████

███████████████, are willing to impale a public official, if only for the opportunity it gives them to do some ███████ writing about █████ wrigglings. It is cruel vivisection, in and ███ itself. And this is exactly what happened to me before I was aware of the technique. It goes to show what a greenhorn ██ was.

I was plugging along, trying to build up my ██████████; trying to achieve an *esprit de* ████████ which, after ██████████ and one or two ██████████, was at a low ebb; trying to do an honest day's work and to see that those under me did likewise. For all of my curmudgeonly ways, I was not conscious that there were newsmongers preparing to █████ up on me.

Some of the columnists began to operate on me. Some of these were just ██████████ ██████████ who had no credit with the public, but only a smelling ██████████. But there were a few able to do real harm because they had built up reputations of ██████████████████. It was one such who touched off the fireworks, so far as ██ was concerned.

I had never known Ernest ██. Lindley. I had never even heard of him. Perhaps that was ████ offense. But the fact is that he meant no more to me than a cub ███████████████ the ██████████ *Beacon*. And he ██████████ now. But Lindley had to get news. He wanted to bay at the head of the pack. So, he began uttering libels concerning my ██████████, utilizing as convenient targets and ██████████ at me two important men in Interior—First Assistant Secretary Ebert ██. Burlew, and Louis ██. Glavis. The ██████████ ██████████ in ██████ York was printing his ██████—██████████ is the word. The day came when Burlew and Glavis felt that they had had enough bruises ██████████ the belt and that it was up to them to hit back. I assured them that I had no objection to their filing libel suits. They consulted one of the best libel lawyers in ██████████ who assured them that they had strong cases.

Then ██████████ came to my office. He was █████ about the gills, and oh! ██ █████████████. He didn't want anything to do with a libel suit, nor did he want ████ newspaper that was paying him to be assessed possibly ████████ damages. He pleaded with me to help him out of his jam. His ████████ and ██████████ and ████████████ and ██████ and ██████ ██ resulted in my sending for Burlew ████████████████ was prepared to go to court, and asking him as a favor to me to drop the proceedings that were about to get under way.

For all of this, ████████████ has continued to ██████████ ████████████████████████—not viciously, but persistently, and for no other known reason. He can't somehow bring himself to forgive the man who put him under at least the obligation to be fair, because that man was instrumental in keeping him out of court. His ████████ moved me, but they never would again.

I was near to ████████████ then, and in ███████ I was nearer it. I had been putting on a good show as Public Works Administrator (but I am getting ahead ████████ story.)

CHAPTER FIFTEEN

WE GIRD FOR WAR

Better build schoolrooms for "the boy" than cells and gibbets
for "the man."
—ELIZA COOK.

OW THAT I AM in Washington, not only by my own admission, but by uncommon dissent, this ought to be the
place to inhale a long breath and take down my hair. I recently celebrated my tenth anniversary as Secretary of the
Department of the Interior, but I heard no clanging of bells
or tooting of horns on that occasion, despite the fact that it
was a double celebration in that I have broken all records
for longevity in this particular job. Of course I didn't expect
a national holiday to be declared. I didn't even look forward to special exercises in the schools where happy little
children would recite original odes written in my honor.
If there is anything that I have learned during the four and
one-half decades since I first hesitantly thrust my big toe into
turgid political waters to test the temperature, it is never to
expect anything except the unexpected.

If the reader suspects that I am saying nothing at all when
I might be saying something, I will willingly enter a plea of
nolo contendere or even of "guilty," if that be insisted upon.

I am not even fooling myself. Perhaps I have done my "public" a grievous wrong in leading it through fourteen discursive chapters while holding out the carrot of hope that some time I would get down to cases and discuss how crummy or even wormy is the public record of some of my associates in Washington as compared with my own incomparable one!

I will not quarrel with anyone who becomes peeved, as it dawns upon him that instead of disinterring a few corpses I have resolved myself into a sepulchral silence. All that I can plead in my own defense is that, for once in my curmudgeoningly career, I mean well. I even wrote a chapter during the inscribing of which I realized that I could not print it while still a member of President Roosevelt's official family. Then I essayed a censoring of it which I thought might get it by. What I have done to the previous chapter is nothing compared with my operations on that candid canvas. But in the end, I realized that the very appearance of the chapter would be a challenge to the ingenious or even to the disingenuous. There might even appear a pretended elucidation by someone of sharp wit but ill will and so I decided that that chapter had better go into my safe-deposit box for future reference.

It is beside the point, but for whatever light it may inject into this darkness, I may say here that, although it may not be generally known, I have twice submitted my resignation to the President—the first time in 1936, after he had been re-elected, and again in 1940, ditto. In making this admission I am innocent of any desire to start an uprising against the President for his failure on either of these occasions to perform a popular act by taking advantage of the opening that I gave him. What I am trying to sidle up to is the fact that it isn't altogether my fault that I cannot season this particular dish with mustard and cayenne pepper and tabasco sauce as you may have expected me to do. You are like a guest who has been invited to what you had at least some reason to believe might be a Lucullan feast only to find yourself served with ham and eggs and one cup of coffee brewed according to the President's formula—if you can call that coffee.

What I have been determinedly circumlocuting about is that while logical continuity at this point calls for at least some account of my sayings and doings vis-à-vis other officials during the past ten years, I will have to disappoint you, with the promise (or threat) that maybe some day I will write a sequel—a bloody one!

I have referred too briefly to the Public Works Administration (some day it will rate a book of its own, but not of my authorship) and how it nearly drove me into voluntary retirement. The PWA constitutes such an exciting and satisfying chapter of my Washington experience that my story would be incomplete (it is statical enough as it is) if nothing more were to be said of it. So I offer this comment because, in view of the war, it is particularly timely.

In one of his recent fireside chats, the President raised this question: ". . . where would we be today if the Government of the United States had not begun to build many of its factories . . . more than two years ago—more than a year before war was forced upon us at Pearl Harbor?"

The President might have asked an even more dramatic question. He might have inquired where we would be if, despite the earnest, if misguided, hell-raising both by Congress and by the press, and by large bodies of public opinion, we had not started to get ready for war when we did *nearly ten years ago!*

Yes, we did start girding our loins for war early in 1933,

and it is important that we do not lose sight of the fact if we want a clear focus, as of today.

The armed forces of the country now have merely to hint to Congress that they need money for war purposes to have their wants satisfied. The wealth of the nation is being poured out for the use of the Army and the Navy and the Marine Corps with no questions asked and no strings attached. All of us may be grateful for this.

I hope that it is not ungenerous of me to recall the days when Congress not only would not vote the money to build up the Army and the Navy, but publicly rebuked those who found a perfectly legitimate and honorable way to do so without specific authorization. In those days the Navy was an unwanted child. The Army was in a higher caste because it was scattered about in fragmentary posts that meant business for many a Congressman's "constits." Pray God that no Congress of the future will be a flash-back to the Congress of those dingy (stingy) days. Less than ten years ago, it was a race between a Navy-minded President and a penny-foolish Senate and House. Fortunately for the United States, and the Allied cause, the President had the wit to win.

None of us who lived through that dank period, especially in Washington, needs to have recalled the fearsome hour when Franklin D. Roosevelt was sworn in as President, and proceeded, almost with the same breath, to close every bank in the country on the theory that it was the only way to save some of them. And so it proved to be. Panic was in the air. Millions of people were half-fed, shred-barely clothed, and living more like kennelless dogs than human beings. It became the new President's most important job to see to it that people were provided with at least a minimum of food, clothing, and shelter; to save as many tottering banks and wobbly industries as he could.

Most of us will remember how boldly he attacked the most desperate problem that ever faced a Chief Executive, not excepting the one that had confronted Abraham Lincoln nearly seventy-five years before.

The "business administrations" that had been going on in Washington under three Presidents had ruined virtually everybody in the country (as well as their own reputations) and the day when the mortgage fell due had at last arrived.

Spurred by an existing national emergency, a panicky Congress lost no time in passing, among other pieces of remedial legislation, the National Industrial Recovery Act, hereinafter refered to as the NIRA. Congress, it seemed, could move faster in those days than it did subsequently, when it developed a slow, painstaking, and supercritical streak, which it continued to maintain even when the Nazi dogs were ready to spring at our throats. But in 1933 Congress quickly turned into flour the grist that came to it in the form of the NIRA.

First off, it appropriated the then staggering sum of $3,300,-000,000 to be spent on permanent public works, and it gave the Administrator, to be appointed by the President, the right to set up a Public Works Administration. The President honored me with that appointment.

I wonder how many people remember that the first allotment out of what, up to that time, was the largest single appropriation ever made by this or any other government, was the sum of $237,000,000 to the Navy for the building of warships. Many of those who may not remember it will at least recall that twenty-five years ago we fought "a war to end war." So autointoxicated were we with our clever and idealistic phraseology that some of us actually believed that there would be no more wars. How could there be a war after Congress had passed, and the President had signed, an act *outlawing* war? (It was like saying that there will be no more murders because there's a law against them.) And if there were to be no more wars, why spend good money building naval vessels? Why even finish the ships that were in course of construction? (Better, I suppose the reasoning was, to throw it away on the stock market as we had done, to our sorrow, in the late '20's.)

So the statesmen of the world, with Americans well in the lead, called a conference of the victorious nations, to be held in Washington, where the boutonniered and gray-spatted wisenheimers produced a brain child and named it Naval Ratio—little Rollo Naval-Ratio. What a cute child it was. Its paternity was variously boasted by the United States, Great Britain, Japan, and France with Italy blushing slightly too. And since all of the assembled diplomats were gentlemen and represented countries that could be trusted—especially in the case of Japan, where they lived by the uncompromising and lofty code of "Bushido"—there was no doubt at all in anyone's mind that, for the duration of the resulting treaty, everybody would be an Alphonse to someone's else Gaston.

Certainly the United States made no attempt to evade. With our flare for emotional goodwill it was a wonder that we didn't go far beyond the terms of the treaty and not only sink everything that smelled of gunpowder, but dismantle our Navy yards and arsenals and blow up all of the machinery that had so wickedly been making armor plate.

We didn't quite do that—we simply determined to let them rot and rust. But we did tow to a safe distance offshore all unfinished dreadnoughts and battleships, finished and in course of construction, of various categories, and there blew them to hell. Remember? It was a practical application of the good old Pollyanna "peace-at-any-price" doctrine of the Republicans and the Pacifists who hadn't liked the way the first World War had been managed and who were going to lead civilization by the hand into the "never-never" land that they had "discovered" and "colonized."

We didn't even have sense enough (I use the editorial "we" because, in the interest of unity, I desire not to say "they") to put the acetylene torch to that great store of steel scrap and save it against possible urgent use in the future. If we had thought that salvage was more worth while than destruction, we would probably have sold the scrap to Japan anyhow just to prove that we were not kidding. Those dear little "Nordics!" The excuse for sending the ships to Davy Jones' locker was that it would give valuable target practice to the few ships that we were saving!

But why should we have engaged in target practice if there were to be no more wars? I don't believe that I can answer that one myself.

What greater proof could the American people have asked that there would never be another war—especially for us—than the junking of a great new American Navy? There couldn't very well be, could there, with nothing left to fight with? The enemy might blow us to smithereens and steal all of our possessions, but if we had nothing to fight with, how could there be a war? It always had taken and always would take two to make a fight, even although it requires only one to accomplish a massacre. Hats off to Frank B. Kellogg who "outlawed" war in so many words, and to the State Department that "implemented" the peace pact by persuading the United States and our principal naval allies to scuttle their ships and go and build no more.

Those little Japs of loving kindness! We were getting an *hors d'oeuvres* of their "Bushido" and didn't know it. While Uncle Sam was mooning over the serenity and security of life without a battleship on the place, the Japs were beginning to get ready for Pearl Harbor!

Germany would be a pacifist for a good long time—at least until it was again strong enough to bear arms!

Well, it was true, there might not be another war, but we failed to take into account that hell could pop even in peace. And hell did pop, believe me, when the newspapers screamed in headlines to the people of the country that "that warmonger" in the White House was squandering $237,000,000 of *their* money on the rebuilding of a Navy that the Republicans had scuttled—to make sure that there would never be another war—enough money to employ many thousands of faithful Democrats and starving Republicans to rake leaves and cut grass. What was he thinking about, anyway? Hadn't he heard of the International Conference, the law to outlaw war, or of little Rollo Naval-Ratio? Didn't he know that there wasn't going to be any more war because all of our warships—or most of them—were on the bottoms of the oceans? Was that F.D.R.'s idea of a two-ocean Navy?

I cannot say what the President was thinking, because I am no mind-reader. It is hard to believe that he saw from that distance the war clouds that were still below the horizon. He may have had a trick periscope that permitted him to "peek see," but I doubt it. Maybe it was that being congenitally, as well as by choice, Navy-minded, this former Assistant Secretary of the Navy just couldn't bear the thought that we had nothing worth calling a fleet. And Congress, without realizing, as it sometimes doesn't, what it was doing, had adopted language in the NIRA which made it legally possible for the President to spend money in this and other directions by way of shocking the "Milquetoasts" of the Nation. So, there was nothing that could be done at the moment to interrupt the project, however much the newspapers might cry and Congress cuss and rage. It didn't even change the situation when Senator Nye went out to discuss the outrage in level tones and with cultured vehemence before women's clubs! The money had been appropriated and a healthy chunk of it was being spent to give us a Navy.

As recently as 1940, prominent citizens were orating and newspapers were declaiming that if Roosevelt was so smart and knew that Europe was suddenly to break out in a white heat of war that would threaten even us, WHY HADN'T HE DONE SOMETHING ABOUT IT INSTEAD OF SITTING DOWN THERE IN THE WHITE HOUSE INDULGING IN FIRESIDE CHATS?

These were the same voices that had screamed themselves into a state of chronic laryngitis in 1933 when Roosevelt, entirely on his own, had proceeded to do just that. If he had not, we would have been caught absolutely flatfooted without a Navy and lacking many another bit of important fighting equipment.

Wind and wave may destroy a Navy, and wind alone may stop one from being built, but not in this instance. Without debating the issue or asking anyone's leave, the President, through the Navy, and on the strength of the $237,000,000 nest egg, proceeded to get the nation ready for whatever might befall—as indeed it did in its own good time. The pacifists could blow up the Navy later, if they needed more target practice, but so far as he was concerned, we were going to have a Navy while he was President. And before the country realized what was doing, down the ways slid two air-craft carriers—the *Yorktown* and the *Enterprise*.

In passing, let us salute the *Yorktown*, glorious casualty of Midway! I thrill to the story of how she was fighting her way to port and safety when overtaken by a Jap submarine that put two bombs into her listing hulk and finished her. The *Yorktown*, like the *Enterprise*, was built to take punishment —built out of PWA make-work funds—and who cannot take pride in the way she took it?

In addition to the two aircraft carriers, the Navy, with the money allocated by PWA, fabricated 4 cruisers, 4 heavy de-stroyers, 16 light destroyers, 4 submarines, 2 gunboats, and more than 130 combat planes, which then represented about one-fifth of the Navy's first-line combat air force, not to men-tion innumerable new instruments, engines, radio equip-ment, docks, shop buildings, piers, bulkheads, dikes, cause-ways, cranes, timber shipways, and many other naval devices. And the faster we built them the more abscessed became the disposition of the press and the Congress.

The result was that when war came, America, thanks to an apple-cheeked PWA and to a Navy-minded President, had the greatest peacetime Navy in her history—a fleet which, ac-cording to certain strategic pulpiteers and newspaper "ad-mirals," wasn't ever going to have anything to do except to sail leisurably on practice tours to perfect itself in arts that it would never be called upon to exercise.

I may not be making myself popular—not that I care—by recalling sundry wailings and gnashings of teeth, even as lately as two years ago, by seers who, having gazed into their crystal balls, predicted confidently and loudly that there would never be another war, certainly none in which we would become involved. But the President, it seems to me, is entitled, in all fairness, to some credit to counterbalance the invectives and slurs that were hurled at him from all directions back in 1933 when he was way ahead of his time. And who is in a better position than I am to tell the tale?—I, who was scorched somewhat myself by the sulphurous language that was used, much of it on the floor of Congress, by those who actually believed that the richest and fattest and softest country in the world had no need to be able to defend itself—"because it would never be attacked."

So we are entitled to insist now that our stars were lucky in that we had a President who was not afraid of an apoplectic Congress—a President who dared to be misunderstood by the people and by the press, and who, until Congress screamed that he mustn't do it any more, permitted the Public Works Administrator to spend one out of every six dollars to gird the nation's loins for war.

And I would like to see the color of the eyes of the man who would venture to assert that the remaining five dollars did not go, for the most part, into projects that are today doing their part in this titanic struggle to dominate the thinking of the world for at least the next century.

From Horatius Cocles to George Washington to Franklin Delano Roosevelt, it has been axiomatic that the time to prepare for war is in time of peace. Most of this philosophy is written into the wartime literature of the ages. The President's, whether he intended it to be so or not, is expressed in terms of fighting equipment eked out of make-work appropriations. If we had not been given these armaments, Japan and Germany would today be nursing brighter hopes of victory than they are.

It isn't so many months ago that what I consider to be the best newspaper in the country was lambasting the President for his "failure to provide mechanization of the Army out of relief funds"!!! It even charged that the President willfully disregarded a "mandate" in the NIRA under which he was duty-bound to do so—and didn't!

The history of this war will tell posterity that, over the roar of angry legislators, the din of a belligerent press section, and the groans of appeasers, PWA went ahead with its program. The 75th Congress, by this time in a lather, whipping up a public opinion which it itself led, rose up in its wrath and put a stop to such squanderings. If it hadn't, how do we know that we wouldn't have been all set for Pearl Harbor, Guam, and Wake Island? If the Congress hadn't, with its wetted fingers, snuffed out our light, I suspect that we might have done something about these vital strategic outposts, in addition to the ships that we built for the Navy.

I derive some personal satisfaction also from the fact that when the records of hearings before the Appropriations Committee become public property, they will show that the PWA argued vigorously for the policy of lump appropriations, leaving it to the Executive to determine what projects should be eligible for grants and how the money should be apportioned as between different projects.

At the ▮▮▮ of being called on ▮▮ ▮▮▮▮ even now I will venture the assertion that ▮▮▮ ▮▮▮▮▮ hadn't ▮▮▮ ▮▮▮▮ ▮▮▮▮ ▮▮▮ it did, we would have had ▮▮▮ and ▮▮▮▮ and ▮▮▮ and other strategic ▮▮▮▮▮ in better shape than they ▮▮▮ ▮▮▮ ▮▮▮▮ ▮▮▮▮ ▮▮▮▮ ▮▮ ▮▮▮▮ pocket edition of ▮▮▮▮.

There is a good laugh in the reflection that four years after PWA had been ordered by Congress to quit spending money for defense, Congressmen were actually boasting about our

Navy—the very one that had been built up to its greatest peacetime strength over the opposition of Congress—and using it as an argument for voting down a $5,000,000 appropriation for the dredging of the harbor preliminary to the fortification of Guam.

Cunning little Japan had already served notice that we simply *must not* fortify Guam, Wake, or the Enderberry Islands, and that we must demilitarize Pearl Harbor!

The cheek of them! And yet, under Congressional hectoring, we were falling in line with these incredibly insolent suggestions as fast as we could. Having already put a stop to the PWA program of preparedness, Congress, four years later, was still grousing.

As one Congressman ably, but unconvincingly, stated to his colleagues: "Defenses are never a threat to the peace of the world. Defenses cannot be provocative. Defenses cannot be objectionable to foreign countries, unless such foreign countries plan hostile activities against us. Therefore, are we not very foolish to be influenced by such protests?"

Had we taken seriously Ogden Nash's silly verse—

> "How courteous is the Japanese;
> He always says, 'Excuse it, please!'
> He climbs into his neighbor's garden
> And smiles and bows and begs his pardon.
> He bows and smiles a friendly grin,
> And calls his hungry family in,
> He smiles and bows a friendly bow!
> 'So sorry! This my garden now.' " *

—if, I say, we had been awake to the fact that there was more

---

* From "The Face Is Familiar" by Ogden Nash. Reprinted by permission of Little, Brown & Co.

truth than poetry in that little verse, PWA might have been allowed to carry on, in which case the Japs would never have stepped a foot inside of our garden.

To the chapter in history which will be devoted to the Public Works Administration, I suggest a footnote telling how people used to trail expectantly the Public Works Administrator—one Ickes by name—hoping to be on hand when —it was only a question of time—an avenging Providence would mow him down for building bombers when one brooklet in every congressional district could have been getting a permanent wave.

Naturally, I tingle with pride when I review what PWA was actually able to do before a majority of Congressmen got mad and wrote, in the Relief Appropriation Act of 1935, that "no part of the appropriation made by this joint resolution shall be expended for munitions, warships, or military or naval material. . . ." This was the money for which we have been chided by the *New York Times* and others for not making available for defense or war purposes.

To make it even more certain that we would not spend money for the Army and Navy, Congress went so far as to earmark the 1935 appropriations, specifying with great particularity the purposes for which the money could and could not be used. It even catalogued amounts for the different categories of projects.

In the circumstances, is it any wonder that, when an Administration critic (yes, there are such) rises up, as he so frequently does, and castigates it for not spending more PWA money when it was "available" and when there was still time to get ready for war, we who were put through the wringer of public disapproval back in those dark and gloomy wash-

Here you see a picture of the first patent ever issued on a flower. It took some doing, but I got it.

Plant Pat. 19

THE UNITED STATES OF AMERICA

TO ALL TO WHOM THESE PRESENTS SHALL COME:

Whereas   HAROLD L. ICKES,
of
Hubbard Woods,   Illinois,

PRESENTED TO THE **Commissioner of Patents** A PETITION PRAYING FOR
THE GRANT OF LETTERS PATENT FOR AN ALLEGED NEW AND USEFUL IMPROVEMENT IN

DAHLIAS,

A DESCRIPTION OF WHICH INVENTION IS CONTAINED IN THE SPECIFICATION OF WHICH
A COPY IS HEREUNTO ANNEXED AND MADE A PART HEREOF, AND COMPLIED WITH THE
VARIOUS REQUIREMENTS OF LAW IN SUCH CASES MADE AND PROVIDED, AND

Whereas UPON DUE EXAMINATION MADE THE SAID CLAIMANT is
ADJUDGED TO BE JUSTLY ENTITLED TO A PATENT UNDER THE LAW.

NOW THEREFORE THESE **Letters Patent** ARE TO GRANT UNTO THE SAID

Harold L. Ickes, his heirs   OR ASSIGNS
FOR THE TERM OF SEVENTEEN YEARS FROM THE DATE OF THIS GRANT

THE EXCLUSIVE RIGHT TO MAKE, USE AND VEND THE SAID INVENTION THROUGHOUT THE
UNITED STATES AND THE TERRITORIES THEREOF.

In testimony whereof, I have hereunto set my
hand and caused the seal of the Patent Office
to be affixed at the City of Washington
this nineteenth day of July,
in the year of our Lord one thousand nine
hundred and thirty-two, and of the
Independence of the United States of America
the one hundred and fifty-seventh.

Attest:

S. C. ____
Law Examiner.

Thomas E. Robertson
Commissioner of Patents.

By Talburt

AND HE NEVER TOOK A LESSON IN HIS LIFE!

HIS OWN HORN

ICKES

EVERYBODY ELSE'S BUSINESS

Talburt

"If there had been a band, I would have been *it*, too. And it would have been brass." *Chap. 6.*

PUBLIC WORKS RESTAURANT

SAVE YOUR APPETITE FOR HARRY'S FREE LUNCH

H. ICKES, MGR.

FREE LUNCH

BOONDOGGLING CAFE

FEDERAL RELIEF ADMINISTRATOR HARRY HOPKINS PROPRIETOR

PUBLIC WORKS SERVE YOURSELF PROJECT CAFE

ICKES

TOUGH COMPETITION

days of the early and middle thirties should come out a bit irritated?

When the "hindsighters" wring their hands over what they call the "bungling" of today, they conveniently forget the "procrastination and short-sightedness" of yesterday. The reason is that they were the shortsighted ones who were doing the procrastinating.

But before a nearsighted and irritated Congress, which would not permit another to do what it didn't have the sense itself to do, could interfere in its business to the point of putting a stop to enterprising preparedness, PWA had to its credit not only the building of our greatest peacetime Navy, it had run up many other marks that caused many a Congressman and newspaper publisher to froth at the mouth, and doves of peace to molt.

PWA gave the Army Air Corps the money with which to buy more than 100 planes, including training, bombing, and pursuit craft for training and experimental purposes.

It supplied $25,000,000 to be spent in the construction of revenue cutters for the Treasury. The Navy has them now and is making good use of them. These were the best boats that we had ever had.

It allocated $10,000,000 to the Army for the renovation and preservation of ammunition, the modernization of ordnance, the improvement of arsenals, and *to the speeding up of the motorization and mechanization of the Army through* the purchase of cars, motorcycles, trucks, tractors, scout cars, and other power vehicles.

PWA financed the building of more than 50 military airports throughout the country, among them the great Mc-

Chord Field in the State of Washington, the Sand Point Field near Seattle, and the Corry Field near Pensacola, Florida.

It provided enough money for the improvement of the 32 permanent U. S. Army posts so that more than 12 per cent of the enlisted men were provided with new quarters.

With financial help from the same source, the Army was able to lay out and build a network of 74,000 miles of strategic highways. Did I hear someone say that good roads are not essential to national defense? If I did, it wasn't the voice of the man who knows that the roads of France saved Paris from the Germans in 1915. Nor was it the voice of Hitler, whose first big undertaking after emerging from his beer hall was to build throughout Germany trunk highways over which his mechanized forces could rush to overwhelm Holland, Belgium, and France.

PWA money was spent to build an air tunnel in which to test the effect of winds on airplanes. Harbors and rivers were dredged, canals were built, hospitals went up. Certainly hospitals have their uses, in war as well as in peace. One hospital for the exclusive use of Negroes was erected in St. Louis, and when I went through it at the time of its dedication I decided that it was the finest building of its kind that I had ever seen.

I confess that I wasn't able to do everything that I thought should be done—particularly to construct a new building for the War Department and a new Naval hospital. I once had a cherished dream of building modern new hospitals in all parts of the land. I wish now that I, or someone else, had done this.

Between the early days of 1933 and the passage of the Relief Appropriation Act of 1935, more than one billion dollars had been invested in these and other types of "permanent public works" that the NIRA permitted, but which Congress, in its wisdom, had never thought of. In any event they were "permanent public works" unless and until they were destroyed by accident or by enemy action. And this could happen to the Interior building which was also built as a PWA project and which none would deny belongs in the category of "permanent public works."

One thousand million dollars, and then some, that might have, I grant you, been used to hire grown men to chase tumbleweed on windy days!

One thousand million dollars stood between what was a defenseless nation ten years ago and the cruel enemy that we were at least able to stand off yesterday until we could get ready to fight him today!

I have attempted to sketch briefly PWA's direct contribution to national defense. Because of the leeway that it had under the law to make grants to cover the entire cost of Federal projects, PWA was able to undertake some others that, while useful in peacetime, are just as important for war purposes as are munitions themselves.

I particularly have in mind hydroelectric power developments. Where would we be today with a scarcity of power already making itself felt, and a greater lack facing us during the next few years, if we had not gone in for the most stupendous program of power development in history?

We claim no credit for the conception of Boulder Dam or of the TVA. But we hurried Boulder Dam to completion after we came in in 1933 and finished it two years ahead of schedule. The power now being generated there is indispensable to the war. And while the main credit for the TVA must gratefully go to that really fine elder statesman, George W. Norris, the records will show that it was PWA encouragement—encouragement in the form of coin of the realm—that gave it not only the means but the opportunity to expand into the vitally important project that it is.

Then take Grand Coulee Dam, unquestionably the greatest edifice ever built by the hand of man. It used to be referred to by the scoffing as "Roosevelt's folly." Occasionally, I was flattered by having it denominated "Ickes' folly." If Hitler had had anything to do with either its conception or its construction, I would be willing to have it called "Hitler's folly." After all, perhaps Hitler did fail to take into account certain mighty forces of the Americas that he had marked as his prey long before he embarked on the rape of Austria. There "could never possibly be found a market for the enormous amount of power that can be developed at Grand Coulee," vociferated the apoplectic critics.

The fact is that today we cannot supply enough power from Grand Coulee, or from all of our great hydroelectric plants combined, to satisfy the demand.

At the Bonneville project also is being produced electric power for the manufacture of war materials that we cannot do without if we are to overcome the Nazis. Parker Dam, Shasta and Keswick Dams, the addition to Hetch Hetchy Dam, the Seminoe Dam on the Kendrick Project, and others, must be named in any enumeration of the greatest hydroelectric development in all history.

The cost of these dams, which are producing, or will produce, huge quantities of electric power so cheaply that it can be sold at low cost to small businesses, to farmers, and to other users, will be amortized over a period of years. In addition to power, many of them, such as those in the Central Valley of California and Grand Coulee, are storing and will continue to store enough water to irrigate millions of acres of rich desert land which is capable of raising abundant and varied foodstuffs. Grand Coulee will irrigate an area, larger than the State of Delaware, of land that is said to be as rich as can be found anywhere on earth. Many thousands of farmers will be able to build happy homes on those irrigated acres and add to the Nation's food supply. Be it remembered that food, too, is a *sine qua non* if we are to win the war, so that, in the final analysis, by providing more land and water for the raising of it, PWA will have contributed directly and again to Hitler's forthcoming downfall.

The record would be inexcusably incomplete if I did not mention the $200,000,000 loaned by PWA (in some cases under protest, mind you!) to 32 American railroads that are today carrying troops and oil, and munitions of war closer and ever closer to the fighting front. It may not be generally remembered, but it was the Public Works Administration that within six months of its creation had loaned to the Pennsylvania Railroad the millions of dollars required to complete the barely begun electrification of its line between Washington and New York. You may thank the same "Santa Claus" for the streamlined trains upon which you can now travel and for taking many "kinks" out of railroad systems so as to make the ride swifter, safer, and more comfortable.

Don't talk to me about a want of preparedness—unless you are thinking of Congress. Trace the record for yourself and your eyes will be opened (reluctantly in some notable instances) to the fact that had not Franklin D. Roosevelt come along when he did with his PWA cornucopia in 1933, we might today be doing the goose step.

NOTE—Before the ink runs out I would like to mention one of God's creatures (my first-born used to call it "God's screecher") who won't mind, I am sure, if I confer upon him a suitable sobriquet. I refer to Martin Dies—Congressman Martin Dies, of Orange, Texas—who has achieved distinction in a field of his own, one in which Congress regularly supports him with hardly wrung public cash, even although some of the war program may have to wait its turn until Dies is loaded. Dies even expects Congress to dip into the Federal Treasury to pay the cost of libelous statements which he may make when inadvertently when wearing something other than his Congressional immunity uniform. For his unmitigated gall, for his long-winded yammerings that seemingly go "babbling" on forever, and for the strange power that he appears to have over Congress, I christen him "Bubble Dancer" Dies who cavorts lumberingly on the Congressional stage with nothing but a toy balloon with which to hide his intellectual nudity. To my mind the most contemptible human being in public life is the one who will recklessly smear another's character and then wrap himself tightly in his Congressional immunity.

CHAPTER SIXTEEN

"THE OILY BOID"

Give me another horse! Bind up my wounds!
—SHAKESPEARE.

CONTINUING TO SPEAK of oil, because that is what I want to do: So changeable is our petroleum problem that what one may say about it today may sound even sillier tomorrow. But it couldn't be more idiotic than what most of the papers and commentators were chattering about it a year ago. Some newspapers are still hoping to prove that an unholy mess has been made of it, but even they are becoming short of breath. By the time that we go to press, even they may be flatter than day-before-yesterday's pancakes.*

Therefore, in discussing petroleum in its relation to our national life, it is going to be difficult, if not positively dan-

---

* I was lambasted so hard, as Petroleum Coordinator, that I cannot refrain from gloating a bit over two pipe lines—two 1,400 mile systems from Texas to the East Coast—one of which nears completion and the other one assured. If these had been started when I urged them, a year and a half earlier, our petroleum problem today would not be as painful as it is. Fortunately, I am not bothered by criticism, so that I haven't been slowed up by it in my efforts to get the materials for pipe lines that many critics swore up and down that we didn't need. I have been more than passing successful—no thanks to some people whom I might blame—with the result that the immediate future, so far as petroleum is concerned, looks better than it did, even if it is not yet anything to cheer about.

gerous, to venture away from the safe ground of history. Forecasts that may be fly-specked before the next cold snap are nothing to rely upon—few people take stock in them anyway—so that predictions, for all present purposes, are definitely out.

With the sky black with war clouds, I one day found myself reading a letter from the President appointing me Petroleum Coordinator for National Defense (the whole thing changed later to Petroleum Administrator for War), and telling me what my duties were. Not only had I not solicited this appointment, I had not even discussed it with the President, although I knew that my name had been suggested to him. More than any other Government official, I knew about oil in its broader aspects and I had had much to do with the administration of oil policies. After all, I had been Oil Administrator under the NIRA Code and I had a small Oil Conservation Division as one of the permanent adjuncts of the Department of the Interior. Notwithstanding all of this, I did not believe that the President would appoint me Petroleum Coordinator. But he did, in May 1941.

I knew at once whom I wanted as Deputy Coordinator. It was Ralph K. Davies, ranking vice president of the Standard Oil Company of California. In two personal interviews that I had had with him, on neither occasion having in mind any imminent possibility of our involvement in war, I had been impressed by his ability. I liked his attitude toward the whole problem. Davies accepted this appointment without demur as a full-time Government employee. I have never made a better guess. With my full support, he has built up a staff of outstanding experts. I do not believe that the greatest oil company has a staff better in quality, although it may be larger in numbers.

We took a quick look at the over-all petroleum situation and we saw a cloud on the horizon—"a scowl of cloud" that was frightening. As we regarded it anxiously we could read its meaning. It meant that, with tankers being sunk by German submarines, which fact, in its turn, meant that more tankers would have to be diverted from our fleet to the British service, we would not have enough to supply the normal demands of the Eastern states. It did not need much acumen to discover that if 95 per cent of the petroleum supplies were carried to the East coast by tankers, and if 35 per cent to 50 per cent, or even more, of that fleet were diverted to the service of our Allies, we might find ourselves caught up short. There was plenty of transportation for either gasoline or fuel oil, but not enough for both. Our fear was that we would run short of fuel oil, particularly the fuel oil that is used to heat homes. We believed that the public ought to be apprised of this situation at once. We were convinced that it would understand. And the public would have understood if the newspapers and the commentators—in many cases deliberately, I have always thought—had not misrepresented or twisted the facts.

We went to the public with our first premise, namely, that there was a shortage of transportation. As a result of this shortage the oil companies could not send in all of the petroleum products that would be needed along the Atlantic coast. We had to prefer one product to another, and our distinct preference was *fuel oil*. We did not like to think of people being cold because of a lack of oil to heat their homes. Men could walk to work and, in doing it, keep warm, but old people and helpless babies were something else again. Neither did we relish the thought of war industries in New

England, New York, New Jersey, and Pennsylvania closing for lack of heavy fuel oil.

So we suggested a voluntary curtailment in the use of gaso-line by the owners of automobiles. We pointed out that if less gasoline were used, it would mean that we could bring in more fuel oil. Simple enough, wasn't it? At least this is what went forth from the office of the Petroleum Coordina-tor, but it was not what appeared in the newspapers, neither was it what was said on the air by the commentators. When people began perversely to use *more* gasoline instead of less there was but one course left open to us—to curtail deliveries to the filling stations. Then hell broke loose!

According to the blatant *New York Daily News,* which would rather rant than reason, Harold Ickes was a war-monger. Worse still, he was going to see to it that there would be no Congressional elections in 1942. (It might have helped at that if someone had prevented some of them.) Other newspapers insisted that I was trying to scare the peo-ple—to make them war-conscious—and that there was no shortage either of gasoline or of transportation. In this way they were half right. There was no shortage of gasoline—nor is there. We have said it over and over again. Let me say it once more—there has been no shortage of gasoline but there has been, and is, a shortage of transportation. These same newspapers averred that I was drunk with power. I was a faker of every known quality and variety. The Senate set up a committee to investigate the "Ickes shortage," announcing before its first meeting that there was not any shortage either of product or of transportation, a prognostication that it had no difficulty bringing in as a verdict after a "full and fair" hearing.

I have been assailed by newspapers in my time. And

plenty! I know what it is to "cower like a belabored hound beneath his master's lash." Or do I? Anyway, the belaboring and the pummeling that I took in the early days as Petroleum Coordinator beat anything that I have ever been through. For months it dragged on—and it's still dragging, although there isn't much life in it any more. It almost seemed as if by common consent the newspapers had agreed among themselves, "Here is a God-sent opportunity at last to destroy this man Ickes and drive him from public life." After all, the newspapers have never forgotten, and perhaps they will not forget, at least for a long, long time, that while I have maintained that the American press is the best in the world and has more liberty than it knows what to do with properly, I have also contended that the American press is far from perfect. To question the perfectibility of the American press is no doubt a monstrous and unpardonable sin. It is an affront to the "most high." At all costs, such a skeptic must be destroyed.

But fate continued to stitch. We of the Petroleum Office knew that such a shortage would manifest itself and that it would come in such a way that not even the editor of the *New York Daily News* could deny that it was here. Because of the warmest autumn in the Northeastern states in the history of the Weather Bureau, storage stocks of fuel oil held up for a long time. But as the winter of 1941-42 turned into spring, stocks began to diminish rapidly. Then the oil companies began to send their men to Washington to insist that gasoline be rationed—again not because there wasn't enough gasoline to go around, but because there wasn't enough transportation to supply at one time all of the gasoline and all of the heating oil needed in the East coast states.

Some newspapers then began to admit meekly that there *was* a shortage of transportation. That is, all except the *New*

York Herald Tribune, which, apparently, adopted the creed: "We will be damned before we admit any such thing because it was Ickes who persisted in saying that there *was* a shortage." To be sure, most of the newspapers picked up the "news" about a transportation shortage as though they had never heard about it before. They did not propose to admit that they had been wrong and that I had been right.

And while I have been fighting off the newspapers—thousands of them—I have also been beleaguered by certain of the magazines. Several months ago I was, for instance, hauled in by the editors of *Liberty* on a trumped-up charge of being an Alarmist. Irrelevant matter was thrown into the summons and complaint, from which it was made to appear that I was lucky not to be deprived of my citizenship and deported. It made me feel almost as unwelcome as Harry Bridges.

True, I could have asked for a change of venue, but I hoped that, by pleading guilty to the less serious offense of being a Realist, I would get off with a light sentence. The principal difference between an Alarmist and a Realist is that the former is considered by many to be a Menace, particularly in wartime, and is "shushed" at a great deal, while not everybody wants to listen to the latter because his views are generally unpleasant and hard to take. As I dislike very much being "shushed" at, you will see that there wasn't much choice for me as between the two. To make a long story short, *Liberty* gave me exactly seven minutes and thirty seconds in which to prove that I ought not be sent to the guardhouse for the duration.

I did the best I could in the circumstances, considering the fact that the editors of *Liberty* stood over me tolling off the seconds, and also that my disposition has always been to shrink in the presence of my traducers. (Happily I am overcoming that weakness and am already looking forward eagerly to the day when I may be able to stand my ground like a man.)

Dragging myself to the bar, I denied the allegation that had been made in amended pleadings that I was a Scaremonger, or at best a Pessimist, but admitted between sobs that I was a Realist—that I had been one all of my life and had never been able to shake it off. Under the cruel fire of cross-examination I became unruly and stated that if, as my accusers charged, I had what it took to be an Alarmist, I would not hesitate to be one when and if the occasion, such as a public emergency, demanded it. That apparently didn't help my case any because the impression was allowed to go forth that I had broken down and confessed. *Liberty* even showed some attempt at judicial clemency by saying that I had at least "been man enough" to *apologize* for what it called "the bogus oil shortage." (Imagine *me* apologizing—especially when I'm right!)

. In the gloom of solitary confinement I have since had an opportunity to reconstruct the circumstances of my case, and I am now in a position to say, in the light of new evidence, that I was jobbed. Smart prosecutors took advantage of my timorous nature and convicted me on the incompetent testimony and the inexpert opinion of newspapermen without .giving me the opportunity to locate my witnesses.

Furor fit laesa saepius patentia!

I must admit that at the time it probably did look bad for me, but is that any good reason why I should have been railroaded? Why did the mills of the gods have to make an exception in my case and grind both fast and exceeding fine? Just because it was Harold Ickes at the bar was no reason why the Constitution had to be scrapped. I know now how Alfred Dreyfus must have felt.

And so in my fancy I sat in a Court of Justice. My Chief Counsel was addressing the Court.

My Counsel. If Your Honor please—and whether you do or not it still goes—I have been asked to appear here for this poor soul and to ask that his case be reopened for the purpose of introducing new evidence.

The Court. How much time will you require?

My Counsel. Just enough, Your Honor, to prove that my client is actually smarter than he looks.

The Court (stroking his whiskers and sizing up the defendant). H-m-m! I wonder. Looks like quite a job if you ask me, but who am I to judge? Snap it up.

My Counsel. Thanks, Judge. I will call as our first witness the *Miami* (Florida) *News.*

[*Witness called and sworn.*]

My Counsel. Your full name is—

Witness. The *Miami* (Florida) *News.*

My Counsel. You claim to be the leading newspaper of Florida?

Witness. Who else?

My Counsel. I'll ask the questions. You answer them. Where were you on the afternoon of May 16 last?

Witness. I was in Miami.

My Counsel. Can you be more specific?

Witness. Well, I have a lot of friends in the country districts, if that's what you mean. According to the latest Audit Bureau of Circulation report I have—

My Counsel. Never mind the commercial. Let me put it another way. Were you on the streets of Miami, Florida, on the afternoon of May 16, 1942?

Witness. I most certainly was.

My Counsel. Doing what?

Witness. My stuff, of course.

My Counsel. Just what is your "stuff," as you call it?

Witness. Are you kidding?

My Counsel. No, I am not kidding. You're a newspaper, I take it.

Witness. You said it.

My Counsel. I'll show you this clipping. Are you able to identify it?

Witness. I certainly can. It's one of my editorials.

My Counsel. Did you have it on your person on the afternoon of May 16, 1942?

Witness. I did.

My Counsel. It purported to be what?

Witness. My views on the petroleum situation.

My Counsel. I ask the witness to read aloud the title of the editorial.

Witness. Can't you read?

My Counsel. Certainly I can read, but I want it read aloud for the purposes of the record.

Witness. Oh! The title is "Time Bore Him Out."

My Counsel. To whom does it refer? Who is "him"?

Witness. That guy sitting over there—Ickes.

My Counsel. My client?

Witness. As though you didn't know.

My Counsel. Will you read a few lines from the editorial —make it loud.

Witness (reading). "Secretary Ickes rates a bow from the numerous pre-Pearl Harbor critics who so lustily berated his early notions of what should be done to assure the country's gasoline supply—and who succeeded in blocking the recommendations which would have helped ease the rationing strain now."

[*Defendant Ickes jumps up and takes a bow. The Court gives him a dirty look and bangs the gavel.*]

My Counsel. Yes, yes, go on.

Witness. "He rates it first for his foresight. Nine months ago he told us what was ahead. The—"

[*The prisoner whispers excitedly in his counsel's ear.*]

My Counsel. Pardon me. Will you repeat that last line, please. I didn't quite catch it.

Witness. "*Nine months ago he told us what was ahead.* The shortage was not of gas but of facilities to move it. Tankers largely depended upon for transportation to the East coast would be increasingly diverted from that service to our own and Britain's military needs. Ickes called for a new pipe line to help close the gap. The most he could get was a gas curfew in the East. Even that didn't last when a Senate Committee saw only 'unnecessary alarm' and no—"

[*Prisoner again whispers excitedly in council's other ear.*]

My Counsel. What was that again? "Unnecessary" what?

Witness. "Alarm," sir, "unnecessary alarm."

[*The prisoner stands up and glowers at the magazine editors huddling like mice in a corner.*]

My Counsel. Continue, please.

Witness. "Even that didn't last when a Senate Committee saw only 'unnecessary alarm' and no 'oil shortage' and recommended lifting the restrictions."

My Counsel. It that all?

Witness. No, there is one thing more. (*Reads*) " 'The whole thing,' Ickes said then, 'is in the lap of time and time will tell the story.' Time has told it, all right. Despite rationing and utmost utilization of existing transportation facilities

When I got out this picture for inclusion in the book, I noticed for the very first time that it was a good picture of my wife (right center, looking and laughing at the cameraman). She should have had her eyes on me as I laid the cornerstone of the new Interior Building. The man standing behind me should need no introduction.

Herr Dr. Hugo Eckener did his utmost to talk me out of 18 million cubic feet of helium for Herr Schickelgruber, but I didn't go for it.

Many times I have let someone else try out the oysters at the start of the season, and if he survives—then I have some!

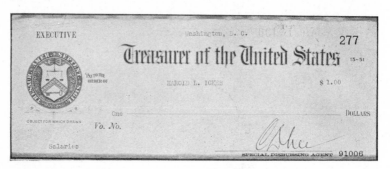

It has long been a source of curmudgeonly satisfaction to me that by my failure to cash this check, I have made it impossible for the Treasurer of the United States to balance his books for a quarter of a century. He is bound to have been a dollar over, and although he probably knows by this time that the check, issued to me for "salaries" in connection with my work in World War I as the Illinois representative of Creel's Committee on Public Information, is the one that is out, the fact remains that his bank statement will never jibe.

now the East will yet be 200,000 barrels short of its daily essential requirements.' "

My Counsel. All right. That will be all. At this point I wish to put my client on the stand.

[*The prisoner sworn—not sworn at.*]

My Counsel. You heard the last witness?

H. L. I. I did.

My Counsel. Mention was made of an estimated daily shortage of 200,000 barrels of oil in the East. Does that figure still hold?

H. L. I. It's approximately 400,000 barrels now.

My Counsel. Then as a matter of fact when, as the witness said, you told us nine months ago what was ahead, you only told us half of it? Is that right?

H. L. I. You might say so, I suppose.

My Counsel. That's all.

The Court. May I ask Counsel if he has any more witnesses?

My Counsel. Have I! The antechamber is full of them.

The Court. Anybody I know?

My Counsel. All of them, no doubt—*Wall Street Journal; Printer's Ink; Springfield* (Ohio) *News; Akron* (Ohio) *Beacon-Journal; Washington Post,* and many others.

The Court. Hm! *(Looks at his watch)* I have no desire, Counsel, to shut off any testimony that you desire to introduce, but I have a golf match on this afternoon and an "A" rationing card which means that I have to hoof it to the links. It has just occurred to me that if the testimony of the other witnesses is similar to the testimony that we have just heard, there isn't much use in going all over it again. Personally I have heard enough, but just to be on the safe side you might call another witness or two—good lookers if you have them.

My Counsel. Call *Printer's Ink.*

[*The witness blushes becomingly and is sworn.*]

My Counsel. Where do you live?

Witness. New York.

My Counsel. Do you know the defendant in this case?

Witness. Do I have to answer that question?

The Court. I'm afraid you do.

Witness. Will it be used against me?

The Court. Never mind. Answer the question.

Witness. Yes, I know him.

My Counsel. How well do you know him?

Witness. As well as I know any of my public servants.

My Counsel. Have you ever bawled him out in front of people?

Witness. And how! Only last summer we got into a fight over the matter of gasoline supply. He said that what this country needed more than a good five-cent cigar was a pipe line between Texas and the East Coast, and I said that he was nuts.

My Counsel. Do you still think so?

Witness. I do not. I have already publicly admitted that he was right and that I didn't know what I was talking about.

My Counsel. That's all. Do you want to hear any more, Your Honor?

The Court. Have you any younger witnesses?

My Counsel. One. The *Washington Post* of July 23, 1942.

The Court. What will that witness testify to?

My Counsel. It will testify as to "how painfully correct has been Petroleum Coordinator Ickes when he called the turn on the gasoline situation last year."

The Court. That's enough. Prisoner to the bar. (*The pris-*

oner crawls forward.) Mr. Ickes, I am of the opinion that you have been done a serious injustice. Moreover, I am convinced that nothing that I might say now will make up to you the sleepless nights and tasteless meals that you have been through. However, I feel that it would only be a waste of good white paper to continue this inquisition. In turning you loose, I want to say that I will order *Liberty* to cancel my subscription which still has about three months to run. Court is adjourned. Fore!

CHAPTER SEVENTEEN

"HEARTS AND FLOWERS"

Hard-boiled, unbroken egg, what can you care
For the enfolded passion of the Rose?
—H. PHELPS PUTNAM.

ISANTHROPES ARE OFTEN unpredictable. And what is true of them applies to the hardy curmudgeon as well. For all of their much-vaunted spleen, the misanthrope and the curmudgeon sometimes have soft spots in their characters, for which, I suppose, there is no biological accounting.

I, for instance, am supposed to be the essence of all that is dispositionally disagreeable in a human being. And yet, if we probe carefully under my elephant hide of meanness, what do we find?

Like Ferdinand the Bull, I love flowers! I always have. I won't say that I would rather be a florist than a fighter, and yet I wouldn't want the choice put up to me in earnest. I have spent many moons mooning over the beauties of my dahlias (I hold the first dahlia patent ever issued), my acre or two of naturalized mertensia and narcissi, and my gorgeous peonies. One fall, I planted fifteen thousand crocus bulbs in the circle within the Ickes driveway in Winnetka, and after they had come to full bloom and were glorious in their bright

312

colors, a heavy, clinging May snow swept from across Lake Michigan and killed them. My disposition took a nose dive then and there.*

On other occasions I have had rare moments of mellowness. One of the most important of these I made use of to scoop the world. This was one time in my long experience with the press of the nation that I did *not* come off second best. It is a prize memory, second only to the event itself. To give the newspapers credit, they seemed to enjoy the "beat" almost as much as I did.

In 1938, after the death of my first wife in an automobile accident on the Santa Fe-Taos Road in New Mexico, I fell in love with and became engaged to Jane Dahlman, who had recently been graduated from Smith College with honors. For reasons that I have never been able to understand (despite her generally admitted good looks, she is a sensible

---

* Speaking of hobbies, I feel under internal pressure to confess that I have been, and am, a common garden variety of stamp collector. My first disposition was to suppress this information, or at least not to divulge it voluntarily. Somehow it doesn't fit into my self-portrayal as a curmudgeon. Admittedly, a man can be a grouch and a garden addict because he can always find weather or insects or moles or something else at which to curse. But stamp collectors, as I have known them, are a friendly and philosophical lot in general. They can admire another collection without being jealous of the collector. They are home bodies practicing their hobby quietly and contentedly. So this will explain why I thought it just as well not to admit being a stamp collector. I am still one (at least in theory) but I hesitated to say so because I was afraid I would only make it more difficult to persuade my readers what a surly and cross-grained creature I really am. I would not want anyone to conclude that as a curmudgeon I am a first-rate boon-doggler. However, I am confident that I have made such a strong case for myself that I can make this simple admission without prejudice. Philately has for many years been a great comfort to me, and I wouldn't have missed the excitement of it for twice the money and effort that it has cost me. Some people still think stamp collecting is child's play. Maybe so, but if it is a symptom of juvenility then there are several million of us who have never grown up. A good red-blooded philatelist would commit mayhem for a rare stamp—call it child's play if you want to.

body, ambitious neither for money—fortunately so in this instance; nor for social estate—also fortunately so), she agreed to marry me. I knew what would happen if the newspapers got wind of it. So we decided to keep it deeply secret.

I am no national hero, thank God, but I was a member of the Cabinet and there was a discrepancy in age between Jane and me that the gossips—both male and female—would roll under their tongues.

It was our conclusion that despite the interest that it was anticipated the public would show in this event, our marriage was primarily a matter personal to ourselves. We did not want to have to jump off with newspaper sharks and cameramen in swift pursuit. We wanted to be married quietly and without ostentation. Marriage should not be made a "holy show." Both of us wanted to escape attention and be on our own for a few weeks.

So it was arranged that Jane should go to Dublin, Ireland, to visit her uncle, John Cudahy, who was then American Minister there. I was to follow her in April. But when April came, I was held in Washington by an appropriation bill for public works. After what seemed to be endless delays, the bill finally passed the House. Over in the Senate, the committee holding the hearings was under the chairmanship of the late Alva B. Adams of Colorado. Without telling him why, I asked him to put me on as the first witness. He did. Then I went to the President to break the news to him. He knew Jane and congratulated me warmly. I cautioned him to tell no one. I reminded him that there was quite a difference in our ages. He waved that aside as not worthy of consideration. There had been a considerable difference in the ages of his father and mother.

The President graciously called Secretary Cordell Hull

and me to his office together. He told the Secretary that I was
going abroad on a confidential matter. The passport was
quickly arranged for. So far, so good. But Ireland was a long
way off, and it is not an easy matter to slip out of a Cabinet
office and get all of the way to Ireland and safely married and
hidden away before the news hounds are heard baying along
the trail.

I sent for Mike Straus, Director of Information. Handing
him a short prepared release announcing the marriage, I told
him to give it out upon cabled advice from me. Mike's remark was: "Boss, you'll never get away with it." My reply
was: "Don't be so damned pessimistic. Maybe I can't, but we
can at least try."

Then I called in Harry Slattery, Under Secretary of the
Interior. He devised ways and means by which I might be
able to get across the Atlantic incognito on the *Normandie*.
Passage was secured for me. Harry knew an inspector in New
York who was attached to the State Department. He could be
trusted. The inspector got in touch with an employee of the
French Line.

So, early one day, I got off the Pennsylvania train in New
York. I had it figured out that if I made my getaway on a
Wednesday, only a couple of days would have to elapse before the end of the week, and I reasoned that if my absence
weren't suspected until the week end, it might be assumed
that I was in Chicago. I went to the trouble to write to the
caretaker of my house in Winnetka telling him to say to anyone inquiring if I were in Chicago that I had been out to
Winnetka, but that he didn't, at the moment, know where I
could be located. What a liar I was willing to make out of
him! But I thought the cause a good one.

The *Normandie* was to sail about noon. I went quietly

aboard via a gangway over which kitchen supplies were being taken on. The purser was in the know. He showed me to my stateroom, which faced the dock. We pulled down the shades and we were well down the harbor before I ventured on deck. In the meantime, I had scanned the passenger list. It was a small one, and I recognized no names except those of Mr. and Mrs. John D. Rockefeller, Jr., who, however, at the last moment had decided to go across on another ship. But people whom I did not know might recognize me, even from the unflattering newspaper pictures that had appeared from time to time. So it was arranged for me to have my meals in a private dining cabin to which I could have access through a little-used corridor, instead of in the main dining salon. There I took my meals early, which gave me a chance for walks on the deck while the other passengers were feeding at more conventional hours. After the first day, I felt that I would be safe until Southampton, but I doubted whether I could escape detection there by the ship reporters. Secretary Hull, at the suggestion of the President, had cabled across to have the Consul at Liverpool meet a Mr. So-and-So, arriving on the *Normandie*.

Two men came out to meet and to offer their services to Mr. So-and-So, but neither one knew me. I made myself as inconspicuous as possible during disembarkation, and fortunately everyone was busy with his own affairs, especially because of a retarding fog that we had encountered out of Southampton. We were late, which meant that the boat train would be late, which meant that I would have to stretch my legs if I were to catch the Liverpool train at Euston station in London. And I had to catch that train, because Jane would be waiting for me at the pier in Dublin early the next morning.

Again I had luck. I was not recognized either on the landing boat or at the pier. An official of the French Line had come down from London. The purser introduced me to him in *mea propria persona*. This French Line official saved my life. He saw me safely on the ship train with my baggage properly bestowed. Then, just before we reached London, he came to my compartment to say that if I were to catch the Liverpool train, it would be by an eyelash. He offered to take me across town. I had never been to London and it would be so easy for me to miss connections. We jumped into a taxi, told the driver to hurry, and I had my first glimpse of the Thames Embankment and the Houses of Parliament from a scurrying vehicle that might have broken down at any moment. The French Line official got me through the gates at Euston Station at a dogtrot. A porter scurried along with my bags and I finally sat down panting in the train, just five minutes before it pulled out.

At Liverpool, I boarded the crowded packet that would run across that night to Dublin. I found myself stuffed into a small cabin that had no outside opening except the door. Fortunately, I am not subject to claustrophobia, but at that I don't like to be shut up in a cubbyhole without air or natural light.

We reached Dublin about six o'clock the next morning, and there was Jane waiting for me. She had already arranged for Dr. Hanna, minister of the Presbyterian Church, to marry us at ten. I went to the hotel that was said to be the best one in Dublin, but which, if it was, didn't look the part. And not a newspaperman yet!

After he had pronounced us man and wife, Dr. Hanna took us into his office. He had been in the United States, having spent a year at Princeton. We liked the kindly little old man, with his snow-white mop of hair. Making entries in his records, he asked me my employment. I started to say "lawyer." Then I switched to "civil servant." He hadn't the foggiest notion who I was until late that day, when the news hounds, finally in full cry, interviewed him. The letter that Dr. Hanna wrote us subsequently showed that the experience had been an exciting one to him, as it certainly had been to me.

Back at the hotel, we were toasted with champagne by some of Jane's friends from the Legation who had come to congratulate us. In order further to cover our tracks, Jane had hired what, in Cobh, passed for an automobile. This had driven over for us. Our belongings were already packed. After lunch in the dining room, we settled ourselves in the automobile for a drive to a quiet summer resort near Cobh that had very few guests and was not on a main track. Then I suddenly remembered that I had sent no word to Mike Straus, although we had been married for almost five hours. That was rubbing it in on the newspapers with a vengeance. We stopped at the post office and I cabled Mike to let go of the release. He did so, with the result that the news of our wedding was cabled back to Dublin from Washington.

I confess that I was just a little proud of this exploit. We got to our hotel, and there we hid ourselves out for a few peaceful days. Meanwhile, a mad hunt was on by the news agencies and by correspondents who were trying to locate a very happy and, at least temporarily, noncurmudgeonly bridegroom, and his wife. The search was directed by telephone to our hotel but the management protected us. There were only two or three guests. They smelled out who we were and entered into the spirit of the occasion. Our plan was to go to London soon, and I finally sent out word as to where and when we could be met up with.

On the little boat that we took out of Cobh, one local correspondent found us. In the main, our cargo consisted of pigs, as to which our senses of sight, smell, and sound could testify. Landing at Fishguard, Wales, we boarded a train to London, where, it seemed, every newspaperman of the city, together with his "sisters, his cousins, and his aunts," had turned out at Paddington Station to meet us.

I had not expected such a mob. We had decided to give them all the time that they wanted. At the end, I asked whether anyone wanted to ask any additional questions or to take any more pictures. The negative was unanimous. Then I remarked that we had been glad to help out but that we were going to be in London for a short time only and would they do us the favor of not seeking us out any further? There was a general agreement but we had gone no more than a couple of blocks when our eagle-eyed taxi driver slipped word back to us that we were being followed by a string of cars.

Near Hyde Park I told our driver to stop. Five or six taxis, laden with correspondents and cameramen, were on our trail. Climbing out, I stood on the sidewalk and waited for them to gather about. Then I said: "Now I have told you everything that there is to tell. Mrs. Ickes and I are on our wedding trip. You can understand that we would like to be permitted to come and go freely. If there is anything more that we can do, we will be happy to do it. Won't you then really let us alone?" They were good sports about it and told us that if we would walk out to the traffic bobby at the next street crossing and ask him for some direction that he could point out while they took a picture of us, they would really let us alone, and they did.

Joseph P. Kennedy was our Ambassador to the Court of St. James's at the time. He was very hospitable, placing an automobile at our disposal while we were in London. We were guests at a big state dinner at the Embassy in honor of the Duke and Duchess of Kent. Ambassador and Mrs. Kennedy had already had us as their guests at a wonderful Toscanini concert at Victoria Music Hall. Kennedy took me to the office of Lord Halifax, who was then Foreign Minister. He arranged for us to call on the Lord High Chancellor and have a peek at the Law Lords hearing a noted patent case. We met Churchill, Chamberlain, and other men high in the Government and in British social life. I recall that at the Embassy dinner, Lady Stanley sat on my left. Her husband was Home Secretary in the Chamberlain Cabinet. She asked me if I were not the man who had refused to permit the sale of helium to Germany. When I told her that I was, she congratulated me warmly and said that my act had been widely applauded in England. I remarked that there had been no such cheering in my own country.

After the dinner, Lord Stanley sought me out. The United States had just taken over those three infinitesimal but, now in the days of airplane travel, immensely valuable atolls in the far Pacific—Howland, Baker, and Jarvis islands. These were under the jurisdiction of my Department through the Division of Territories and Island Possessions. The British had claimed but had not exercised sovereignty as to these. After we had planted the American flag on them the British became interested. The President had told me that I might say, unofficially, to any member of the British Government who inquired that there would be no difficulty if the British wished to work out with us an agreement for a free joint use of the islands. This greatly reassured Lord Stanley, and the result was a quick and altogether harmonious understanding between the British Government and our own.

In London, and later in Paris, we had long, serious talks about the Nazi threat. In London, Lord Wedgewood, then Colonel Josiah Wedgewood, whom I had met over here, invited us to a small dinner at the House of Commons. Clement R. Attlee was there and so was Sir Archibald Sinclair. David Lloyd George was entertaining a small party at an adjoining table and we had the pleasure of meeting that old lion whose roar was so throaty twenty-five years ago. After dinner we went into the office of the leader of the Labour party. Members of Parliament are not furnished with offices and all that goes with them, as members of Congress are. Only party leaders have such appurtenances.

The group that met in that room saw a world catastrophe lowering not far off on a black horizon. Bitterly they protested Chamberlain's appeasement policy. They saw nothing but grave trouble ahead as the result of it.

We had a thoroughly good time in London. We saw the House of Commons in session and visited Oxford, where my own university had gone for many of its architectural ideas. Mr. and Mrs. John D. Rockefeller, Jr., who had attended the Embassy dinner (along with another well-known American, Arthur H. Sulzberger, publisher of the *New York Times*), graciously invited us to dinner in their hotel apartment and were our hosts subsequently at the theater.

We flew to Paris in a rattletrap airplane. As I looked down at the Channel, really as smooth as a fishpond, I regretted that I wasn't on a boat. I was becoming more and more uncomfortable, as I am likely to do when bumping about in the air, and I reached Le Bourget field just in time. Ambassador William C. Bullitt had interested himself in our whereabouts and had had advance notice of our arrival. He met us with a big touring car and we were driven at a dizzy speed to the charming château, located on a ten-thousand-acre "lot" at Chantilly, which he had leased for ten years. The Huns are now his unbidden and unwelcome guests. After we had spent a night there, he found us just the hotel that we wanted in Paris. Jane had never been in Paris. She had left London somewhat regretfully, because she knew London and liked it, but no one ever fell harder for delightful Paris than she did. I had loved it from my first visit in 1911.

Time flew all too swiftly for us. We did not venture out of the city except on two occasions. We visited Versailles, and one Sunday we drove to the thrillingly beautiful Cathedral of Chartres. Another Sunday morning found us at Notre Dame, where I saw the most colorful religious service of my Spartan Presbyterian career.

We sought out famous restaurants and gorged ourselves with the best French cooking and wines in Paris. If there is better cooking any otherwhere than in Paris when Paris is Paris, then I don't know where it is.

Bill Bullitt was pessimistic about the war. He clearly saw it coming and when Bullitt sees anything clearly he does not put on smoked glasses. As he sized things up, a mighty struggle was in certain prospect between Germany and Italy on one side, and France and England, principally, on the other, but supported by a group of small free nations whose lives too would be in jeopardy. He had no more idea of the futility of the Maginot Line than did Marshal Gamelin, whom we met at a dinner given at our Paris Embassy. As Bullitt looked ahead, he saw the possibility of these two mighty contestants bleeding each other white. He did not know whether America could keep out of it, but he thought that if we could we should, so that there would be one civilized nation left whole to help to bind up the wounds of the stricken and to carry on the torch of civilization. But that there would be war, and that soon, Bullitt did not have the slightest doubt. Nor had the Britishers with whom we had talked. They were for joining sharp issue with Hitler without delay. Why make strong an enemy who must be fought in the end anyway?

We had hoped to visit Prague, but Bill Bullitt and John Cudahy thought that it would be unwise in view of my well-known opposition to Hitler and his Nazi gangsters. The situation in Prague, they said, was too critical. The slightest incident might precipitate the crisis that could not be long postponed in any event.

There were many places that I wanted to revisit in France and new interests that we wished to discover, but the Congress had appropriated another considerable sum for public works and duty called. At Le Havre we boarded the *Paris*. We promised ourselves that we would come back to France one day. And we wanted to see Scotland—my romantic Scotland, which I have never seen—and Scandinavia. But as we looked back at the disappearing French coast, Jane said sadly: "I don't believe that either of us will ever see France again. There won't be any France to see."

As our ship snuggled into her berth at the French Line pier in New York Harbor, we saw another regiment of newspapermen with clicking cameras awaiting us. A customs inspector expedited our baggage, and we were soon on our way to Headwaters Farm near Olney, Maryland.

That was nearly five years ago. I was to discover, to my grateful surprise, that the young woman who had been born and bred in Milwaukee and whose hardest manual labor had been put forth at Smith College on the tennis courts, the basketball floor, and the hockey field, was at heart a farmer. She loves Headwaters Farm. I love it. At once, we set ourselves to working seriously to become practical farmers. Instead of ordering chicken fried *à la Maryland* at a restaurant, or sniffing appraisingly at the eggs before putting them into the pan, Jane orders her chickens as "chicks" in the early spring—several thousand of them at a time, and out of them raises broilers, and roasters, and fryers, and capons, and laying hens, the latter of which, as a result of her personal attention and intelligent care, produce eggs for which she is able to obtain a premium in an appreciative market that she cannot satisfy, thanks, at least in part, to freely contributed but ungenerously intended newspaper advertising on the part of the Washington lady who snoops to conquer.

In the fields of Headwaters Farm and of more recently acquired Limestone Farm, tractors plow, and cultivate, and reap. We have put in a few sheep and are going into the breeding and marketing of Hampshire hogs—in a rather substantial way. We boast of a few pure-bred Jerseys. We are acquiring some feeders. In short, we are putting in all of our energy and Jane's goodwill (she is the farmer), in an attempt to earn from the land an economic independence that will assure the future, whatever may befall, not only of Jane, but of our two little blessed events.

It remains to be seen how long even a confirmed curmudgeon can refrain from reverting to type in such surroundings.

CHAPTER EIGHTEEN

A PEOPLE'S PEACE

> We have learned by hard experience that peace is not to be
> had for the mere asking; that peace, like other great privileges,
> can be obtained only by hard and painstaking effort.
> —FRANKLIN D. ROOSEVELT.

*F*OR ALMOST AS MANY YEARS as I have been able to stand
on a platform without holding on desperately to my
shaking knees, I have been giving voice to certain inborn
convictions concerning basic rules of conduct, by observing
which our democratic country might remain free and independent, and its people, regardless of color or creed, be assured the fullest possible measure of liberty.

It may be characteristic of a curmudgeon that, once he is
convinced of something, he rarely changes front on it. This
standpattism does not apply to all members of the human
race, who are, I find, frequently unpredictable. I have been
fooled many times, for better or for worse, both by the male
and by the female of the species.

I have already confessed, penitentially, in these pages that
once I was too quick to agree that we Americans could hiber-
nate smugly on our segment of the Western Hemisphere and
never be afraid that an enemy could reach us. I have lived

to see that theory ripped into shreds by the acetylene torch of war.

I lay no claim to originality—only to consistency—when I record that civil liberties cannot possibly exist under an absolute form of government *(New York, December 8, 1937),** and those same civil liberties I have been among the first and, of course, the loudest to defend.

For untold generations *(Detroit, October 23, 1934)* man has fought for the right to live in peace and harmony and understanding, not only in the world of the spirit, but with his fellow men. Above all other things he has aspired to and striven for liberty—liberty to live his life in his own way, subject only to the right of other men also to live their lives in their own way; liberty to worship according to the dictates of his own conscience; liberty to adapt the social customs that have come down to him from his forefathers to whatever new environment he may choose for himself; liberty to think his own thoughts and give free expression to them; liberty to find for himself in the social order the niche for which he is best adapted, regardless of race, or creed, or color; liberty to work at any task, suitable to his abilities and agreeable to his taste, for a sufficient wage to support himself and his family in reasonable comfort, with a modest surplus over for his periods of leisure and to carry him in decency and security through the years of his old age; liberty to follow freely his own political convictions; liberty to keep his children in school until they are fully equipped in their turn to put their abilities and their talents to the highest service of the State and of society.

The desire for liberty has been one of the consuming pas-

---

* References are to dates and places of speeches in which I have stated my position on the matter referred to.

sions of the human heart. Paradoxically enough, there has
dwelt side by side with a love of liberty, a contempt for it.
We want liberty for ourselves, but we have, too often, little
interest in liberty for others. In fact, it would seem that to
some people liberty is desirable to the degree that its possession represents a restriction of the liberties of others.

There are self-appointed champions of our liberties *(Detroit, December 4, 1935)* who would return to the old order.
Either they possess great wealth themselves or they are "little
brothers of the rich," men who have abased themselves before
wealth in the possession of others. But I warn them that they
are putting a lighted match to a keg of powder when they
insist upon returning to the old order. These critics would
meet a political crisis with a slogan, a serious argument with
a shibboleth. They are the modern exponents of do-nothingism. They do not want the patient restored to health if it
has to be done by new methods of surgery. They believe that
if their incantations should fail, it would be better for the
patient to die. In that event, he would at least die respectably
and "constitutionally."

I was one of the first *(Detroit, December 4, 1935)*, if not
the very first man in public life, to denounce and to warn
against the evils of fascism. It is the fascist-minded men of
America who are the real enemies of our institutions by reason of their solidarity, their common interest in seizing more
power and greater riches for themselves, and their ability and
willingness to turn the wealth of America against the welfare
of America. It is these men who, pretending that they would
save us from dreadful communism, would superimpose upon
our political institutions equally dreadful fascism.

We are not in this world *(Philadelphia, November 3,
1933)* to work like galley slaves for long hours at toilsome

tasks in order to accumulate in the hands of 2 per cent of the population 80 per cent of the wealth of the country. We are not here merely to endure a purgatorial existence in anticipation of a beatific eternity after the grave closes on us. We are here with hopes and aspirations and legitimate desires that we are entitled to have satisfied to at least a reasonable degree.

So long as I can remember I have been in the lists against special privilege parading in the verisimilitude of benevolence and democratic concern for the common man. In other words, hypocrisy reduced to its most detested form—men who "have" exploiting, under a cloak of friendly interest, men who "have not" in order that they themselves might have more! Out of this war will come—I hope—among other things, a spiritual and not a literal interpretation of the promise that to him that hath (character and goodwill) shall be given (opportunities to exercise his gifts in the service of mankind).

I have long urged universal education as a *sine qua non* to intelligent self-government. Ignorance is incompatible with free institutions that are the carefully reasoned choice of the people themselves. Every child should be given every possible opportunity in the schools to unfold to his utmost intellectual and spiritual capacity, regardless of where along the long road of education any particular child should stop (*Chicago, July 6, 1933*).

All of which leads to the view that schools, since they are specialized in scientific institutions, should be managed by specialists. (*Chicago, May 24, 1935.*) For businessmen generally, or for men of other than the teaching profession, to think that success in other fields, especially if that success is measured by money, qualifies them to run schools, is based on an egotism that properly subjects them to ridicule. There seems to be an unhallowed tradition among certain groups in America that a man's intellectual attainments are in exact proportion to the number of dollars that he has been able to acquire or was fortunate enough to inherit. Yet a bulging bank account and a cultivated mind are not synonymous. Nor ever will be.

I have insisted *(Chicago, February 26, 1936)* that no race, or creed, or color should be denied that equal opportunity under the law about which we are so eloquent on the Fourth of every July and concerning which so many of us are indifferent at all other times. Times have changed for all of us. Conditions which we and our fathers learned how to face in the past no longer exist. If we are to enjoy the rights and privileges of citizenship in the different world that lies ahead of us, we must share its obligations as well as its responsibilities. This principle applies to all of us, Caucasian and Asiatic and Negro.

We must build up our national defenses *(Cleveland, May 26, 1940)* to the point that they will be an adequate protection not only for ourselves, but for those other countries of the new and better world, whose immunity from foreign invasion we have underwritten. This we cannot hope to accomplish unless we achieve national unity to a degree that we have never before had it in this country. Economic security, social justice, equal opportunity under the law—these constitute the trinity to be set above the altar of the Temple of Liberty that America must build and maintain for its citizens. With these as our inspiration, we need not fear for our national unity, which will be our guarantee, both of immunity from attack and of the ability and the means to repel attack.

And be it said also that I hold very firm convictions on the subject of peace, a subject that is now suggesting itself for consideration.

What this sixty-nine-year-old, self-made, porcupinish churl who has come up "the hard way" knows about a global war depends entirely upon what he has learned, if anything, from the present one, this being the first all-wool-and-a-yard-wide global war since there has been a globe. I might have learned something from World War I if that had indeed been an honest-to-god World War. At the time we thought that it was, but, viewed in retrospect and brought into comparison with this one, it shrinks into a mere skirmish that we financed out of our change pocket. And although I had some fairly intimate contacts with it, I didn't draw much on World War I for additions to my curmudgeonly qualities, although undoubtedly it added to my ability to snork. There wasn't sufficient time left after we had gone in for me greatly to expand my mean streak, and, besides, I was much younger, which makes a difference. I know now that even then I was on my way to pre-eminence as a curmudgeon, but my goal was still a long way off. For one thing, the newspapers hadn't spotted me, and while I had had my baptism of fire in politics, it was more or less desultory. It was of the flintlock era rather than of the grenade.

But had times been different, and had I stood out even then as a "terrible-tempered Mr. Bangs," I suspect that I would have done exactly what I am doing now—I would have stepped out of character long enough to say something about the peace that was to follow. I couldn't have made the situation any worse than it turned out to be, no matter what I had said, although I might have added something to my stature as the snarlingest creature that ever went to bed with his boots on.

And so, nearly a quarter of a century later, I am changing my role so as to speak my piece about the peace (blessed little am I supposed to know about peace!) that is to follow this ghastly war. For there will be a peace, regardless of how or when it may come. The end may not be in sight—if it is I can't see it—but it is there across the wide horizon just the same and some day it will appear in all of its rising-sun glory. We can be as sure of this as we are that peace always has followed every war, (be it thirty years long or one hundred in span), just as the hillbilly knew that it was going to stop raining because it always had.

To my way of thinking, it is high time that we were beginning to think about the peace. We don't want to be caught off our guard as we were twenty-five years ago. Then the people who had poured out their treasure and their blood "to end war" were too quick to relax. Guilelessly, they permitted the power-statesmen of Europe, who got us into that unnecessary conflict, to return to their pleasant little game of international penny ante. Or would duplicate power-politics be a better name for it? Are they going to do it again with Hitler sitting in as the banker? I can't read the thoughts of all of them, but my suspicions are that a goodly number will want to revive the old international racket. They have never done anything else, therefore it is only natural that they should want to draw cards in a game that they love and to which they have been devotees in the past, but never to the point of playing a deciding rubber.

War will inevitably break out again in a generation or two if the flowering of this war unfolds merely as a variety of the Versailles Treaty. And this time we really don't want any more wars. We know what this one is doing to our brothers and sons, and we want to protect our grandchildren from being engulfed in what, if it does come, will be an even more cruel and devastating conflict than the present one.

So it were well to mistrust those who advise that we wait until we have won the war before we undertake to discuss, or even to think about, the peace. Such counselors have an ax to grind. I suspect that an appropriate name for it would be the *"status-quo-ante"* ax. Some are hungrily looking forward to a newer and bigger crop of war millionaires from whose tables a casual crumb might drop into the ragged lap of Lazarus. Some are sharpening their knives to cut their "piece" out of the same sort of pie that was carved at Versailles. These, too, would keep the minds of the common people off of the peace by exhorting them to direct their gaze toward the war. They hope to outwit us while distracting our attention. They are as wrong now as they were when they insisted that we should not prepare for this inevitable war because "there could be no war." There might be a little "disturbance" in Europe, but we would be safe anyhow even if the flare-up across the Atlantic were more than a little one. Hitler couldn't possibly strike across the Atlantic, even if we wanted to. Hadn't he said so himself? And hadn't we had freely offered and incontrovertible testimony to the same effect from our "flying hero"? As for Japan, its intentions were honorably pacific. Those dear little Hitlerian Nordics loved us as brothers—about as Cain loved Abel!

We should have an awareness for the peace, just as we should have had an awareness for the war during the days when the appeasers were trying to bribe the Whore of Munich with lands that belonged to others. We should have a *be*wareness of those who are trying to soothe us to sleep about the peace, and of those who may urge us to take part in a negotiated peace.

No peace would be worth the writing that is not a peace dictated to Hitler on the soil of Germany itself by the victorious armed forces of the United Nations.

This time Germany must know and acknowledge that she has been given the licking of her life. The United Nations must dictate a permanent peace in the interest of humanity and they must see to it that, by whatever necessary measures, that peace will be properly and effectively policed.

As a curmudgeon *in absentia,* I would like to make it known, although I have tried to keep it under cover up to this point, that I have had more than a passing interest, amounting almost to a passionate belief, in the dignity of the human being. This is the reason that I have regarded with such aversion the Gymnophiona that constitute the majority of the "Special Committee to Investigate Un-American (sic) Activities." This accounts for my participation in the long-continued "Battle of Bertie," which, by its very nature, has had to be a running fight. I have been brought up, and I have brought up myself, to respect that line of Burns that all of us ought to keep at the masthead of our lives: "A man's a man for a' that." I respect a man (used generically) not because he is white or black or brown or yellow, but because he is a man. I am even sentimentally foolish enough to believe in what Thomas Jefferson wrote in the Declaration of Independence. If the assurances of freedom that shine with brilliance from our Bill of Rights, as the diamond radiates from a platinum ring, were not already our solemn assurances of freedom, without which man could not live except in hopeless despair, I would be willing to shed the last drop of my blood for their enactment.

So far as the United Nations are concerned, this is a people's war. With the sole exception of the Union of Soviet Republics, which, by reason of its close proximity to both Germany and Japan, of necessity was required to build up and maintain a large standing army, the United Nations mustered only skeletonized armies—nuclei to which could be attached citizens called from civil life. Even that former mistress of the seas, Great Britain, had yielded to the pleas of peaceful America, and had reduced her navy. What gave the Huns such a big start was the fact that while they had been training an army for years, we had not been doing that here. Nor had Great Britain. Literally, we had to beat our plowshares into bayonets. We had to exchange our peacetime economy for a wartime spending spree. Move as quickly and as determinedly as we could, this, of necessity, took precious time.

We had to call the cream of our manhood from field and factory and college to be trained and hardened for the test of muscle and nerve which we must win if we were to continue to live. And to pay for our murderous and expensive toys, we went deep into our pockets. We operated on our incomes. We drew upon our savings. Our generals and our admirals, whom we had trained at our expense to serve the nation in time of war, might lead because they were our experts in armed conflict, but they would have had nothing to lead if it had not been for our cheerful willingness to throw all of our possessions into the conflict and to expose our lives in defense of the institutions that we cherish.

And if, as I have said, this is a people's war, so must the peace to which, in due course, it will give bloody birth, be a people's peace.

And such a peace must not be permitted to be written by

power politicians, by *status-quo-ante* entrepreneurs. It must be written by the people themselves, a people determined no longer to defer to selfish interests that will not hesitate to embroil us in another war when they can the better be served that way. The peace must be written in a deeply religious spirit by men and women who passionately desire for themselves and their children such a peace as cannot be riven, no matter how rough the road that it may be called upon to travel.

A people's peace will, of necessity, be founded upon certain elementary principles. These are:

First: The right to think and speak and print freely.

Second: The right to worship according to the dictates of one's own conscience.

Third: The right of freedom from discrimination on account of race or creed or color.

Fourth: The right of adult citizenship, which means the right to vote on terms of equality with all others.

Fifth: The right to work at a fair wage that will provide a living, with something over for leisure and modest luxuries.

Sixth: The right to an education up to one's ability to absorb and use that education.

Seventh: The right to create for oneself such happiness as may be within one's capacity.

Eighth: The right to move freely and to act independently, consistent with the same rights in others.

Ninth: The right to security—to financial security and to physical security, including the right of preventive and of curative medicine.

Tenth: The right to justice without fear or favor and at the lowest possible cost.

Eleventh: The right to a free government of one's own choosing.

Twelfth: The right to freedom from servitude to unfair and undemocratic special privilege.

Thirteenth: The right to be taxed fairly for the support of the government on an equitable basis as between the richest and the poorest.

Fourteenth: The right to an equal opportunity under the law.

Fifteenth: The right to bring international criminals before the bar of an international court.

Sixteenth: The right to live while recognizing the obligation to let live.

These are the roughly hewn but irrefragable timbers that will go into the building of a people's peace, which alone can hold out any hope of being a permanent one. Only the people themselves can build such a peace, because only they are interested in it. And when they have builded it, they must guard it, as they will guard it, because it is their own handiwork, their own ark of the political covenant. It must be so protected as to be safe from assault from without, so guarded that even termites cannot eat away at it from within.

All of the rights that I have enumerated (and the list is by no means exhausted) are important. Most of them speak eloquently for themselves. They are the warp and the woof of which the pattern of our American life has been woven, although at times, alas, imperfectly. But along with the writing of a people's peace we must build the determination to live together in understanding and mutual acceptance. These qualities must leaven all dealings as between individuals, as well as between nations. The supreme rule of life, both individual and collective, must be that utterance of Jesus which is truly the foundation stone of liberty and civilization: "Therefore, all things whatsoever ye would that men should do to you, do ye even so to them."

If each of us should accept this as the North Star of his behavior, there would be no occasion for worry that we might be bringing up our children only to offer them as bloody sacrifices upon the altar of another war Moloch. If those of us who call ourselves Christians really believed in the Christ with the ardor that we profess, the treaty of peace that is to write "finis" to this war would inscribe itself not upon parchment, but upon the indestructible conscience of man.

And if "Therefore, all things whatsoever ye would that men should do to you, do ye even so to them," we must begin with our physical possessions.

In the past, there have been wars between feudalists, wars of revenge, wars over religion, wars for territory, wars because a lady smiled or refused to smile. More modern wars have been wars for natural resources. In a sense, they, too, have been wars of territorial aggrandizement. But if a country needs oil *for nonmilitary purposes,* why can't it be managed short of an invasion at the cost of billions of dollars and the expenditure of hundreds of thousands of lives? If a country needs coal, why not exchange it for something of which another country has a surplus? And so on. Remove the barriers to an equitable distribution of indispensable natural resources and the cause, or even the excuse, for war will be gone. The conventional justification for mighty armadas and invading millions will cease to exist.

In the matter of the availability of raw materials, on an equitable basis, for those who require them, the protective tariff is of primary importance. We can thank our own greedy selves for pushing tariffs higher and again higher until other nations could discover no way to prevent economic strangulation except by going into the business of tariff-making on their own account. For many years, the American people had it dinned into them that "the foreigner pays the tax," when it was a tariff impost. Partisan campaign textbooks indulged in many and persuasive dissertations upon this thesis. In true Yankee spirit we relished the thought that we were out-trading others. Campaign orators—I have heard them myself—were able to wax more eloquent upon this theme than upon any other. I have heard even United States Senators exult, in what they represented as the fact, that a tax of, say, 50 per cent on cloth for men's clothing was not paid by the man who bought the suit, but by the merchant in London who sold the goods. I am afraid that there have been some instances when Senators have actually believed this intellectual hogwash.

For his clear-eyed conception of this subject and for undertaking to do something to abate the evil, Secretary of State Cordell Hull has made an outstanding contribution to our economic life and to international relationships in general. His idea of reciprocal trade agreements and his persistence in having it adopted as a national policy will be recorded in history as a notable achievement. Unfortunately, he came too late, although a future fruitage of his planting is still possible. The rising tide of nationalistic fanaticism, inspired by Hitler, could not be held back by hardly and therefore slowly achieved trade agreements.

The principle of the reciprocal trade agreement must be widely and quickly extended after the war. As a matter of fact, this concept should give way to the broader one of a general international agreement that would, in effect, waive the right of a nation to tax goods coming into it, except for revenue and other bona fide reasons. Just how much protective tariffs have contributed to this war, I do not undertake to assess, but to the degree that they have had anything to do with it, the United States is more responsible than any other. In the beginning, we imposed tariffs to protect "infant" industries—such "infant" industries, if you please, as the steel trust, the sugar trust, and other "babies" of industrial and financial giantism. We have even gone to the extent of "protecting" ourselves against products that, if they could be grown or manufactured here at all, could be so only in adverse circumstances and at greater cost.

Access, on a fair basis, to the natural resources of the earth ought to go far toward equalizing the opportunities of peoples everywhere, as it would contribute to the elimination of economic abscesses that burst into war. The countries that have rare resources, or more common ones in great quantities, ought to be willing to share them on fair terms with those which need them. This would encourage commerce and keep the factories going. Such a course would flower into work and work would mean wages and wages would mean comfort and security.

We should never forget that, in an era of unrest, a demagogue even as fantastic as Hitler first appeared to be can develop at such a pace that, before we realize it, he is beyond our catching. There are men here, and in England and in France as well, who believe in their hearts that a dictatorship is more desirable than democratic self-government. Given a brutal dictator such as Hitler, union labor could be "put in its place and kept there." In the thought of some of our prominent citizens, including persons inside of Congress, and even within our administrative agencies, the "place of labor" is at a machine for long hours at a bare subsistence wage. A dictator would also make short shrift of the farmers who think that they ought to have at least a decent living out of their long hours of sweaty toil. There are those among us who, without compunction, would reduce free-born farmers to the serfdom to which Hitler has consigned, in Europe, men who live on and by the land.

That types of American big business and concentrated wealth are not afraid of a dictatorship, even such a one as Hitler's, is attested by recent shocking disclosures with respect to secret and intimate business alliances between them and German big business—alliances that deliberately strike at the common man.

During the last World War, our Government took over all German businesses in this country. These were put into the hands of an Alien Property Custodian and by him sold, supposedly at least, to American investors. The most valuable of these enterprises had to do with chemical processes. When we found ourselves at war with Germany again in 1941, officials in Washington were shocked to discover that these same industries that Germany had "lost" twenty-five years ago, and which, it was supposed, were reposing safely in the hands of patriotic Americans, were once more in the possession of the Germans. So we had to undertake to go over the same ground again. Will we be futile dupes of big business a second time?

The people ought not to permit a repetition of such a scandalous state of affairs.

Nor was this all. We discovered some of our mightiest financiers and industrialists shamefully in bed with German interests. It seems that they had, in this instance, that "passion for anonymity" that they had so derided. And how they squirmed for some shred with which to cover their revealing nakedness! The cartel system, they called it! American businessmen had been dealing on the closest and most intimate terms with Hitler and his creatures. It was almost like cutting an umbilical cord to separate them. Even after Hitler had broken faith as to important international matters over and over again; even after he had demonstrated himself to be the most abundant liar of all time, American businessmen continued to share their secrets and their loot with him (but not always he with them). They clung to him even after the rape of Austria. They loved him even after his brutal seizure of Czechoslovakia. They were not disturbed when Norway and Denmark and all of the Low Countries found themselves stricken unto death.

Our traditional and cherished friend, France, might fall and England find herself in danger of her life—such things might happen while surreptitious, illegal, and sinister cartel machinations were indulged in by American and Nazi industrialists. The record discloses the willingness of Americans to enter into unholy bargains with treacherous Nazis that were to the distinct disadvantage of their own country, even on the military front. It was more pleasing to share a guilty understanding with Hitler, and to guard against its disclosure, than it was to bring our rubber and certain other industries abreast of the most scientific discoveries.

And if a just peace, a people's peace, a resources-sharing peace is not compatible with a system of international cartels, neither can a just people's peace, in our own land, dwell side by side with such monopolistic practices as we have endured in the past.

It appeals delightfully to my sense of humor to hear monopolists sound off stentoriously about "individual initiative" and "free American enterprise." Free American enterprise and monopoly are mutually exclusive. Both cannot occupy the same space at the same time. It has not been the little businessmen, nor has it been the liberals in this country, who have destroyed free enterprise or even hindered it. It has been the monopolists, men who go about pounding their "individualistic" chests, who have been trying their busy best to destroy initiative while loudly, if at times hypocritically, vaunting this American institution to death.

To assure ourselves of the right kind of a peace we must take the mocking undertones out of "individual initiative" and "free American enterprise." It is one of the fundamentals that we must be sincere in these expressions and no longer degrade them into sneers. (If there is a stronger individualist in the country than he who is writing this, I would like to be introduced to him. No one could hope to be a curmudgeon who is not hopelessly individualistic, both instinctively and by choice. And look at the curmudgeon that I am, even when I step out of character!) The truth is that many of those in whose vocabularies these fine, full words stand out in large blocked letters, although they may not know it, are paying verbal tribute at the gravestone of "individual initiative" and "free American enterprise." Nor, to mix my metaphors, are they courting either of these American beauties with the thought of honorable marriage in their minds.

If we want wholeheartedly a "people's peace," as Vice-President Wallace so pregnantly phrased it, we can have it. But it will not be handed to us on a platter of ease. We must go and get it, and after we shall have gotten it we must protect and cherish it. Evil may, and often does, befall in unexpected ways and at unscheduled times. The good things of life may come, without being striven for, to unheedful individuals, but there are only a negligible few of these. Good never comes to a nation without striving and travail and bitter birth. So it will be as to the peace that lies somewhere behind the dense black clouds just over the horizon. The people must reach out for that peace and take it if it is to be theirs. They can count upon it that if they leave the issue to the power-politicians who call themselves statesmen, or to those who have greedily grabbed and hoarded the natural resources of the world for their own selfish purposes, they (the people) will not find themselves in full enjoyment of their own peace. They will have to be satisfied, until the next world catastrophe inevitably befalls, with a piece of a peace.

It is with these things in mind that I urge Americans to be alert and to *organize now* for peace.

THE END

INDEX

Adams, Alva B., 314
Adams, John T., 180
Addams, Jane, 107, 122, 167f
Ade, George, 43
Adkinson, Elmer W., 74f
Akron Beacon-Journal, 309
Allen, Henry J., 198ff, 203, 205ff, 233f
Allen, Robert, 274
Alschuler, Samuel, 42
Altgeld, John P., 81
Attlee, Clement R., 321
Axelson, Gus, 79

Baker, Alfred L., 177
Ballinger, Richard A., 153 and note, 154
Bancroft, Edgar A., 177, 219
Bannard, Otto T., 86
Barkley, Alben W., 68
Bartzen, Peter, 256
Baruch, Bernard, 269
Bass, John F., 150, 160f, 166
Bass, Robert P., 150
Bean, Edna, 32
Beck, Teddy, 31f
Bell, Laird, 109 note
Beveridge, Albert J., 260
Bingham, Henry, 130
Blaine, Mrs. Emmons, 107, 129
Blaine, James G., 73f
Blake, James B., 109 note, 177
Blount, Fred M., 34, 41, 91
Bonneville Project, 296
Borah, William E., 222, 227, 238
Boston Herald, 70
Boulder Dam, 295
Bourne, Jonathan, Jr., 157
Bower, Commander R. T., 68f, 71
Boyd, Harry, 70
Braden, Tom, 34

Brennan, George E., 36f, 130ff, 190, 235, 240f, 247f, 254f
Brennan, John, 37, 140
Bridges, Harry, 304
Bright, Orville T., 74
Browne, Edward E., 262
Browne, Lee O'Neill, 145
Brundage, Edward J., 130
Bryan, William Jennings, 47ff, 53f, 77ff, 88, 253, 261; Mrs. William Jennings, 50
Buck, Robert, 126
Bullitt, William C., 322f
Burke, Robert E. ("Bobby"), 35, 90
Burlew, Ebert, 277f
Busse, Fred A., 34, 49, 92ff, 108ff, 115, 117, 119ff, 123ff, 127, 129, 132, 134, 137, 142, 255
Busse, William, 143, 238, 259
Butz, Otto C., 177

Canton Evening Repository, 80
Cardozo, Benjamin N., 272
Carey, Robert D., 224
Carey, Tom, 35
Carpenter, Benjamin, 177
Carpenter, George A., 93
Carter, E. C., 193f, 199, 248
Carter, Orrin N., 39f, 177
Carter, Zina R., 89
Cedar Rapids (Iowa) *Gazette*, 70
Cermak, Anton J., 254ff
Chamberlain, Neville, 320f
Chicago Chronicle, 91
Chicago Daily News, 36, 85, 119, 126, 150, 219
Chicago Evening Post, 36
Chicago Record, 27f, 31f, 34, 43, 47, 52, 56, 62, 76, 84f, 90ff
Chicago Times-Herald, 36, 49, 91

Chicago Tribune, 26, 30ff, 36, 58ff, 69, 75f, 81, 93, 108f, 111, 115, 146, 149, 167, 179, 255
Churchill, Winston, 68, 320
Clapp, Moses E., 155
Cleveland, Grover, 73
Colby, Everett, 180
Collier, John, 265f, 273
Congressional Record, 67
Coolidge, Calvin, 65, 118, 126, 233, 235f, 248ff, 261
Corry Field, 294
Costigan, Edward P., 266
Coughlin, "Bathhouse" John, 35, 140
Courtney, Thomas J., 259, 263, 265
Cox, George B., 148
Cox, James M., 241f, 261
Crane, Charles R., 119, 122ff, 128, 138, 141
Crane, Murray, 46, 179, 218, 232
Creel, George, 190f
Creiger, DeWitt C., 14
Crocker, William H., 180
Cudahy, John, 314, 323
Culver, Helen, 129
Cummins, Albert, 74
Cunningham, Bill, 70
Curtis, William E., 43
Cutting, Bronson, 253, 266ff, 270

Dane, Lawrence, 70
Daugherty, Harry, 232, 245
Davenport, Homer C., 51
Davies, Ralph K., 300
Davis, John W., 252, 261
Dawes, Charles G., 95, 146, 193
Delano, Frederic A., 105, 114, 142
Denby, Edwin, 243, 245
Deneen, Charles S., 34, 75, 115ff, 120, 125, 128f, 131, 134f, 142ff, 148, 158, 164, 172ff, 237ff
Dennis, Charles H., 54
Dever, William E., 107, 247f, 254
Dewey, Chauncey, 162, 166
Dewey, Admiral George, 44
De Young, Mike, 182
Dies, Martin, 298 note
Dixon, Arthur, 34
Dobyns, Fletcher, 148, 238

Dolliver, Jonathan P., 155f
Dolliver, Victor, 51
Dover, Elmer, 51
Drake, Marion, 176
Dreyfus, Alfred, 306
Duffy, Sherman R., 30ff
Dunne, Edward F., 101f, 104ff, 111, 115, 131, 139, 164
Durkin, Jimmy, 32
Dyer, John Napier, 262

Eckhart, Bernard A., 173, 177
Eldred, Fred, 35
Elkus, Charles de Y., 265
Emmerson, Louis L., 228f, 233
Enderberry Islands, 291
Estabrook, F. W., 180
Ettelson, Sam, 233

Fall, Albert B., 243, 245
Farley, James A., 262, 264
Farwell, John V., Jr., 177
Fertich, Roscoe, 260ff, 268
Field, Marshall, I, 87
Field, Marshall, III, 31
Fish, Hamilton, Jr., 248
Fisher, Walter L., 107, 177
Fletcher, Eugene, 98
Foster, Stephen A., 177
Frye, William P., 51
Funk, Frank H., 162, 164

Gahan, Tom, 35
Gamelin, General Maurice, 322
Garfield, James A., 74
Garfield, James R., 152f, 180, 185, 187f, 224, 234
George V, King, 213, 221, 247
Gilmore, Mabel, 126
Glass, Carter, 78
Glavis, Louis, 277f
Gorman, Arthur P., 78
Grand Coulee Dam, 296
Grant, Ulysses S., 235
Grayson, Admiral Carey, 225
Grosscup, Peter S., 111ff
Guam, 58, 290f

Hague, Frank, 255f

Haley, Margaret A., 108
Halifax, Lord, 320
Hall, Ross, 37
Hanecy, Elbridge, 39ff, 89
Hanna, Dr., 316f
Hanna, Mark, 46, 49ff, 80, 167
Hard, William, 149
Harding, Warren G., 9, 45, 107, 132, 229ff, 240ff, 245f, 249, 253, 261
Harlan, Alderman, 84
Harlan, James S., 85, 104
Harlan, John Marshall, 8
Harlan, John Maynard, 37, 82, 85ff, 111ff, 120, 134, 155, 257; Mrs. John Maynard, 96, 112, 114
Harper, William Rainey, 11, 20, 25, 118
Harrison, Benjamin, 35, 56
Harrison, Carter H., Sr., 35 and note, 36ff
Harrison, Carter H., Jr., 35 and note, 84f, 87ff, 100f, 131ff, 137ff, 142, 248; Mrs. Carter H., Jr., 139
Hays, Will, 189, 223f
Hemenway, James A., 180
Heney, Francis, 264
Hert, Alvin T., 180
Hert, "Tobe," 187f, 229, 232f
Hertz, Henry L., 34, 93
Hertz, John D., 32
Hetch Hetchy Dam, 296
Hill, David B., 78
Hill, William, 85
Hirohito, Emperor, 111
Hitchcock, Frank, 249f
Hitler, Adolf, 184f, 222, 235, 245, 294, 296f, 323, 332f, 338ff
Hoover, Herbert, 45, 190f, 218, 235, 244ff, 253, 261, 263f, 270
Hopkins, Albert L., 117
Hopkins, John P., 36f, 49, 90, 110, 131ff, 190, 248
Houghteling, James L., 262
Howard, Roy, 211
Howell, Robert B., 180
Hughes, Charles Evans, 114, 152, 178, and note, 179 and note, 180ff, 183 and note, 184ff, 188f, 232, 245, 253, 261

Hull, Cordell, 270, 314ff, 338

Ickes, Anna Wilmarth, 143, 148, 178, 203, 242, 259, 262f, 265, 313
Ickes, Felix, 105
Ickes, Dr. George, 73
Ickes, Harold L., youth, 3ff, reporter, 27ff; political beginnings, 72ff; Chicago politics, 82ff, 172ff, 218ff, 247f, 254ff; first marriage, 148; Progressive movement, 151ff, 234; World War I, 184ff; post-war presidential campaigns, 222ff, 240ff, 248ff; Secretary of Interior, 265ff; Petroleum Coordinator, 299ff; second marriage, 312ff; on People's Peace, 325ff
Ickes, Jane Dahlman, 313f, 316ff
Ickes, Jessie B. W., 5ff
Ickes, Martha Ann McCune, 5ff, 10, 72ff
Ickes, Raymond, 178
Igoe, Mike, 254
Indianapolis News, 91
Insull, Samuel, 49, 83, 111, 190, 233
Inter-Ocean, 36

Jamieson, T. N. ("Doc"), 34, 39, 41, 93, 129
Jefferson, Thomas, 333
Jenkins, Newton D., 265f
Johnson, Hiram W., 163, 181f, 222f, 225f, 228ff, 233ff, 238, 246, 248ff, 264ff, 270f
Jones, David, 91
Jones, Thomas, 91
Jones, Walter Clyde, 148ff, 158, 221
Judah, Lieutenant Colonel Noble B., Jr., 198
Judson, Harry Pratt, 117f

Kansas City Journal, 63, 64 note
Kellogg, Frank B., 285
Kelly, Edward J., 255ff
Kenna, "Hinky Dink," 35, 106, 140
Kennedy, Joseph P., 320
Kent, Duke of, 320
Kent, William, 83, 86, 129
Keswick Dam, 296
Knight, Thomas J., 222

Knox, Frank, 31
Knox, Philander C., 176
Koenig, Samuel, 246
Kohlsaat, H. H., 91, 93

LaFollette, Robert M., Sr., 122, 155, 252, 261
LaFollette, Robert M., Jr., 252, 266f, 270
Lampert, Nelson N., 177
Landis, Kenesaw Mountain, 219
Lasker, Albert D., 224, 230, 249ff
Lawson, Victor, 28f, 31, 33, 37, 85, 91, 93, 97, 129f, 219
League of Nations, 241, 246
Lewis, James Hamilton, 107, 166, 239
Liberty Magazine, 304f, 311
Lincoln, Abraham, 283
Lindley, Ernest K., 277f
Little, Richard Henry ("Dick"), 30f
Lloyd George, David, 321
Loeffler, Billy, 101
Long, Huey, 173
Longworth, Alice, 233, 244
Lorimer, William, 34, 39, 41f, 89, 92f, 116f, 129, 131, 134f, 142, 145ff
Lowden, Frank O., 189, 222f, 225ff; Mrs. Frank O., 227
Lueder, Arthur C., 247
Lundin, Fred, 172f

McAndrew, William, 248
MacChesney, Nathan W., 177
McChord Field, 294
McCormick, Alexander, 177, 219f
McCormick, Cyrus H., 129
McCormick, Harold F., 129
McCormick, Medill, 50, 126, 149f, 160ff, 166f, 170, 178, 192, 230, 236ff
McCormick, Robert R., 30f, 58ff, 65, 93, 108ff, 149, 163, 167, 179, 192, 255f, 333
McCormick, Ruth Hanna, 50f, 149, 167, 239
McCune, Samuel, 18, 75
McCutcheon, John T., 43
McDowell, Malcolm, 33, 42, 49
McKinley, William, 43, 45, 48f, 54, 56, 78ff, 242, 261

McMahon, Mrs., 139
MacVeagh, Franklin, 155
Madden, Martin B., 82, 87
Magerstadt, Ernest J., 136f
Magill, Hugh S., 148ff, 158
Maher, John G., 262
Malone, William H., 227f
Manly, Basil, 252, 260f
Mansfield, Richard, 32
Margold, Nathan R., 266, 273
Martin, Alvah H., 180
Mary, Queen, 213
Masaryk, Thomas G., 211
Mellon, Andrew W., 235
Meriam, Lewis, 266
Merriam, Charles E., 117ff, 127ff, 148, 150f, 158f, 167, 172, 174, 177, 219ff, 238, 255, 257, 270; Mrs. Charles E., 139
Miami News, 306ff
Mills, Ogden L., 224
Mills, Wiley W., 107
Moley, Raymond, 267, 270f
Moses, George H., 236
Mosser, Stacy C., 81
Moulton, William B., 120
Mullaney, Bernard J., 36, 48f, 52ff, 108, 111, 127
Mullen, Arthur F., 262, 268
Municipal Voters' League, 37, 84
Murphy, Frank W., 262
Mussolini, Benito, 213

Nash, Pat, 257
National Industrial Recovery Act, 283, 286, 290, 295, 300
Nelson, Congressman, 252
Nelson, Murry, 177
Newman, Harry, 63 and note 63f, 65
New York Daily News, 61, 302f
New York Herald, 52, 56, 62
New York Herald Tribune, 62, 304f
New York Times, 292, 321
Nightingale, Harry F., 161
Norris, George W., 155, 267, 270, 296
Norton, Charles D., 155f
Noyes, La Verne, 129, 162f, 177
Nye, Senator Gerald P., 253, 266, 287

Ogden (Utah) *Standard-Examiner,* 70
Oglesby, John, 190
Olson, Harry, 174f
O'Malley, "Black," 37
O'Malley, "Red," 37

Panama Affair, 243
Parker, John M., 171
Parker Dam, 296
Patterson, Eleanor, 61f, 65, 237 and note
Patterson, Joseph, 31, 61f, 65, 93, 104f, 108f
Patterson, Mrs., 149
Pearl Harbor, 281, 286, 290f, 307
Pearson, Drew, 274
Pease, James, 34, 93
Peek, George N., 262, 268
Penrose, Boies, 46, 179, 218, 230ff
Périgord, Captain Paul, 191
Perkins, Dwight H., 177
Perkins, Frances, 270
Perkins, George W., 168, 171, 180, 188
Perkins, S. Albert, 180
Pershing, John J., 207, 211
Persons, Herbert, 180
Pinchot, Gifford, 153, 170, 224, 234, 253
Platt, Tom, 45
Pond, Allen B., 83
Poppenhusen, Conrad W., 177
Porter, George F., 177
Printer's Ink, 309f
Proctor, Colonel William, 226ff
Progressives and Progressive Party, 10, 75f, 143, 151ff, 174ff, 178ff, 185, 188f, 224, 227f, 234, 236ff, 241, 250, 252, 254, 259
Public Works Administration (PWA), 278, 281, 283, 288, 290ff, 297

Quay, Matthew S., 45f
Quinn, Jimmy, 35

Rapid City (S.D.) *Journal,* 70
Reeves, Congressman, 39f
Reid, Ogden Mills, 62
Reinecke, George W., 126

Relief Appropriation Act of 1935, 292, 294
Revell, Alexander H., 99f, 108, 177
Richberg, Donald C., 177, 187f, 190, 193, 220f, 224, 234, 239, 252
Ringer, Charles, 126
Robertson, David B., 262
Robertson, Dr. John Dill, 247
Robins, Raymond, 107f, 123, 170, 173, 224, 226, 234
Robinson, Theodore W., 177
Rockefeller, John D., Jr., 316, 321
Rogers, Walter S., 122, 124f
Ronald, W. R., 262
Roosevelt, Archibald, 231, 244
Roosevelt, Franklin D., 64, 69, 142, 240f, 243f, 253, 256, 260f, 263ff, 280ff, 286ff, 296f, 300, 314ff, 320, 325
Roosevelt, Kermit, 169, 244f
Roosevelt, Quentin, 210, 244
Roosevelt, Theodore, 43ff, 54f, 147, 151ff, 169, 176f, 179, 183ff, 210, 216f, 225f, 236, 240, 243, 261, 276
Roosevelt, Theodore, Jr., 231, 242ff
Root, Elihu, 176
Rosenwald, Julius, 123f, 128, 131, 136, 138, 141, 177
Rowell, Chester H., 180, 182, 224

Sand Point Field, 294
Saturday Evening Post, 271
Sawyer, J. H., Jr., 58 note
Schaefer, J. G., 220
Schaffer, John C., 177
Schaffner, Joseph, 237
Schlesinger, Elmer J., 237 and note, 238
Sears, Amelia, 220
Sears, Nathaniel C., 84, 87f, 94
Seattle Times, 64f
Seminoe Dam, 296
Sergel, Charles H., 174ff
Seversky, Alexander P. de, 70
Shanahan, David E., 190
Shasta Dam, 296
Sherman, Lawrence Y., 166, 170, 179f
Shouse, Jouett, 69
Shuster, Dr. George N., 70

Sikes, George C., 118, 220
Siman, John, 120, 174ff
Simpson, James A., 83
Sinclair, Sir Archibald, 321
Singleton, Shelby M., 120
Slattery, Harry, 315
Smith, Alfred Emanuel, 162, 244, 252f, 261
Smith, Delavan, 91
Smoot, Reed, 46, 179, 218, 232
Smulski, John F., 128ff
Smyth, John M., 34, 41
Snyder, Ralph, 262
Sonsteby, John J., 107
Springfield (Ohio) *News,* 309
Stagg, Amos Alonzo, 25
Stanley, Lord, 320f
Steinbrecher, Paul, 220
Stepina, James F., 120
Stewart, Graeme, 34f, 94, 98ff, 108
Straus, Mike, 315, 318
Straus, Oscar S., 180
Sullivan, Roger C., 36f, 49, 91, 131ff, 170, 190, 247f
Sulzberger, Arthur H., 321
Sutherland, George, 114
Sweitzer, Robert M., 176, 221

Taft, William H., 45, 107, 151ff, 160, 253, 261
Tanner, John R., 81
Taylor, Bert Leston, 30
Taylor, Thomas, Jr., 177
Teapot Dome affair, 243, 245
Teller, Henry M., 78
Tennessee Valley Authority (TVA), 295
Thompson, John R., 129, 131
Thompson, William Hale, 143, 146, 172ff, 179f, 185f, 219ff, 228f, 233f, 247f, 254f
Thomson, Charles M., 125, 163, 177
Toscanini, Arturo, 320
Traub, Major-General Peter E., 201, 206, 209

Trohan, Walter, 69
Tumulty, Joseph, 274

Upham, Frederick W., 132

Vail, Charles W., 129
Vaughan, L. Brent, 76f
Versailles Treaty, 225, 331f
Victor Emmanuel III, King, 213
Vittum, Harriet E., 224

Wake Island, 290f
Walker, Frank C., 262
Wallace, Henry A., 262, 342
Wallace, Henry M., 262
Wall Street Journal, 309
Walsh, John R., 34, 91
Walsh, Thomas J., 242, 268, 270
Warren, Charles B., 180
Washington, George, 289
Washington News, 69
Washington Post, 309f
Washington Times-Herald, 32, 57, 61
Watterson, Henry, 71
Weber, William H., 238
Wedgewood, Josiah, 321
West, Roy O., 118, 127, 129f, 135, 172ff
Wetten, Emil C., 257
Wheeler, Felix, 75
White, William Allen, 199, 223f, 234
Wile, Frederic W., 33
Wilhelm II, Kaiser, 156f, 184ff
Willcox, William R., 188
Williams, Ralph E., 180
Wilson, Billy (William Otis), 25
Wilson, Woodrow, 36, 42, 122, 182, 183 and note, 184, 186, 188f, 213f, 216f, 225f, 241; Mrs. Woodrow, 225
Wood, General Leonard, 44, 225ff, 230f
Woodruff, Harvey T., 32
Wrigley, William, Jr., 230, 249, 251

Yates, Richard, 39ff, 117
Yerkes, Charles T., 12, 38, 83ff, 87, 89, 100, 111f